WITHDRAWN

# Castles and Chateaux of Old Touraine
and the Loire Country

# THE SPELL SERIES

*Each volume with one or more colored plates and many illustrations from original drawings or special photographs. Octavo, decorative cover, gilt top, boxed.*
*Per volume, $3.75*

By Isabel Anderson
 **THE SPELL OF BELGIUM**
 **THE SPELL OF JAPAN**
 **THE SPELL OF THE HAWAIIAN ISLANDS AND THE PHILIPPINES**

By Caroline Atwater Mason
 **THE SPELL OF ITALY**
 **THE SPELL OF SOUTHERN SHORES**
 **THE SPELL OF FRANCE**

By Archie Bell
 **THE SPELL OF CHINA**
 **THE SPELL OF EGYPT**
 **THE SPELL OF THE HOLY LAND**

By Keith Clark
 **THE SPELL OF SPAIN**
 **THE SPELL OF SCOTLAND**

By W. D. McCrackan
 **THE SPELL OF TYROL**
 **THE SPELL OF THE ITALIAN LAKES**

By Edward Neville Vose
 **THE SPELL OF FLANDERS**

By Burton E. Stevenson
 **THE SPELL OF HOLLAND**

By Julia DeW. Addison
 **THE SPELL OF ENGLAND**

By Nathan Haskell Dole
 **THE SPELL OF SWITZERLAND**

By Frank Roy Fraprie
 **THE SPELL OF THE RHINE**

By André Hallays (Translated by Frank Roy Fraprie)
 **THE SPELL OF ALSACE**
 **THE SPELL OF THE HEART OF FRANCE**
 **THE SPELL OF PROVENCE**

By Will S. Monroe
 **THE SPELL OF SICILY**
 **THE SPELL OF NORWAY**

## L. C. PAGE & COMPANY
(INCORPORATED)
**53 Beacon Street**          **Boston, Mass.**

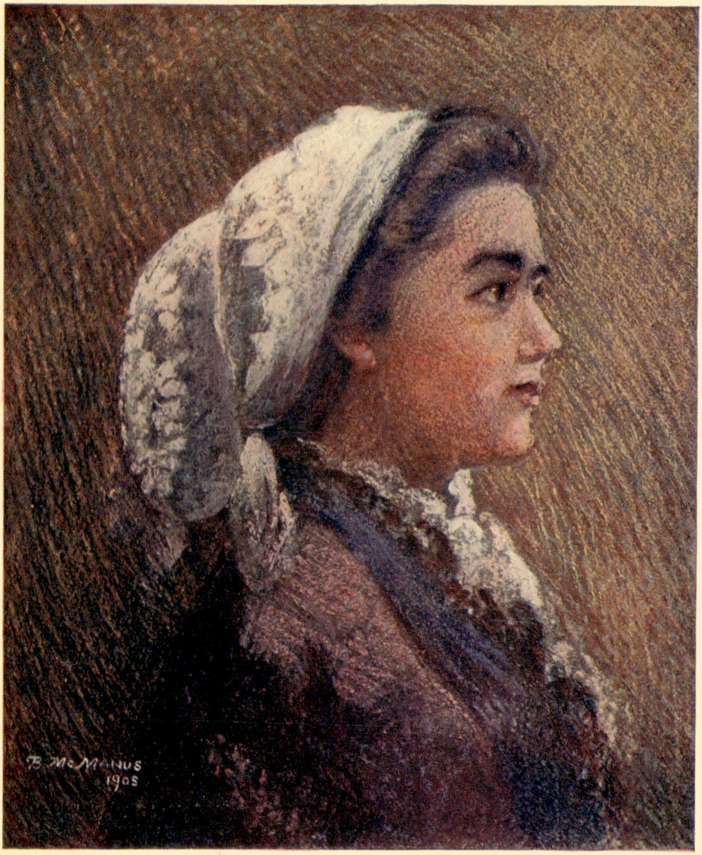
B. McMANUS
1905

# Castles and Chateaux
## OF
# OLD TOURAINE
## AND THE LOIRE COUNTRY

By FRANCIS MILTOUN, pseud.

Author of "Rambles in Normandy," "Rambles in Brittany,"
"Rambles on the Riviera," etc.

*With Many Illustrations*
*Reproduced from paintings made on the spot*

By BLANCHE McMANUS

Milburg Francisco Mansfield

BOSTON
**L. C. PAGE & COMPANY**
(INCORPORATED)

Publishers

DENISON UNIVERSITY
LIBRARY

*Copyright, 1906*
By L. C. PAGE & COMPANY
(INCORPORATED)

*All rights reserved*

New Edition, July, 1923

Made in U.S.A.

PRINTED BY C. H. SIMONDS COMPANY
BOSTON, MASS., U. S. A.

# By Way of Introduction

This book is not the result of ordinary conventional rambles, of sightseeing by day, and lying by night, but rather of leisurely wanderings, for a somewhat extended period, along the banks of the Loire and its tributaries and through the countryside dotted with those splendid monuments of Renaissance architecture which have perhaps a more appealing interest for strangers than any other similar edifices wherever found.

Before this book was projected, the conventional tour of the château country had been "done," Baedeker, Joanne and James's "Little Tour" in hand. On another occasion Angers, with its almost inconceivably real castellated fortress, and Nantes, with its memories of the "Edict" and "La Duchesse Anne," had been tasted and digested *en route* to a certain little artist's village in Brittany.

On another occasion, when we were headed due south, we lingered for a time in the upper valley, between " the little Italian city of Nevers " and " the most picturesque spot in the world " — Le Puy.

But all this left certain ground to be covered, and certain gaps to be filled, though the author's note-books were numerous and full to overflowing with much comment, and the artist's portfolio was already bulging with its contents.

So more note-books were bought, and, following the genial Mark Twain's advice, another fountain pen and more crayons and sketch-books, and the author and artist set out in the beginning of a warm September to fill those gaps and to reduce, if possible, that series of rambles along the now flat and now rolling banks of the broad blue Loire to something like consecutiveness and uniformity; with what result the reader may judge.

# Contents

| CHAPTER | | PAGE |
|---|---|---|
| | BY WAY OF INTRODUCTION | v |
| I. | A GENERAL SURVEY | 1 |
| II. | THE ORLÉANNAIS | 30 |
| III. | THE BLAISOIS AND THE SOLOGNE | 56 |
| IV. | CHAMBORD | 94 |
| V. | CHEVERNY, BEAUREGARD, AND CHAUMONT | 110 |
| VI. | TOURAINE: THE GARDEN SPOT OF FRANCE | 128 |
| VII. | AMBOISE | 148 |
| VIII. | CHENONCEAUX | 171 |
| IX. | LOCHES | 188 |
| X. | TOURS AND ABOUT THERE | 203 |
| XI. | LUYNES AND LANGEAIS | 221 |
| XII. | AZAY-LE-RIDEAU, USSÉ, AND CHINON | 241 |
| XIII. | ANJOU AND BRETAGNE | 273 |
| XIV. | SOUTH OF THE LOIRE | 301 |
| XV. | BERRY AND GEORGE SAND'S COUNTRY | 313 |
| XVI. | THE UPPER LOIRE | 330 |
| | INDEX | 337 |

# List of Illustrations

|  | PAGE |
|---|---|
| A Peasant Girl of Touraine | *Frontispiece* |
| Itinerary of the Loire (Map) | facing 1 |
| A Lace-maker of the Upper Loire | facing 4 |
| The Loire Châteaux (Map) | 9 |
| The Ancient Provinces of the Loire Valley and Their Capitals (Map) | 15 |
| The Loire near La Charité | facing 18 |
| Coiffes of Amboise and Orleans | facing 20 |
| The Châteaux of the Loire (Map) | facing 30 |
| Environs of Orleans (Map) | 39 |
| The Loiret | facing 42 |
| The Loire at Meung | facing 46 |
| Beaugency | facing 50 |
| Arms of the City of Blois | 58 |
| The Riverside at Blois | facing 58 |
| Signature of François Premier | 60 |
| Cypher of Anne de Bretagne, at Blois | 62 |
| Arms of Louis XII. | 65 |
| Central Doorway, Château de Blois | facing 66 |
| The Châteaux of Blois (Diagram) | 71 |
| Cypher of François Premier and Claude of France, at Blois | 72 |
| Native Types in the Sologne | 89 |
| Donjon of Montrichard | facing 92 |
| Arms of François Premier, at Chambord | 99 |
| Plan of Château de Chambord | 103 |
| Château de Chambord | facing 104 |

# List of Illustrations

|   | PAGE |
|---|---|
| CHÂTEAU DE CHEVERNY . . . . . facing | 110 |
| CHEVERNY-SUR-LOIRE . . . . . . | 113 |
| CHAUMONT . . . . . . . facing | 116 |
| SIGNATURE OF DIANE DE POITIERS . . . . | 118 |
| THE LOIRE IN TOURAINE . . . . facing | 134 |
| THE VINTAGE IN TOURAINE . . . . facing | 142 |
| CHÂTEAU D'AMBOISE . . . . . facing | 148 |
| SCULPTURE FROM THE CHAPELLE DE ST. HUBERT facing | 164 |
| CYPHER OF ANNE DE BRETAGNE, HÔTEL DE VILLE, AMBOISE . . . . . . | 168 |
| CHÂTEAU DE CHENONCEAUX . . . facing | 178 |
| CHÂTEAU DE CHENONCEAUX (DIAGRAM) . . . | 179 |
| LOCHES . . . . . . . . | 189 |
| LOCHES AND ITS CHURCH . . . . facing | 192 |
| SKETCH PLAN OF LOCHES . . . . . | 198 |
| ST. OURS, LOCHES . . . . . facing | 198 |
| TOURS . . . . . . . facing | 202 |
| ARMS OF THE PRINTERS, *AVOCATS*, AND INN-KEEPERS, TOURS . . . . . . | 205 |
| SCENE IN THE QUARTIER DE LA CATHÉDRALE, TOURS . . . . . . facing | 208 |
| PLESSIS-LES-TOURS IN THE TIME OF LOUIS XI. | 213 |
| ENVIRONS OF TOURS (MAP) . . . . | 219 |
| A VINEYARD OF VOUVRAY . . . . facing | 222 |
| MEDIÆVAL STAIRWAY AND THE CHÂTEAU DE LUYNES . . . . . . facing | 224 |
| RUINS OF CINQ-MARS . . . . . facing | 228 |
| CHÂTEAU DE LANGEAIS . . . . facing | 232 |
| ARMS OF LOUIS XII. AND ANNE DE BRETAGNE . | 237 |
| CHÂTEAU D'AZAY-LE-RIDEAU . . . . facing | 244 |
| CHÂTEAU D'USSÉ . . . . . facing | 248 |
| THE ROOF-TOPS OF CHINON . . . . facing | 252 |
| RABELAIS . . . . . . . . | 255 |
| CHÂTEAU DE CHINON . . . . . facing | 258 |
| CUISINES, FONTEVRAULT . . . . . | 265 |

# List of Illustrations

|  | PAGE |
|---|---|
| CHÂTEAU DE SAUMUR | facing 276 |
| THE PONTS DE CÉ | facing 284 |
| CHÂTEAU D'ANGERS | facing 288 |
| ENVIRONS OF NANTES (MAP) | 297 |
| DONJON OF THE CHÂTEAU DE CLISSON | facing 306 |
| BERRY (MAP) | 313 |
| LA TOUR, SANCERRE | 317 |
| CHÂTEAU DE GIEN | facing 318 |
| CHATEAU DE VALENÇAY | facing 322 |
| GATEWAY OF MEHUN-SUR-YEVRE | facing 324 |
| LE CARRIOR DORÉ, ROMORANTIN | 325 |
| ÉGLISE S. AIGNAN, COSNE | 331 |
| POUILLY-SUR-LOIRE | facing 332 |
| PORTE DU CROUX, NEVERS | facing 334 |

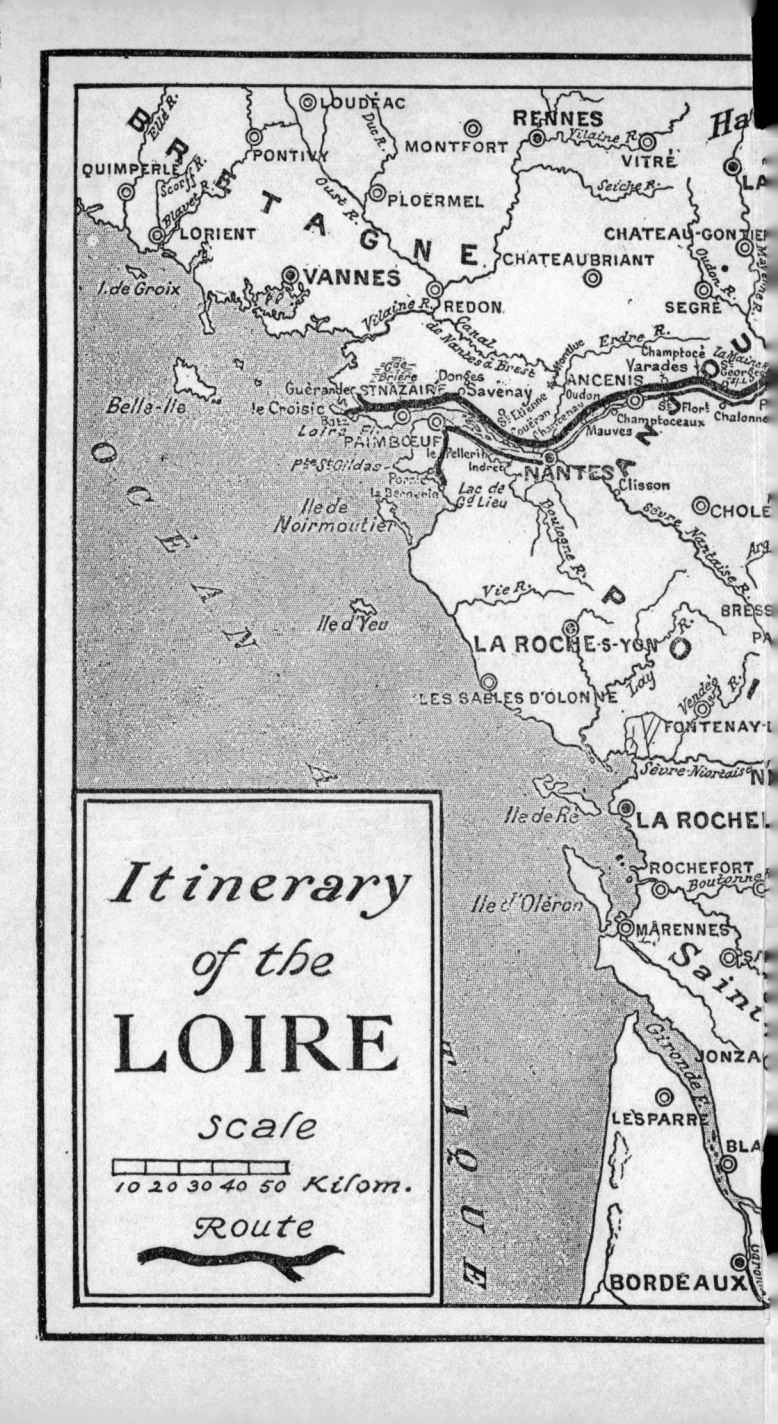

*Itinerary of the* **LOIRE**

*scale*

10 20 30 40 50 *Kilom.*

*Route*

# Castles and Chateaux of Old Touraine

## and the Loire Country

## CHAPTER I.

**A GENERAL SURVEY**

ANY account of the Loire and of the towns along its banks must naturally have for its chief mention Touraine and the long line of splendid feudal and Renaissance châteaux which reflect themselves so gloriously in its current.

The Loire possesses a certain fascination and charm which many other more commercially great rivers entirely lack, and, while the element of absolute novelty cannot perforce be claimed for it, it has the merit of appealing largely to the lover of the romantic and the picturesque.

A French writer of a hundred years ago dedicated his work on Touraine to "Le Baron de Langeais, le Vicomte de Beaumont, le Marquis de Beauregard, le Comte de Fontenailles, le Comte de Jouffroy-Gonsans, le Duc de Luynes, le Comte de Vouvray, le Comte de Villeneuve, *et als.;*" and he might have continued with a directory of all the descendants of the *noblesse* of an earlier age, for he afterward grouped them under the general category of "*Propriétaires des fortresses et châteaux les plus remarquables — au point de vue historique ou architectural.*"

He was fortunate in being able, as he said, to have had access to their "*papiers de famille,*" their souvenirs, and to have been able to interrogate them in person.

Most of his facts and his gossip concerning the personalities of the later generations of those who inhabited these magnificent establishments have come down to us through later writers, and it is fortunate that this should be the case, since the present-day aspect of the châteaux is ever changing, and one who views them to-day is chagrined when he discovers, for instance, that an iron-trussed, red-tiled wash-house has been built on the banks of the Cosson before the magnificent château of

Chambord, and that somewhere within the confines of the old castle at Loches a shopkeeper has hung out his shingle, announcing a newly discovered dungeon in his own basement, accidentally come upon when digging a well.

Balzac, Rabelais, and Descartes are the leading literary celebrities of Tours, and Balzac's "Le Lys dans la Vallée" will give one a more delightful insight into the old life of the Tourangeaux than whole series of guide-books and shelves of dry histories.

Blois and its counts, Tours and its bishops, and Amboise and its kings, to say nothing of Fontevrault, redolent of memories of the Plantagenets, Nantes and its famous "Edict," and its equally infamous "Revocation," have left vivid impress upon all students of French history. Others will perhaps remember Nantes for Dumas's brilliant descriptions of the outcome of the Breton conspiracy.

All of us have a natural desire to know more of historic ground, and whether we make a start by entering the valley of the Loire at the luxurious midway city of Tours, and follow the river first to the sea and then to the source, or make the journey from source to mouth, or vice versa, it does not matter in the least. We traverse the same ground and we meet the same varying conditions as we advance a hundred kilometres in either direction.

Tours, for example, stands for all that is typical of the sunny south. Prune and palm trees thrust themselves forward in strong contrast to the cider-apples of the lower Seine. Below Tours one is almost at the coast, and the *tables d'hôte* are abundantly supplied with sea-food of all sorts. Above Tours the Orléannais is typical of a certain well-to-do, matter-of-fact existence, neither very luxurious nor very difficult.

Nevers is another step and resembles somewhat the opulence of Burgundy as to conditions of life, though the general aspect of the city, as well as a great part of its history, is Italian through and through.

The last great step begins at Le Puy, in the great volcanic *Massif Centrale,* where conditions of life, if prosperous, are at least harder than elsewhere.

Such are the varying characteristics of the towns and cities through which the Loire flows. They run the whole gamut from gay to earnest and solemn; from the ease and comfort of the country around Tours, almost sub-tropical in its softness, to the grime and smoke of busy

*A Lace-maker of the Upper Loire*

St. Etienne, and the chilliness and rigours of a mountain winter at Le Puy.

These districts are all very full of memories of events which have helped to build up the solidarity of France of to-day, though the Nantois still proudly proclaims himself a Breton, and the Tourangeau will tell you that his is the tongue, above all others, which speaks the purest French, — and so on through the whole category, each and every citizen of a *petit pays* living up to his traditions to the fullest extent possible.

In no other journey in France, of a similar length, will one see as many varying contrasts in conditions of life as he will along the length of the Loire, the broad, shallow river which St. Martin, Charles Martel, and Louis XI., the typical figures of church, arms, and state, came to know so well.

Du Bellay, a poet of the Renaissance, has sung the praises of the Loire in a manner unapproached by any other topographical poet, if one may so call him, for that is what he really was in this particular instance.

There is a great deal of patriotism in it all, too, and certainly no sweet singer of the present day has even approached these lines, which are eulogistic without being fulsome and fervent without being lurid.

The verses have frequently been rendered into English, but the following is as good as any, and better than most translations, though it is one of those fragments of " newspaper verse " whose authors are lost in obscurity.

> "Mightier to me the house my fathers made,
>   Than your audacious heads, O Halls of Rome !
> More than immortal marbles undecayed,
>   The thin sad slates that cover up my home;
> More than your Tiber is my Loire to me,
>   More Palatine my little Lyré there;
> And more than all the winds of all the sea,
>   The quiet kindness of the Angevin air."

In history the Loire valley is rich indeed, from the days of the ancient Counts of Touraine to those of Mazarin, who held forth at Nevers. Touraine has well been called the heart of the old French monarchy.

Provincial France has a charm never known to Paris-dwellers. Balzac and Flaubert were provincials, and Dumas was a city-dweller, — and there lies the difference between them.

Balzac has written most charmingly of Touraine in many of his books, in " Le Lys dans la Vallée " and " Le Curé de Tours " in particular; not always in complimentary terms, either, for he has said that the Tourangeaux will not even inconvenience themselves to go in search of pleasure. This does not bespeak indolence so much as philosophy, so most of us will not cavil. George Sand's country lies a little to the southward of Touraine, and Berry, too, as the authoress herself has said, has a climate " *souple et chaud, avec pluie abondant et courte.*"

The architectural remains in the Loire valley are exceedingly rich and varied. The feudal system is illustrated at its best in the great walled château at Angers, the still inhabited and less grand château at Langeais, the ruins at Cinq-Mars, and the very scanty remains of Plessis-les-Tours.

The ecclesiastical remains are quite as great. The churches are, many of them, of the first rank, and the great cathedrals at Nantes, Angers, Tours, and Orleans are magnificent examples of the church-builders' art in the middle ages, and are entitled to rank among the great cathedrals, if not actually of the first class.

With modern civic and other public buildings, the case is not far different. Tours has a gorgeous Hôtel de Ville, its architecture being of the most luxuriant of modern French

Renaissance, while the railway stations, even, at both Tours and Orleans, are models of what railway stations should be, and in addition are decoratively beautiful in their appointments and arrangements, — which most railway stations are not.

Altogether, throughout the Loire valley there is an air of prosperity which in a more vigorous climate is often lacking. This in spite of the alleged tendency in what is commonly known as a relaxing climate toward *laisser-aller*.

Finally, the picturesque landscape of the Loire is something quite different from the harder, grayer outlines of the north. All is of the south, warm and ruddy, and the wooded banks not only refine the crudities of a flat shore-line, but form a screen or barrier to the flowering charms of the examples of Renaissance architecture which, in Touraine, at least, are as thick as leaves in Vallambrosa.

Starting at Gien, the valley of the Loire begins to offer those monumental châteaux which have made its fame as the land of castles. From the old fortress-château of Gien to the Château de Clisson, or the Logis de la Duchesse Anne at Nantes, is one long succession of florid masterpieces, not to be equalled elsewhere.

The true château region of Touraine — by which most people usually comprehend the Loire châteaux — commences only at Blois. Here the edifices, to a great extent, take on these superfine residential attributes which were the glory of the Renaissance period of French architecture.

Both above and below Touraine, at Mont-

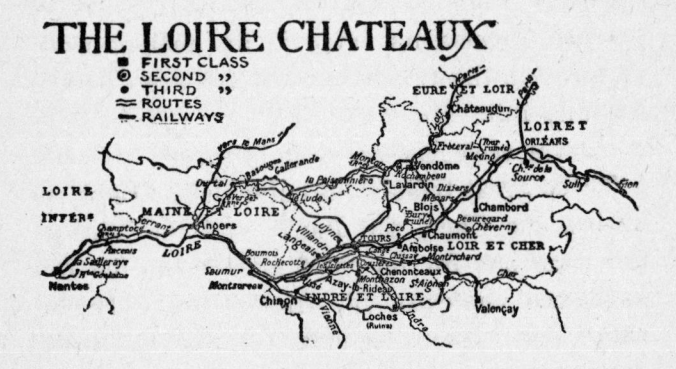

richard, at Loches, and Beaugency, are still to be found scattering examples of feudal fortresses and donjons which are as representative of their class as are the best Norman structures of the same era, the great fortresses of Arques, Falaise, Domfront, and Les Andelys being usually accounted as the types which gave the stimulus to similar edifices elsewhere.

In this same versatile region also, beginning

perhaps with the Orléannais, are a vast number of religious monuments equally celebrated. For instance, the church of St. Benoit-sur-Loire is one of the most important Romanesque churches in all France, and the cathedral of St. Gatien, with its "bejewelled façade," at Tours, the twin-spired St. Maurice at Angers, and even the pompous, and not very good Gothic, edifice at Orleans (especially noteworthy because its crypt is an ancient work anterior to the Capetian dynasty) are all wonderfully interesting and imposing examples of mediæval ecclesiastical architecture.

Three great tributaries enter the Loire below Tours, the Cher, the Indre, and the Vienne. The first has for its chief attractions the Renaissance châteaux St. Aignan and Chenonceaux, the Roman remains of Chabris, Thézée, and Larçay, the Romanesque churches of Selles and St. Aignan, and the feudal donjon of Montrichard. The Indre possesses the château of Azay-le-Rideau and the sombre fortresses of Montbazon and Loches; while the Vienne depends for its chief interest upon the galaxy of fortress-châteaux at Chinon.

The Loire is a mighty river and is navigable for nearly nine hundred kilometres of its length, almost to Le Puy, or, to be exact, to

# A General Survey

the little town of Vorey in the Department of the Haute Loire.

At Orleans, Blois, or Tours one hardly realizes this, much less at Nevers. The river appears to be a great, tranquil, docile stream, with scarce enough water in its bed to make a respectable current, leaving its beds and bars of *sable* and *cailloux* bare to the sky.

The scarcity of water, except at occasional flood, is the principal and obvious reason for the absence of water-borne traffic, even though a paternal ministerial department of the government calls the river navigable.

At the times of the *grandes crues* there are four metres or more registered on the big scale at the Pont d'Ancenis, while at other times it falls to less than a metre, and when it does there is a mere rivulet of water which trickles through the broad river-bottom at Chaumont, or Blois, or Orleans. Below Ancenis navigation is not so difficult, but the current is more strong.

From Blois to Angers, on the right bank, extends a long dike which carries the roadway beside the river for a couple of hundred kilometres. This is one of the charms of travel by the Loire. The only thing usually seen on the bosom of the river, save an occasional fishing punt, is one of those great flat-bottomed ferry-boats, with a square sail hung on a yard amidships, such as Turner always made an accompaniment to his Loire pictures, for conditions of traffic on the river have not greatly changed.

Whenever one sees a barge or a boat worthy of classification with those one finds on the rivers of the east or north, or on the great canals, it is only about a quarter of the usual size; so, in spite of its great navigable length, the waterway of the Loire is to be considered more as a picturesque and healthful element of the landscape than as a commercial proposition.

Where the great canals join the river at Orleans, and from Chatillon to Roanne, the traffic increases, though more is carried by the canal-boats on the *Canal Lateral* than by the barges on the Loire.

It is only on the Loire between Angers and Nantes that there is any semblance of river traffic such as one sees on most of the other great waterways of Europe. There is a considerable traffic, too, which descends the Maine, particularly from Angers downward, for Angers with its Italian skies is usually thought of, and really is to be considered, as a Loire

town, though it is actually on the banks of the
Maine some miles from the Loire itself.

One thousand or more bateaux make the ascent to Angers from the Loire at La Pointe
each year, all laden with a miscellaneous cargo
of merchandise. The Sarthe and the Loir also
bring a notable agricultural traffic to the
greater Loire, and the smaller confluents, the
Dive, the Thouet, the Authion, and the Layon,
all go to swell the parent stream until, when
it reaches Nantes, the Loire has at last taken
on something of the aspect of a well-ordered
and useful stream, characteristics which above
Nantes are painfully lacking. Because of its
lack of commerce the Loire is in a certain way
the most noble, magnificent, and aristocratic
river of France; and so, too, it is also in respect to its associations of the past.

It has not the grandeur of the Rhône when
the spring freshets from the Jura and the
Swiss lakes have filled it to its banks; it has
not the burning activity of the Seine as it bears
its thousands of boat-loads of produce and
merchandise to and from the Paris market;
it has not the prettiness of the Thames, nor
the legendary aspect of the Rhine; but in a
way it combines something of the features of
all, and has, in addition, a tone that is all its

own, as it sweeps along through its countless miles of ample curves, and holds within its embrace all that is best of mediæval and Renaissance France, the period which built up the later monarchy and, who shall not say, the present prosperous republic.

Throughout most of the river's course, one sees, stretching to the horizon, row upon row of staked vineyards with fruit and leaves in luxuriant abundance and of all rainbow colours. The peasant here, the worker in the vineyards, is a picturesque element. He is not particularly brilliant in colouring, but he is usually joyous, and he invariably lives in a well-kept and brilliantly environed habitation and has an air of content and prosperity amid the well-beloved treasures of his household.

The Loire is essentially a river of other days. Truly, as Mr. James has said, " It is the very model of a generous, beneficent stream . . . a wide river which you may follow by a wide road is excellent company."

The Frenchman himself is more flowery: *" C'est la plus noble rivière de France. Son domaine est immense et magnifique."*

The Loire is the longest river in France, and the only one of the four great rivers whose basin or watershed lies wholly within French

# A General Survey

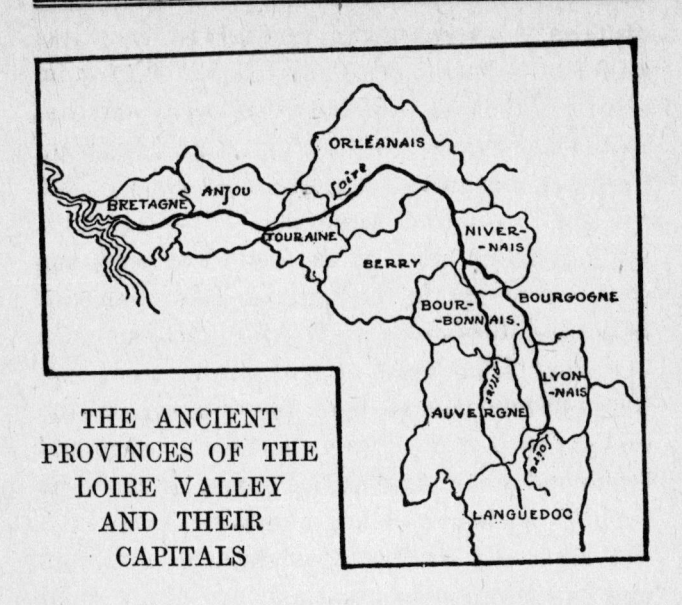

THE ANCIENT
PROVINCES OF THE
LOIRE VALLEY
AND THEIR
CAPITALS

| | |
|---|---|
| Bretagne | Rennes |
| Anjou | Angers |
| Touraine | Tours |
| Orléannais | Orleans |
| Berry | Bourges |
| Nivernais | Nevers |
| Bourbonnais | Moulins |
| Lyonnais | Lyon |
| Bourgogne | Dijon |
| Auvergne | Clermont-Ferrand |
| Languedoc | Toulouse |

territory. It moreover traverses eleven provinces. It rises in a fissure of granite rock at the foot of the Gerbier-de-Jonc, a volcanic cone in the mountains of the Vivarais, a hundred kilometres or more south of Lyons. In three kilometres, approximately two miles, the little torrent drops a thousand feet, after receiving to its arms a tiny affluent coming from the Croix de Monteuse.

For twelve kilometres the river twists and turns around the base of the Vivarais mountains, and finally enters a gorge between the rocks, and mingles with the waters of the little Lac d'Issarles, entering for the first time a flat lowland plain like that through which its course mostly runs.

The monument-crowned pinnacles of Le Puy and the inverted bowl of Puy-de-Dôme rise high above the plain and point the way to Roanne, where such activity as does actually take place upon the Loire begins.

Navigation, classed officially as "*flottable,*" merely, has already begun at Vorey, just below Le Puy, but the traffic is insignificant.

Meantime the streams coming from the direction of St. Etienne and Lyons have been added to the Loire, but they do not much increase its bulk. St. Galmier, the *source* dear to patrons of *tables d'hôte* on account of its palatable mineral water, which is about the only decent drinking-water one can buy at a reasonable price, lies but a short distance away to the right.

At St. Rambert the plain of Forez is entered, and here the stream is enriched by numberless rivulets which make their way from various sources through a thickly wooded country.

From Roanne onward, the *Canal Lateral* keeps company with the Loire to Chatillon, not far from Orleans.

Before reaching Nevers, the *Canal du Nivernais* branches off to the left and joins the Loire with the Yonne at Auxerre. Daudet tells of the life of the *Canal du Nivernais,* in "La Belle Nivernaise," in a manner too convincingly graphic for any one else to attempt the task, in fiction or out of it. Like the Tartarin books, "La Belle Nivernaise" is distinctly local, and forms of itself an excellent guide to a little known and little visited region.

At Nevers the topography changes, or rather, the characteristics of the life of the country round about change, for the topography, so far as its profile is concerned, remains much the same for three-fourths the length of this great river. Nevers, La Charité,

Sancerre, Gien, and Cosne follow in quick succession, all reminders of a historic past as vivid as it was varied.

From the heights of Sancerre one sees a wonderful history-making panorama before him. Cæsar crossed the Loire at Gien, the Franks forded the river at La Charité, when they first went against Aquitaine, and Charles the Bald came sadly to grief on a certain occasion at Pouilly.

It is here that the Loire rises to its greatest flood, and hundreds of times, so history tells, from 490 to 1866, the fickle river has caused a devastation so great and terrible that the memory of it is not yet dead.

This hardly seems possible of this usually tranquil stream, and there have always been scoffers.

Madame de Sévigné wrote in 1675 to M. de Coulanges (but in her case perhaps it was mere well-wishing), "*La belle Loire, elle est un peu sujette à se déborder, mais elle en est plus douce.*"

Ancient writers were wont to consider the inundations of the Loire as a punishment from Heaven, and even in later times the superstition — if it was a superstition — still remained.

In 1825, when thousands of charcoal-burners

*The Loire near La Charité*

(*charbonniers*) were all but ruined, they petitioned the government for assistance. The official who had the matter in charge, and whose name — fortunately for his fame — does not appear to have been recorded, replied simply that the flood was a periodical condition of affairs which the Almighty brought about as occasion demanded, with good cause, and for this reason he refused all assistance.

Important public works have done much to prevent repetitions of these inundations, but the danger still exists, and always, in a wet season, there are those dwellers along the river's banks who fear the rising flood as they would the plague.

Chatillon, with its towers; Gien, a busy hive of industry, though with a historic past; Sully; and St. Benoit-sur-Loire, with its unique double transepted church; all pass in rapid review, and one enters the ancient capital of the Orléannais quite ready for the new chapter which, in colouring, is to be so different from that devoted to the upper valley.

From Orleans, south, one passes through a veritable wonderland of fascinating charms. Châteaux, monasteries, and great civic and ecclesiastical monuments pass quickly in turn.

Then comes Touraine which all love, the

river meantime having grown no more swift or ample, nor any more sluggish or attenuated. It is simply the same characteristic flow which one has known before.

The landscape only is changing, while the fruits and flowers, and the trees and foliage are more luxuriant, and the great châteaux are more numerous, splendid, and imposing.

Of his well-beloved Touraine, Balzac wrote: "Do not ask me *why* I love Touraine; I love it not merely as one loves the cradle of his birth, nor as one loves an oasis in a desert, but as an artist loves his art."

Blois, with its bloody memories; Chaumont, splendid and retired; Chambord, magnificent, pompous, and bare; Amboise, with its great tower high above the river, follow in turn till the Loire makes its regal entrée into Tours. "What a spectacle it is," wrote Sterne in "Tristram Shandy," "for a traveller who journeys through Touraine at the time of the vintage."

And then comes the final step which brings the traveller to where the limpid waters of the Loire mingle with the salty ocean, and what a triumphant meeting it is!

Most of the cities of the Loire possess but one bridge, but Tours has three, and, as be-

*Coiffes of Amboise and Orleans*

comes a great provincial capital, sits enthroned
upon the river-bank in mighty splendour.

The feudal towers of the Château de Luynes
are almost opposite, and Cinq-Mars, with its
pagan " *pile* " and the ruins of its feudal castle
high upon a hill, points the way down-stream
like a mariner's beacon. Langeais follows, and
the Indre, the Cher, and the Vienne, all ample
and historic rivers, go to swell the flood which
passes under the bridges of Saumur, Ancenis,
and Ponts de Cé.

From Tours to the ocean, the Loire comes to
its greatest amplitude, though even then, in
spite of its breadth, it is, for the greater part
of the year, impotent as to the functions of a
great river.

Below Angers the Loire receives its first
great affluent coming from the country lying
back of the right bank: the Maine itself is a
considerable river. It rises far up in the
Breton peninsula, and before it empties itself
into the Loire, it has been aggrandized by
three great tributaries, the Loir, the Sarthe,
and the Mayenne.

Here in this backwater of the Loire, as
one might call it, is as wonderful a collection of
natural beauties and historical châteaux as on
the Loire itself. Châteaudun, Mayenne, and

Vendôme are historic ground of superlative interest, and the great castle at Châteaudun is as magnificent in its way as any of the monuments of the Loire. Vendôme has a Hôtel de Ville which is an admirable relic of a feudal edifice, and the *clocher* of its church, which dominates many square leagues of country, is counted as one of the most perfectly disposed church spires in existence, as lovely, almost, as Texier's masterwork at Chartres, or the needle-like *flêches* at Strasburg or Freiburg in Breisgau.

The Maine joins the Loire just below Angers, at a little village significantly called La Pointe. Below La Pointe are St. Georges-sur-Loire, and three *châteaux de commerce* which give their names to the three principal Angevin vineyards: Château Serrand, l'Epinay, and Chevigné.

Vineyard after vineyard, and château after château follow rapidly, until one reaches the Ponts de Cé with their *petite ville*, — all very delightful. Not so the bridge at Ancenis, where the flow of water is marked daily on a huge black and white scale. The bridge is quite the ugliest wire-rope affair to be seen on the Loire, and one is only too glad to leave it behind, though it is with a real regret that he parts from Ancenis itself.

Some years ago one could go from Angers to St. Nazaire by boat. It must have been a magnificent trip, extraordinarily calm and serene, amid an abundance of picturesque details; old châteaux and bridges in strong contrast to the prairies of Touraine and the Orléannais. One embarked at the foot of the stupendously towered château of King René, and for a *petite heure* navigated the Maine in the midst of great *chalands,* fussy little *remorqueurs* and *barques* until La Pointe was reached, when the Loire was followed to Nantes and St. Nazaire.

To-day this fine trip is denied one, the boats going only so far as La Pointe.

Below Angers the Loire flows around and about a veritable archipelago of islands and islets, cultivated with all the luxuriance of a back-yard garden, and dotted with tiny hamlets of folk who are supremely happy and content with their lot.

Some currents which run behind the islands are swift flowing and impetuous, while others are practically elongated lakes, as dead as those *lômes* which in certain places flank the Saône and the Rhône.

All these various branches are united as the Loire flows between the piers of the ungainly bridge of the Chemin-de-fer de Niort as it crosses the river at Chalonnes.

Champtocé and Montjean follow, each with an individuality all its own. Here the commerce takes on an increased activity, thanks to the great national waterway known as the "Canal de Brest à Nantes." Here at the busy port of Montjean — which the Angevins still spell and pronounce *Montéjean* — the Loire takes on a breadth and grandeur similar to the great rivers in the western part of America. Montjean is dominated by a fine ogival church, with a battery of arcs-boutants which are a joy in themselves.

On the other bank, lying back of a great plain, which stretches away from the river itself, is Champtocé, pleasantly situated on the flank of a hill and dominated by the ruins of a thirteenth-century château which belonged to the cruel Gilles de Retz, somewhat apocryphally known to history as "Barbe-bleu" — not the Bluebeard of the nursery tale, who was of Eastern origin, but a sort of Occidental successor who was equally cruel and bloodthirsty in his attitude toward his whilom wives.

From this point on one comes within the

sphere of influence of Nantes, and there is more or less of a suburban traffic on the railway, and the plodders cityward by road are more numerous than the mere vagabonds of the countryside.

The peasant women whom one meets wear a curious bonnet, set on the head well to the fore, with wings at the side folded back quite like the pictures that one sees of the mediæval dames of these parts, a survival indeed of the middle ages.

The Loire becomes more and more animated and occasionally there is a great tow of boats like those that one sees continually passing on the lower Seine. Here the course of the Loire takes on a singular aspect. It is filled with long flat islands, sometimes in archipelagos, but often only a great flat prairie surrounded by a tranquil canal, wide and deep, and with little resemblance to the mistress Loire of a hundred or two kilometres up-stream. All these isles are in a high state of cultivation, though wholly worked with the hoe and the spade, both of them of a primitiveness that might have come down from Bible times; rare it is to see a horse or a harrow on these "bouquets of verdure surrounded by waves."

Near Oudon is one of those monumental

follies which one comes across now and then in most foreign countries: a great edifice which serves no useful purpose, and which, were it not for certain redeeming features, would be a sorry thing indeed. The "Folie-Siffait," a citadel which perches itself high upon the summit of a hill, was — and is — an *amusette* built by a public-spirited man of Nantes in order that his workmen might have something to do in a time of a scarcity of work. It is a bizarre, incredible thing, but the motive which inspired its erection was most worthy, and the roadway running beneath, piercing its foundation walls, gives a theatrical effect which, in a way, makes it the picturesque rival of many a more famous Rhine castle.

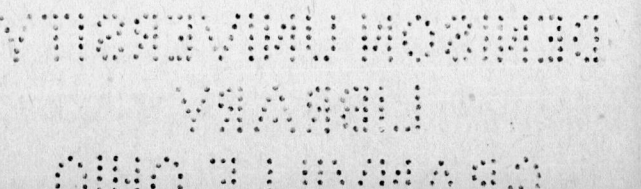

The river valley widens out here at Oudon, practically the frontier of Bretagne and Anjou. The railroad pierces the rock walls of the river with numerous tunnels along the right bank, and the Vendean country stretches far to the southward in long rolling hills quite unlike any of the characteristics of other parts of the valley. Finally, the vast plain of Mauves comes into sight, beautifully coloured with a white and iron-stained rocky background which is startlingly picturesque in its way, if not wholly beautiful according to the majority of standards.

Next comes what a Frenchman has called a "tumultuous vision of Nantes." To-day the very ancient and historic city which grew up from the Portus Namnetum and the Condivicnum of the Romans is indeed a veritable tumult of chimneys, masts, and locomotives. But all this will not detract one jot from its reputation of being one of the most delightful of provincial capitals, and the smoke and activity of its port only tend to accentuate a note of colour that in the whole itinerary of the Loire has been but pale.

Below Nantes the Loire estuary has turned the surrounding country into a little Holland, where fisherfolk and their boats, with sails of red and blue, form charming symphonies of pale colour. In the *cabarets* along its shores there is a strange medley of peasants, seafarers, and fisher men and women. Not so cosmopolitan a crew as one sees in the harbourside *cabarets* at Marseilles, or even Le Havre, but sufficiently strange to be a fascination to one who has just come down from the headwaters.

The "Section Maritime," from Nantes to the sea, is a matter of some sixty kilometres.

Here the boats increase in number and size. They are known as *gabares, chalands,* and *alléges,* and go down with the river-current and return on the incoming ebb, for here the river is tidal.

Gray and green is the aspect at the Loire's source, and green and gray it still is, though of a decidedly different colour-value, at St. Nazaire, below Nantes, the real deep-water port of the Loire.

By this time the river has amplified into a broad estuary which is lost in the incoming and outgoing tides of the Bay of Biscay.

For nearly a thousand kilometres the Loire has wound its way gently and broadly through rocky escarpments, fertile plains, populous and luxurious towns, — all of it historic ground, — by stately châteaux and through vineyards and fruit orchards, with a placid grandeur.

Now it becomes more or less prosaic and matter-of-fact, though in a way no less interesting, as it takes on some of the attributes of the outside world.

This outline, then, approximates somewhat a portrait of the Loire. It is the result of many pilgrimages enthusiastically undertaken; a long contemplation of the charms of perhaps the most beautiful river in France, from its source to its mouth, at all seasons of the year.

The riches and curios of the cities along its banks have been contemplated with pleasure, intermingled with a memory of many stirring scenes of the past, but it is its châteaux that make it famous.

The story of the châteaux has been told before in hundreds of volumes, but only a personal view of them will bring home to one the manners and customs of one of the most luxurious periods of life in the France of other days.

# CHAPTER II.

### THE ORLÉANNAIS

Of the many travelled English and Americans who go to Paris, how few visit the Loire valley with its glorious array of mediæval and Renaissance châteaux. No part of France, except Paris, is so accessible, and none is so comfortably travelled, whether by road or by rail.

At Orleans one is at the very gateway of this splendid, bountiful region, the lower valley of the Loire. Here the river first takes on a complexion which previously it had lacked, for it is only when the Loire becomes the boundary-line between the north and the south that one comes to realize its full importance.

The Orléannais, like many another province of mid-France, is a region where plenty awaits rich and poor alike. Not wholly given over to agriculture, nor yet wholly to manufacturing, it is without that restless activity of the frankly industrial centres of the north. In spite of this, though, the Orléannais is not idle.

Orleans is the obvious *pointe de départ* for all the wonderland of the Renaissance which is to follow, but itself and its immediate surroundings have not the importance for the visitor, in spite of the vivid historical chapters which have been written here in the past, that many another less famous city possesses. By this is meant that the existing monuments of history are by no means as numerous or splendid here as one might suppose. Not that they are entirely lacking, but rather that they are of a different species altogether from that array of magnificently planned châteaux which line the banks of the Loire below.

To one coming from the north the entrance to the Orléannais will be emphatically marked. It is the first experience of an atmosphere which, if not characteristically or climatically of the south, is at least reminiscent thereof, with a luminosity which the provinces of old France farther north entirely lack.

As Lavedan, the Académicien, says: "Here all focuses itself into one great picture, the combined romance of an epoch. Have you not been struck with a land where the clouds, the atmosphere, the odour of the soil, and the breezes from afar, all comport, one with another, in true and just proportions?" This is the Orléannais, a land where was witnessed the morning of the Valois, the full noon of Louis XIV., and the twilight of Louis XVI.

The Orléannais formed a distinct part of mediæval France, as it did, ages before, of western Gaul. Of all the provinces through which the Loire flows, the Orléannais is as prolific as any of great names and greater events, and its historical monuments, if not so splendid as those in Touraine, are no less rare.

Orleans itself contains many remarkable Gothic and Renaissance constructions, and not far away is the ancient church of the old abbey of Notre Dame de Cléry, one of the most historic and celebrated shrines in the time of the superstitious Louis XI.; while innumerable mediæval villes and ruined fortresses plentifully besprinkle the province.

One characteristic possessed by the Orléannais differentiates it from the other outlying provinces of the old monarchy. The people and the manners and customs of this great and important duchy were allied, in nearly all things, with the interests and events of the capital itself, and so there was always a lack of individuality, which even to-day is noticeably apparent in the Orleans capital. The shops, hotels, cafés, and the people themselves might well be one of the *quartiers* of Paris, so like are they in general aspect.

The notable Parisian character of the inhabitants of Orleans, and the resemblance of the people of the surrounding country to those of the Ile of France, is due principally to the fact that the Orléannais was never so isolated as many others of the ancient provinces. It was virtually a neighbour of the capital, and its relations with it were intimate and numerous. Moreover, it was favoured by a great number of lines of communication by road and by water, so that its manners and customs became, more or less unconsciously, interpolations.

The great event of the year in Orleans is the Fête de Jeanne d'Arc, which takes place in the month of May. Usually few English and American visitors are present, though why it is hard to reason out, for it takes place at quite the most delightful season in the year. Perhaps it is because Anglo-Saxons are ashamed of the part played by their ancestors in the shocking death of the maid of Domremy and Orleans. Innumerable are the relics and reminders of the " Maid " scattered throughout the town, and the local booksellers have likewise innumerable and authoritative accounts of the various episodes of her life, which saves the necessity of making further mention here.

There are several statues of Jeanne d'Arc in the city, and they have given rise to the following account written by Jules Lemaitre, the Académicien:

"I believe that the history of Jeanne d'Arc was the first that was ever told to me (before even the fairy-tales of Perrault). The 'Mort de Jeanne d'Arc,' of Casimir Delavigne, was the first fable that I learned, and the equestrian statue of the 'Maid,' in the Place Martroi, at Orleans, is perhaps the oldest vision that my memory guards.

"This statue of Jeanne d'Arc is absurd. She has a Grecian profile, and a charger which is not a war-horse but a race-horse. Nevertheless to me it was noble and imposing.

"In the courtyard of the Hôtel de Ville is a *petite pucelle,* very gentle and pious, who holds against her heart her sword, after the manner of a crucifix. At the end of the bridge across the Loire is another Jeanne d'Arc, as the maid of war, surrounded by swirling draperies, as in a picture of Juvenet's. This to me tells the whole story of the reverence with which the martyred ' Maid ' is regarded in the city of Orleans by the Loire."

One can appreciate all this, and to the full, for a Frenchman is a stern critic of art, even that of his own countrymen, and Jeanne d'Arc, along with some other celebrities, is one of those historical figures which have seldom had justice done them in sculptured or pictorial representations. The best, perhaps, is the precocious Lepage's fine painting, now in America. What would not the French give for the return of this work of art?

The Orléannais, with the Ile de France, formed the particular domain of the third race of French monarchs. From 1364 to 1498 the province was an appanage known as the Duché d'Orleans, but it was united with the Crown by Louis XII., and finally divided into the Departments of Loir et Cher, Eure et Loir, and Loiret.

Like the "pardons" and "benedictions" of Finistère and other parts of Bretagne, the peasants of the Loiret have a quaint custom which bespeaks a long handed-down superstition. On the first Sunday of Lent they hie themselves to the fields with lighted **fagots** and chanting the following lines:

> "Sortez, sortez d'ici mulots!
> Où je vais vous brûler les crocs!
> Quittez, quittez ces blés;
> Allez, vous trouverez
> Dans la cave du curé
> Plus à boire qu' à manger.

Just how far the curé endorses these sentiments, the author of this book does not know. The explanation of the rather extraordinary proceeding came from one of the participants, who, having played his part in the ceremony, dictated the above lines over sundry *petits verres* paid for by the writer. The day is not wound up, however, with an orgy of eating and drinking, as is sometimes the case in far-western Brittany. The peasant of the Loiret simply eats rather heavily of "*mi*," which is nothing more or less than oatmeal porridge, after which he goes to bed.

The Loire rolls down through the Orléannais, from Châteauneuf-sur-Loire and Jargeau, and cuts the banks of *sable,* and the very shores themselves, into little capes and bays which are delightful in their eccentricity. Here cuts in the *Canal d'Orleans,* which makes possible the little traffic that goes on between the Seine and the Loire.

A few kilometres away from the right bank of the Loire, in the heart of the Gatanais, is

Lorris, the home of Guillaume de Lorris, the first author of the "Roman de la Rose." For this reason alone it should become a literary shrine of the very first rank, though, in spite of its claim, no one ever heard of a literary pilgrim making his way there.

Lorris is simply a big, overgrown French market-town, which is delightful enough in its somnolence, but which lacks most of the attributes which tourists in general seem to demand.

At Lorris a most momentous treaty was signed, known as the "Paix de Lorris," wherein was assured to the posterity of St. Louis the heritage of the Comte de Toulouse, another of those periodical territorial aggrandizements which ultimately welded the French nation into the whole that it is to-day.

From the juncture of the *Canal d'Orleans* with the Loire one sees shining in the brilliant sunlight the roof-tops of Orleans, the Aurelianum of the Romans, its hybrid cathedral overtopping all else. It was Victor Hugo who said of this cathedral: "This odious church, which from afar holds so much of promise, and which near by has none," and Hugo undoubtedly spoke the truth.

Orleans is an old city and a *cité neuve*. Where the river laps its quays, it is old but

commonplace; back from the river is a strata
which is really old, fine Gothic house-fronts
and old leaning walls; while still farther from
the river, as one approaches the railway station, it is strictly modern, with all the devices
and appliances of the newest of the new.

The Orleans of history lies riverwards, —
the Orleans where the heart of France pulsed
itself again into life in the tragic days which
were glorified by " the Maid."

" The countryside of the Orléannais has the
monotony of a desert," said an English traveller some generations ago. He was wrong.
To do him justice, however, or to do his ob-
servations justice, he meant, probably, that,
save the river-bottom of the Loire, the great
plain which begins with La Beauce and ends
with the Sologne has a comparatively uninter-
esting topography. This is true; but it is not a
desert. La Beauce is the best grain-growing
region in all France, and the Sologne is now a
reclaimed land whose sandy soil has proved
admirably adapted to an unusually abundant
growth of the vine. So much for this old-time
point of view, which to-day has changed considerably.

The Orléannais is one of the most populous
and progressive sections of all France, and its

inhabitants, per square kilometre, are constantly increasing in numbers, which is more than can be said of every *département*. There are multitudes of tiny villages, and one is

### ENVIRONS of ORLEANS

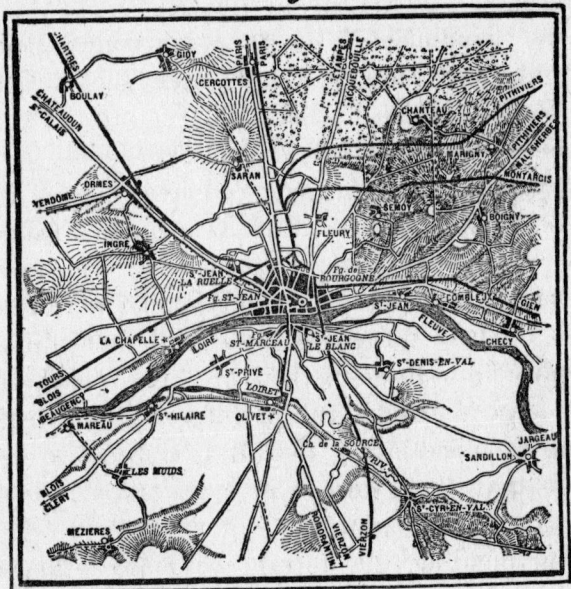

scarcely ever out of sight and sound of a habitation.

In the great forest, just to the west of Orleans, are two small villages, each a celebrated battle-ground, and a place of a patriotic pilgrimage on the eighth and ninth of November of each year. They are Coulmiers and Bacon, and here some fugitives from Metz and Sedan, with some young troops exposed to fire for the first time, engaged with the Prussians (in 1870) who had occupied Orleans since mid-October. There is the usual conventional "soldiers' monument," — with considerably more art about it than is usually seen in America, — before which Frenchmen seemingly never cease to worship.

This same *Forêt d'Orleans*, one of those wild-woods which so plentifully besprinkle France, has a sad and doleful memory in the traditions of the druidical inhabitants of a former day. Their practices here did not differ greatly from those of their brethren elsewhere, but local history is full of references to atrocities so bloodthirsty that it is difficult to believe that they were ever perpetrated under the guise of religion.

Surrounding the forest are many villages and hamlets, war-stricken all in the dark days of seventy-one, when the Prussians were overrunning the land.

Of all the cities of the Loire, Orleans, Blois, Tours, Angers, and Nantes alone show any spirit of modern progressiveness or of likeness to the capital. The rest, to all appearances, are dead, or at least sleeping in their pasts. But they are charming and restful spots for all that, where in melancholy silence sit the old men, while the younger folk, including the very children, are all at work in the neighbouring vineyards or in the wheat-fields of La Beauce.

Meung-sur-Loire and Beaugency sleep on the river-bank, their proud monuments rising high in the background, — the massive tower of Cæsar and a quartette of church spires. Just below Orleans is the juncture of the Loiret and the Loire at St. Mesmin, while only a few kilometres away is Cléry, famed for its associations of Louis XI.

The Loiret is not a very ample river, and is classed by the Minister of Public Works as navigable for but four kilometres of its length. This, better than anything else, should define its relative importance among the great waterways of France. Navigation, as it is known elsewhere, is practically non-existent.

The course of the Loiret is perhaps twelve kilometres all told, but it has given its name to a great French *département,* though it is doubtless the shortest of all the rivers of France thus honoured.

It first comes to light in the dainty park of

the Château de la Source, where there are two distinct sources. The first forms a small circular basin, known as the "Bouillon," which leads into another semicircular basin called the "Bassin du Miroir," from the fact that it reflects the façade of the château in its placid surface. Of course, this is all very artificial and theatrical, but it is a pretty conceit nevertheless. The other source, known as the "Grande Source," joins the rivulet some hundreds of yards below the "Bassin du Miroir."

The Château de la Source is a seventeenth-century edifice, of no great architectural beauty in itself, but sufficiently sylvan in its surroundings to give it rank as one of the notable places of pilgrimage for tourists who, said a cynical French writer, "take the châteaux of the Loire *tour à tour* as they do the morgue, the Moulin Rouge, and the sewers of Paris."

In the early days the château belonged to the Cardinal Briçonnet, and it was here that Bolingbroke, after having been stripped of his titles in England, went into retirement in 1720. In 1722 he received Voltaire, who read him his "Henriade."

In 1815 the invading Prince Eckmühl, with his staff, installed himself in the château, when, after Waterloo, the Prussian and French ar-

*The Loiret*

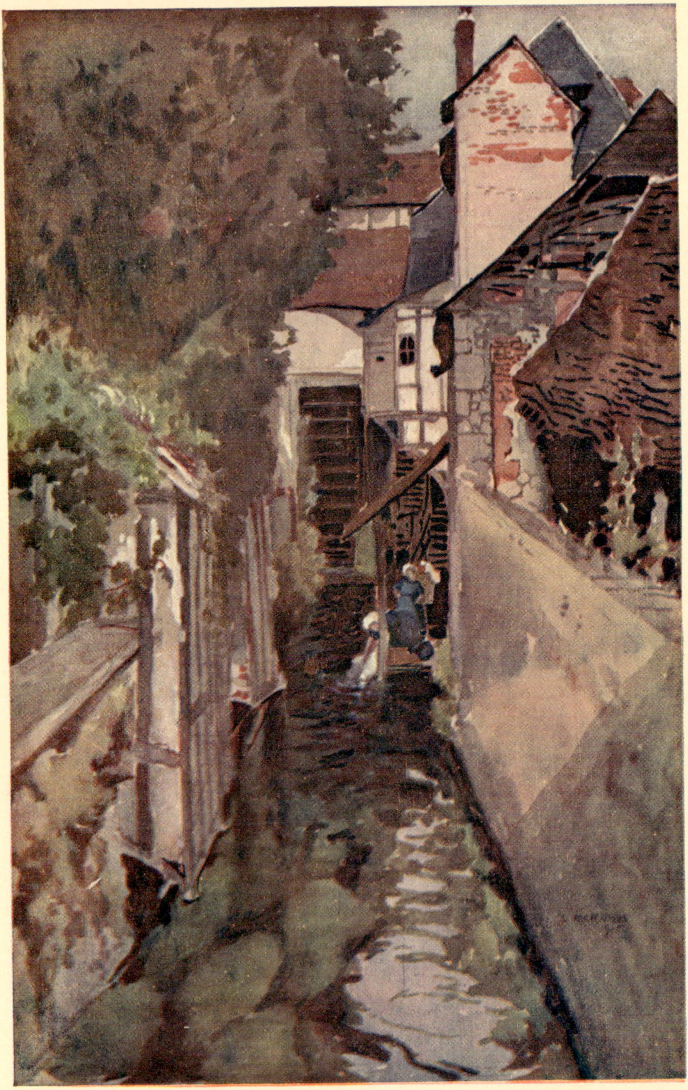

mies were separated only by a barrier placed midway on the bridge at Orleans. It was here also that the Prussian army was disbanded, on the agreement of the council held at Angerville, near Orleans.

There are three other châteaux on the borders of the Loiret, which are of more than ordinary interest, so far as great country houses and their surroundings go, though their histories are not very striking, with perhaps the exception of the Château de la Fontaine, which has a remarkable garden, laid out by Lenôtre, the designer of the parks at Versailles.

Leaving Orleans by the right bank of the Loire, one first comes to La Chapelle-St. Mesmin. La Chapelle has a church dating from the eleventh century and a château which is to-day the *maison de campagne* of the Bishop of Orleans. On the opposite bank was the Abbaye de Micy, founded by Clovis at the time of his conversion. A stone cross, only, marks the site to-day.

St. Ay follows next, and is usually set down in the guide-books as " celebrated for good wines." This is not to be denied for a moment, and it is curious to note that the city bears the same name as the famous town in the champagne district, celebrated also for good wine, though of a different kind. The name of the Orléannais Ay is gained from a hermitage founded here by a holy man, who died in the sixth century. His tomb was discovered in 1860, under the choir of the church, which makes it a place of pilgrimage of no little local importance.

At Meung-sur-Loire one should cross the river to Cléry, five kilometres off, seldom if ever visited by casual travellers. But why? Simply because it is overlooked in that universal haste shown by most travellers — who are not students of art or architecture, or deep lovers of history — in making their way to more popular shrines. One will not regret the time taken to visit Cléry, which shared with Our Lady of Embrun the devotions of Louis XI.

Cléry's three thousand pastoral inhabitants of to-day would never give it distinction, and it is only the Maison de Louis XI. and the Basilique de Notre Dame which makes it worth while, but this is enough.

In " Quentin Durward " one reads of the time when the superstitious Louis was held in captivity by the Burgundian, Charles the Bold, and of how the French king made his devotions before the little image, worn in his hat, of the

Virgin of Cléry; "the grossness of his superstition, none the less than his fickleness, leading him to believe Our Lady of Cléry to be quite a different person from the other object of his devotion, the Madonna of Embrun, a tiny mountain village in southwestern France.

"'Sweet Lady of Cléry,' he exclaimed, clasping his hands and beating his breast as he spoke, 'Blessed Mother of Mercy! thou who art omnipotent with omnipotence, have compassion with me, a sinner! It is true I have sometimes neglected you for thy blessed sister of Embrun; but I am a king, my power is great, my wealth boundless; and were it otherwise, I would double my *gabelle* on my subjects rather than not pay my debts to you both.'"

Louis endowed the church at Cléry, and the edifice was built in the fine flamboyant style of the period, just previous to his death, which De Commines gives as "*le samedy pénultième jour d'Aoust, l'an mil quatre cens quatre-vingtz et trois, à huit heures du soir.*"

Louis XI. was buried here, and the chief "sight" is of course his tomb, beside which is a flagstone which covers the heart of Charles VIII. The Chapelle St. Jacques, within the church, is ornamented by a series of charming sculptures, and the Chapelle des

Dunois-Longueville holds the remains of the famous ally of Jeanne d'Arc and members of his family.

In the choir is the massive oaken statue of Our Lady of Cléry (thirteenth century); the very one before which Louis made his vows. There is some old glass in the choir and a series of sculptured stalls, which would make famous a more visited and better known shrine. There is a fine sculptured stone portal to the sacristy, and within there are some magnificent old *armoires,* and also two chasubles, which saw service in some great church, perhaps here, in the times of Louis himself.

The "Maison de Louis XI.," near the church, is a house of brick, restored in 1651, and now — or until a very recent date — occupied by a community of nuns. In the Grande Rue is another "Maison de Louis XI.;" at least it has his cipher on the painted ceiling. It is now occupied by the Hôtel de la Belle Image. Those who like to dine and sleep where have also dined and slept royal heads will appreciate putting up at this hostelry.

Meung-sur-Loire was the birthplace of Jehan Clopinel, better known as Jean de Meung, who continued Guillaume de Lorris's "Roman de la Rose," the most famous bit of verse produced

The Loire at Meung

by the *trouvères* of the thirteenth century. The voice of the troubadour was soon after hushed for ever, but that thirteenth-century masterwork — though by two hands and the respective portions unequal in merit — lives for ever as the greatest of its kind. In memory of the author, Meung has its Rue Jehan de Meung, for want of a more effective or appealing monument.

Dumas opens the history of "Les Trois Mousquétaires" with the following brilliantly romantic lines anent Meung: "*Le premier lundi du mois d'Avril, 1625, le bourg de Meung, où naquit l'auteur du 'Roman de la Rose.'*" (One of the authors, he should have said, but here is where Dumas nodded, as he frequently did.)

Continuing, one reads: "The town was in a veritable uproar. It was as if the Huguenots were up in arms and the drama of a second Rochelle was being enacted." Really the description is too brilliant and entrancing to be repeated here, and if any one has forgotten his Dumas to the extent that he has forgotten D'Artagnan's introduction to the hostelry of the "Franc Meunier," he is respectfully referred back to that perennially delightful romance.

Meung was once a Roman fortress, known as Maudunum, and in the eleventh century St. Liphard founded a monastery here.

In the fifteenth century Meung was the prison of François Villon. Poor vagabond as he was then, it has become the fashion to laud both the personality and the poesy of Maître François Villon.

By the orders of Thibaut d'Aussigny, Bishop of Orleans, Villon was confined in a strong tower attached to the side of the *clocher* of the parish church of St. Liphard, and which adjoined the *château de plaisance* belonging to the bishop. Primarily this imprisonment was due to a robbery in which the poet had been concerned at Orleans. He spent the whole of the summer in this dungeon, which was overrun with rats, and into which he had to be lowered by ropes. As his food consisted of bread and water only, his sufferings at this time were probably greater than at any other period in his life. Here the burglar-poet remained until October, 1461, when Louis XI. visited Meung, and, to mark the occasion, ordered the release of all prisoners. For this delivery, Villon, according to the accounts of his life, appears to have been genuinely grateful to the king.

At Beaugency, seven kilometres from Meung,

one comes upon an architectural and historical treat which is unexpected.

In the eleventh century Beaugency was a fief of the bishopric of Amiens, and its once strong château was occupied by the Barons de Landry, the last of whom died, without children, in the thirteenth century. Philippe-le-Bel bought the fief and united it with the Comté de Blois. It was made an independent *comté* of itself in 1569, and in 1663 became definitely an appanage of Orleans. The Prince de Galles took Beaugency in 1359, the Gascons in 1361, Duguesclin in 1370 and again in 1417; in 1421 and in 1428 it was taken by the English, from whom it was delivered by Jeanne d'Arc in 1429. Internal wars and warfares continued for another hundred and fifty years, finally culminating in one of the grossest scenes which had been enacted within its walls, — the bloody revenge against the Protestants, encouraged doubtless by the affair of St. Bartholomew's night at Paris.

The ancient square donjon of the eleventh century, known as the Tour de César, still looms high above the town. It must be one of the hugest keeps in all France. The old château of the Dunois is now a charitable institution, but reflects, in a way, the splendour of its fourteenth-century inception, and its Salle de Jeanne d'Arc, with its great chimneypiece, is worthy to rank with the best of its kind along the Loire. The spiral staircase, of which the Loire builders were so fond, is admirable here, and dates from 1530.

The Hôtel de Ville of Beaugency is a charming edifice of the very best of Renaissance, which many more pretentious structures of the period are not. It dates from 1526, and was entirely restored — not, however, to its detriment, as frequently happens — in the last years of the nineteenth century. Its charm, nevertheless, lies mostly in its exterior, for little remains of value within except a remarkable series of old embroideries taken from the choir of the old abbey of Beaugency.

The Église de Notre Dame is a Romanesque structure with Gothic interpolations. It is not bad in its way, but decidedly is not remarkable as mediæval churches go.

The old streets of Beaugency contain a dazzling array of old houses in wood and stone, and in the Rue des Templiers is a rare example of Romanesque civil architecture; at least the type is rare enough in the Orléannais, though more frequently seen in the south of France. The Tour St. Firmin dates from 1530, and is all that remains of a church which stood

*Beaugency*

## The Orléannais 51

here up to revolutionary times. The square ruined towers known as the Porte Tavers are relics of the city's old walls and gates, and are all that are left to mark the ancient enclosure.

The Tour du Diable and the house of the ruling abbot remain to suggest the power and magnificence of the great abbey which was built here in the tenth century. In 1567 it was burned, and later restored, but beyond the two features just mentioned there is nothing to indicate its former uses, the remaining structures having passed into private hands and being devoted to secular uses.

The old bridge which crosses the Loire at this point is most curious, and dates from various epochs. It is 440 metres in length, and is composed of twenty-six arches, one of which dates from the fourteenth century, when bridge-building was really an art. Eight of the present-day arches are of wood, and on the second is a monolith surmounted by a figure of Christ in bronze, replacing a former chapel to St. Jacques. A chapel on a bridge is not a unique arrangement, but few exist to-day, one of the most famous being, perhaps, that on the ruined bridge of St. Bénezet at Avignon.

Altogether, Beaugency, as it sleeps its life away after the strenuous days of the middle ages, is more lovable by far than a great metropolis.

The traveller is well repaid who makes a stop at Beaugency a part of a three days' gentle ramble among the usually neglected towns and villages of the Orléannais and the Blaisois, instead of rushing through to Blois by express-train, which is what one usually does.

Southward one's route lies through pleasant vineyards, on one side the Sologne, and on the other the Coteau de Guignes, which latter ranks as quite the best among the vine-growing districts of the Orléannais.

Near Tavers is a natural curiosity in the shape of the "Fontaine des Sables Mouvants," where the sands of a tiny spring boil and bubble like a miniature geyser.

Mer, another small town, follows, twelve kilometres farther on. Like Beaugency it is a somnolent bourg, and the life of the peasant folk round about, who go to market on one day at Beaugency and on another at Blois, and occasionally as far away as Orleans, is much the same as it was a century ago.

There is a Boulevard de la Gare and a Grande Rue at Mer, the latter leading to a fine Gothic church with a fifteenth-century tower, which is admirable in every way, and forms a beacon by land for many miles around. The primitive church at Mer dates from the eleventh century, the side walls, however, being all that remain of that period. There is a sculptured pulpit of the seventeenth century, and a great painting, which looks ancient and is certainly a masterful work of art, representing an "Adoration of the Magi."

When all is said and done, it is its irresistible and inexpressible charm which makes Mer well-beloved, rather than any great wealth of artistic atmosphere of any nature.

Away to the south, across the Loire to Muides, runs the route to Chambord, through the Sologne, where immediately the whole aspect of life changes from that on the borders of the rich grain-lands of the Orléannais and La Beauce.

All the way from Beaugency to Blois the Loire threads its way through a lovely country, whose rolling slopes, back from the river, are surmounted here and there by windmills, a not very frequent adjunct to the landscape of France, except in the north.

Near Mer is Menars, with its eighteenth-century château of La Pompadour; Suèvres, the site of an ancient Roman city; the lowlands lying before Chambord; St. Die; Montlivault;

St. Claude, and a score of little villages which are entrancing in their old-world aspect even in these days of progress. This completes the panorama to Blois which, with the Blaisois, forms the borderland between the Orléannais and Touraine.

Before reaching Blois, Menars, at any rate, commands attention. It fronts upon the Loire, but is practically upon the northern border of the Forêt de Blois, hence properly belongs to the Blaisois. Menars was made a rendezvous for the chase by the wily and pleasure-loving La Pompadour, who quartered herself at the château, which afterward passed to her brother, De Marigny.

Before the Revolution, Menars was the seat of a marquisate, of which the land was bought by Louis XV. for his famous, or infamous, *maîtresse*. The property has frequently changed hands since that day, but its gardens and terraces, descending toward the riverbank, mark it as one of those *coquette* establishments, with which France was dotted in the eighteenth century.

These establishments possessed enough of luxurious appointments to be classed as fitting for the butterflies of the time, but in no way, so far as the architectural design or the artistic details were concerned, were any of them worthy to be classed with the great domestic châteaux of the early years of the Renaissance.

# CHAPTER III.

### THE BLAISOIS AND THE SOLOGNE

The Blésois or Blaisois was the ancient name given to the *petit pays* which made a part of the government of the Orléannais. It was, and is, the borderland between the Orléannais and Touraine, and, with its capital, Blois, the city of counts, was a powerful territory in its own right, in spite of the allegiance which it owed to the Crown. Twenty leagues in length by thirteen in width, it was bounded on the north by the Dunois and the Orléannais, on the east by Berry, on the south by Touraine, and on the west by Touraine and the Vendomois.

Blois, its capital, was famed ever in the annals of the middle ages, and to-day no city in the Loire valley possesses more sentimental interest for the traveller than does Blois.

To the eastward lay the sands of the Sologne, and southward the ample and fruitful Touraine, hence Blois's position was one of supreme importance, and there is no wonder that it proved to be the scene of so many momentous events of history.

The present day Department of the Loir et Cher was carved out from the Blaisois, the Vendomois, and the Orléannais. The Baisois was, in olden time, one of the most important of the *petits gouvernements* of all the kingdom, and gave to Blois a line of counts who rivalled in power and wealth the churchmen of Tours and the dukes of Brittany. Gregory of Tours is the first historian who makes mention of the ancient *Pagus Blensensis*.

One must not tell the citizen of Blois that it is at Tours that one hears the best French spoken. Everybody knows this, but the inhabitant of the Blaisois will not admit it, and, in truth, to the stranger there is not much apparent difference. Throughout this whole region he understands and makes himself understood with much more facility than in any other part of France.

For one thing, not usually recalled, Blois should be revered and glorified. It was the native place of Lenoir, who invented the instrument which made possible the definite determination of the metric system of measurement.

One reads in Bernier's "Histoire de Blois"

that the inhabitants are " honest, gallant, and polite in conversation, and of a delicate and diffident temperament." This was written nearly a century ago, but there is no excuse for one's changing the opinion to-day unless, as was the misfortune of the writer, he runs up against an unusually importunate vender of post-cards or an aggressive *garçon de café*.

Blois, among all the cities of the Loire, is the favourite with the tourist. Why this should be is an enigma. It is overburdened, at times, with droves of tourists, and this in itself is a detraction in the eyes of many.

Perhaps it is because here one first meets a great château of state; and certainly the Château de Blois lives in one's memory more than any other château in France.

Much has been written of Blois, its counts, its château, and its many and famous *hôtels* of the nobility, by writers of all opinions and abilities, from those old chroniclers who wrote

*The Riverside at Blois*

of the plots and intrigues of other days to those critics of art and architecture who have discovered — or think they have discovered — that Da Vinci designed the famous spiral staircase.

From this one may well gather that Blois is the foremost château of all the Loire in popularity and theatrical effect. Truly this is so, but it is by no manner of means the most lovable; indeed, it is the least lovable of all that great galaxy which begins at Blois and ends at Nantes. It is a show-place and not much more, and partakes in every form and feature — as one sees it to-day — of the attributes of a museum, and such it really is. All of its former gorgeousness is still there, and all the banalities of the later period when Gaston of Orleans built his ugly wing, for the " personally conducted " to marvel at, and honeymoon couples to envy. The French are quite fond of visiting this shrine themselves, but usually it is the young people and their mammas, and detached couples of American and English birth that one most sees strolling about the courts and apartments were formerly lords and ladies and cavaliers moved and plotted.

The great château of the Counts of Blois is built upon an inclined rock which rises above the roof-tops of the lower town quite in fairy-book fashion, —

> ". . . Bâtie en pierre et d'ardoise couverte,
>    Blanche et carrée au bas de la colline verte."

Commonly referred to as the Château de Blois, it is really composed of four separate and distinct foundations; the original château

*Signature of François Premier*

of the counts; the later addition of Louis XII.; the palace of François I., and the most unsympathetically and dismally disposed *pavillon* of Gaston of Orleans.

The artistic qualities of the greater part of the distinct edifices which go to make up the château as it stands to-day are superb, with the exception of that great wing of Gaston's, before mentioned, which is as cold and unfeeling as the overrated palace at Versailles.

The Comtes de Chatillon built that portion just to the right of the present entrance; Louis XII., the edifice through which one enters the inner court and which extends far to the left, including also the chapel immediately to the rear; while François Premier, who here as elsewhere let his unbounded Italian proclivities have full sway, built the extended wing to the left of the inner court and fronting on the present Place du Château, formerly the Place Royale.

Immediately to the left, in the Basse Cour de Château, are the Hôtel d'Amboise, the Hôtel d'Épernon, and farther away, in the Rue St. Honore, the Hôtel Sardini, the Hôtel d'Alluye, and a score of others belonging to the nobility of other days; all of them the scenes of many stirring and gallant events in Renaissance times.

This is hardly the place for a discussion of the merits or demerits of any particular artistic style, but the frequently repeated expression of Buffon's "*Le style, c'est l'homme*" may well be paraphrased into "*L'art, c'est l'époque.*" In fact one finds at all times imprinted upon the architectural style of any period the current mood bred of some historical event or a passing fancy.

At Blois this is particularly noticeable. As an architectural monument the château is a picturesque assemblage of edifices belonging to many different epochs, and, as such, shows, as well as any other document of contemporary times, the varying ambitions and emotions of its builders, from the rude and rough manners of the earliest of feudal times through the

CYPHER OF ANNE D' BRETAGNE. CHÂTEAU DE BLOIS.

highly refined Renaissance details of the imaginative brain of François, down to the base concoction of the elder Mansart, produced at the commands of Gaston of Orleans.

The whole gamut, from the gay and winsome to the sad and dismal, is found here.

The escutcheons of the various occupants are plainly in evidence, — the swan pierced by an arrow of the first Counts of Blois; the ermine of Anne de Bretagne; the porcupine of the Ducs d'Orleans, and the salamander of François Premier.

In the earliest structure were to be seen all the attributes of a feudal fortress, towers and walls pierced with narrow loopholes, and damp, dark dungeons hidden away in the thick walls. Then came a structure which was less of a fortress and more habitable, but still a stronghold, though having ample and decorative doorways and windows, with curious sculptures and rich framings. Then the pompous Renaissance with *escaliers* and *balcons à jour,* balustrades crowning the walls, arabesques enriching the pilasters and walls, and elaborate cornices here, there, and everywhere, — all bespeaking the gallantry and taste of the *roi-chevalier.* Finally came the cold, classic features of the period of the brother of Louis XIII., decidedly the worst and most unlivable and unlovely architecture which France has ever produced. All these features are plain in the general scheme of the Château de Blois to-day, and doubtless it is this that makes the appeal; too much loveliness, as at Chenonceaux or Azay-le-Rideau, staggers the modern mortal by the sheer impossibility of its modern attainment.

In plan the Château de Blois forms an irregular square situated at the apex of a promontory high above the surface of the Loire, and practically behind the town itself. The building has a most picturesque aspect, and, to those who know, gives practically a history of the château architecture of the time. Abandoned, mutilated, and dishonoured from time to time, the structure gradually took on new forms until the thick walls underlying the apartment known to-day as the Salle des États — probably the most ancient portion of all — were overshadowed by the great richness of the fifteenth and sixteenth centuries. One early fragment was entirely enveloped in the structure which was built by François Premier, the ancient Tour de Château Regnault, or De Moulins, or Des Oubliettes, as it was variously known, and from the outside this is no longer visible.

From the platform one sees a magnificent panorama of the city and the far-reaching Loire, which unrolls itself southward and northward for many leagues, its banks covered by rich vineyards and crowned by thick forests.

The building of Louis XII. presents its brick-faced exterior in black and red lozenge shapes, with sculptured window-frames, squarely upon the little tree-bordered *place* of to-day, which in other times formed a part of that magnificent terrace which looked down upon the roof of the Église St. Nicolas, and the Jesuit Church of the Immaculate Conception, and the silvery belt of the Loire itself.

On the west façade of this vast conglomerate

ARMS OF LOUIS XII

structure one sees the effigy of the porcupine, that weird symbol adopted by the family of Orleans.

The choice of this ungainly animal — in spite of which it is most decorative in outline — was due to the first Louis, who was Duc d'Orleans. In the year 1393 Louis founded the order of the porcupine, in honour of the birth of Charles, his eldest son, who was born to him by Valentine de Milan. The legend which accompanied the adoption of the symbol — though often enough it was missing in the sculptured representations — was *Cominus et eminus,* which had its origin in the belief that the porcupine could defend himself in a near attack, but that when he himself attacked, he fought from afar by launching forth his spines.

Naturalists will tell you that the porcupine does no such thing; but in those days it was evidently believed that he did, and in many, if not all, of the sculptured effigies that one sees of the beast there is a halo of detached spines forming a background as if they were really launching themselves forth in mid-air.

Above this central doorway, or entrance to the courtyard, is a niche in which is a modern equestrian statue of Louis XII., replacing a more ancient one destroyed at the Revolution. This old statue, it is claimed, was an admirable work of art in its day, and the present statue is thought to be a replica of it.

It originally bore the following inscription — a verse written by Fausto Andrelini, the king's favourite poet.

*Central Doorway, Château de Blois*

"Hic ubi natus erat dextro Lodoicus Olympo,
　Sumpsit honorata Regia sceptra manu;
Felix quæ tanti fulfit lux nuntia Regis;
　Gallia non alio Principe digna fuit.
FAUSTUS 1498."

According to an old French description this old statue was: "*très beau et très agréable ainsy que tous ses portraits l'ont représenté, comme celui qui est au grand portail de Bloys.*"

Above rises a balustrade with fantastic gargoyles with the pinnacles and fleurons of the window gables all very ornate, the whole topped off with a roofing of slate.

Blois, in its general aspect, is fascinating; but it is not sympathetic, and this is not surprising when one remembers men and women who worked their deeds of bloody daring within its walls.

The murders and other acts of violence and treason which took place here are interesting enough, but one cannot but feel, when he views the chimneypiece before which the Duc de Guise was standing when called to his death in the royal closet, that the men of whom the bloody tales of Blois are told quite deserved their fates.

One comes away with the impression of it

all stamped only upon the mind, not graven upon the heart. Political intrigue to-day, if quite as vulgar, is less sordid. Bigotry and ambition in those days allowed few of the finer feelings to come to the surface, except with regard to the luxuriance of surroundings. Of this last there can be no question, and Blois is as characteristically luxurious as any of the magnificent edifices which lodged the royalty and nobility of other days, throughout the valley of the Loire.

A numismatic curiosity, connected with the history of the Château de Blois, is an ancient piece of money which one may see in the local museum. It is the oldest document in existence in which, or on which, the name of Blois is mentioned. On one side is a symbolical figure and the legend *Bleso Castro,* and on the other a *croix haussée* and the name of the officer of the mint at Blois, *Pre Cistato, monetario.*

The plan of the Château de Blois here given shows it not as it is to-day, but as it was at the death of Gaston d'Orleans in 1660. The constructions of the different epochs are noted on the plan as follows:

ERECTED BY THE COMTES DE CHATILLON

1. Tour de Donjon, Château-Regnault, Moulins, or des Oubliettes.

2. Salle des États.
3. Tour du Foix or Observatory.

### Erected by the Ducs d'Orleans

4. Portico and Galerie d'Orleans. (Destroyed in part by the military.)

5. Galerie des Cerfs. (Built in part by Gaston, but made away with by the city of Blois when the Jardins du Roi were built.)

### Erected by Louis XII.

6. Chapelle St. Calais. (Destroyed in part by the military.)

7. La Grande Vis, or Grand Escalier of Louis XI.

8. La Petite Vis, or Petit Escalier, in one chamber of which the corpse of the Duc de Guise was burned.

9. Portico and Galerie de Louis XII.

10. Portico.

11. Salle des Gardes, — of the queen on the ground floor and of the king on the first floor.

12. Bedchamber, — of the queen on the ground floor and of the king on the first floor.

13. Corps de Garde.

14. Kitchen. (To-day Salle de Réception for visitors.)

### Erected from the Time of Francois I. to Henri III.

15 and 16. Portico and Terrace Henri II. (In part built over by Gaston.)

17. Grand Staircase.

18. Galerie de François I.

19. Staircase of the Salle des États. (Destroyed by the military.)

20. First floor, Salle des Gardes of the queen; second floor, Salle des Gardes of the king.

21. Staircase leading to the apartments of the queen-mother. Here also Henri III. had made the cells destined for

the use of the Capucins, and here were closeted "*pour s'assurer de leur discretion,*" the "*Quarante-Cinq*" who were to kill the Duc de Guise.

22. Cabinet Neuf of Henri III. (Second floor.)

23. Gallery where was held the reunion of the Tiers Etats of 1576.

24. First floor, bedchamber of the king; second floor, bedchamber of the queen.

25. Oratory.

26. Cabinet.

27. Passage to the Tour de Moulins.

28. Passage to the Cabinet Vieux, where the Duc de Guise was struck down.

29. Cabinet Vieux.

30. Oratory, where the two chaplains of the king prayed during the perpetration of the murder.

31. Garde-robe, where was first deposited the body of De Guise.

### Erected by Gaston d'Orleans

32. Peristyle. (Destroyed by the military.)

33. Dome.

34. Pavillon des Jardins.

35. Pavillon du Foix.

36. Petit Pavillon of the Méridionale façade. (Destroyed in 1825.)

37. Terraces.

38. Bastions du Foix and des Jardins.

39. L'Eperon.

40. Le Jardin Haut, or Jardin du Roi.

The interior court is partly surrounded by a colonnade, quite cloister-like in effect. At the right centre of the François I. wing is that wonderful spiral staircase, concerning the in-

The CHATEAUX of BLOIS

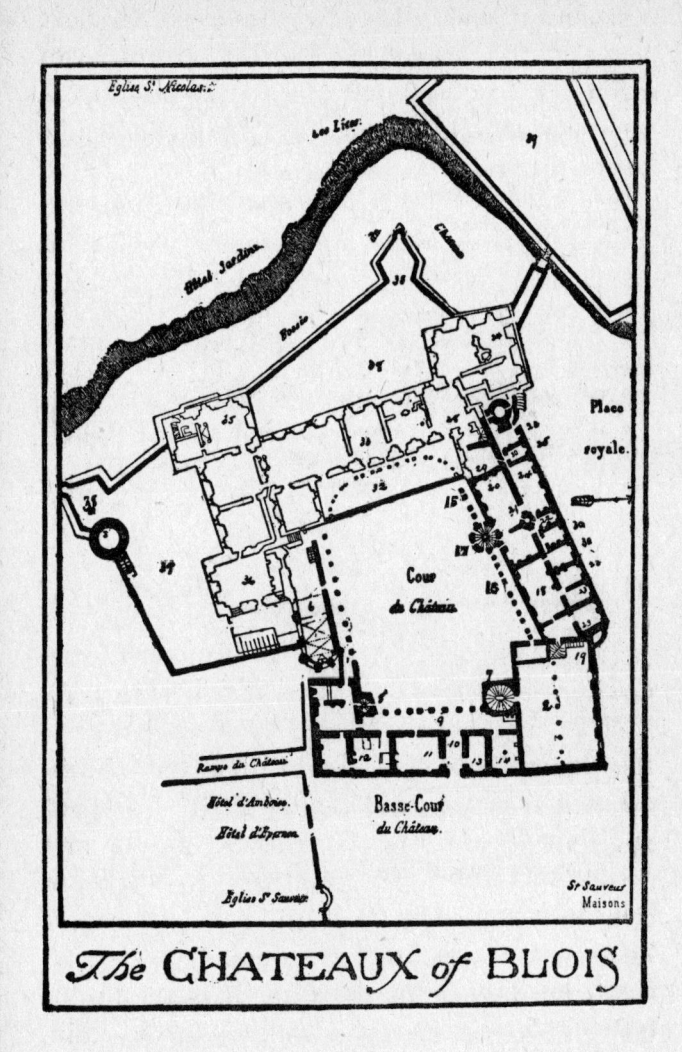

vention of which so much speculation has been launched. Leonardo da Vinci, the protégé of François, has been given the honour, and a very considerable volume has been written to prove the claim.

Within this " *tour octagone* " — " *qui fait à ses huit pans hurler un gorgone* " — is built

*Cypher of François Premier and Claude of France, at Blois*

this marvellous openwork stairway, — an *escalier à jour,* as the French call it, — without an equal in all France, and for daring and decorative effect unexcelled by any of those Renaissance motives of Italy itself. Its ascent turns not, as do most *escaliers,* from left to right, but from right to left. It is the prototype of those supposedly unique outside staircases pointed out to country cousins in the abodes of Fifth Avenue millionaires.

It is as impossible to catalogue the various apartments and their accessories here, as it is to include a chronology of the great events which have passed within their walls. One thing should be remembered, and that is, that the architect Duban restored the château throughout in recent years. In spite of this restoration one may readily enough reconstruct the scene of the murder of the Duc de Guise from the great fireplace on the second floor before which De Guise was standing when summoned by a page to the kingly presence, from the door through which he entered to his death, and from the wall where hung the tapestry behind which he was to pass. All this is real enough, and also the "Tour des Oubliettes," in which the duke's brother, the cardinal, suffered, and of which many horrible tales are still told by the attendants.

Duban, the architect, came with his careful restorations and pictured with a most exact fidelity the decorations and the furnishings of the times of François, of Catherine, and of Henri III. The ornate chimneypieces have been furbished up anew, the walls and ceilings covered with new paint and gold; nothing

could be more opulent or glorious, but it gives
the impression of a city dwelling or a great
hotel, "newly done up," as the house reno-
vators express it.

One contrasting emotion will be awakened
by a contemplation of the two great Salles des
Gardes and the apartments of Catherine de
Medici; here, at least for the moment, is a
relief from the intrigues, massacres, and assas-
sinations which otherwise went on, for one recalls that, at one period, "*danses, ballets et
jeux*" took place here continuously.

In the apartments of Catherine there is much
to remind one of "the base Florentine," as it
has been the fashion of latter-day historians
to describe the first of the Medici queens.
Nothing could be more sumptuous than the
Galerie de la Reine, her *Cabinet de Toilette,*
or her *Chambre à Coucher,* with its secret
panels, where she died on the 5th of January,
1589, "adored and revered," but soon forgotten, and of no more account than "*une
chèvre mort,*" says one old chronicler.

The apartments of Catherine de Medici
were directly beneath the guard-room where
the Balafré was murdered, and that event,
taking place at the very moment when the

"queen-mother" was dying, cannot be said to have been conducive to a peaceful demise.

Here, on the first floor of the François Premier wing, the *reine-mère* held her court, as did the king his. The great gallery overlooked the town on the side of the present Place du Château. It was, and is, a truly grand apartment, with diamond-paned windows, and rich, dark, wall decorations on which Catherine's device, a crowned C and her monogram in gold, frequently appears. There was, moreover, a great oval window, opposite which stood her altar, and a doorway, half concealed, led to her writing-closet, with its secret drawers and wall-panels which well served her purposes of intrigue and deceit. A hidden stairway led to the floor above, and there was a *chambre à coucher*, with a deep recess for the bed, the same to which she called her son Henri as she lay dying, admonishing him to give up the thought of murdering Guise. "What," said Henri, on this embarrassing occasion, "spare Guise, when he, triumphant in Paris, dared lay his hand on the hilt of his sword! Spare him who drove me a fugitive from the capital! Spare them who never spared me! No, mother, I will *not*."

As the queen-mother drew near her end,

and was lying ill at Blois, great events for France were culminating at the château. Henri III. had become King of France, and the Balafré, supported by Rome and Spain, was in open rebellion against the reigning house, and the word had gone forth that the Duc de Guise must die. The States General were to be immediately assembled, and De Guise, once the poetic lover of Marguerite, through his emissaries canvassed all France to ensure the triumph of the party of the Church against Henri de Navarre and his queen, — the Marguerite whom De Guise once professed to love, — who soon were to come to the throne of France.

The uncomfortable Henri III. had been told that he would never be king in reality until De Guise had been made away with.

The final act of the drama between the rival houses of Guise and Valois came when the king and his council came to Blois for the Assembly. The sunny city of Blois was indeed to be the scene of a momentous affair, and a truly sumptuous setting it was, the roof-tops of its houses sloping downward gently to the Loire, with the chief accessory, the coiffed and turreted château itself, high above all else.

Details had been arranged with infinite

pains, the guard doubled, and a company of Swiss posted around the courtyard and up and down the gorgeous staircase. Every nook and corner has its history in connection with this greatest event in the history of the Château of Blois.

As Guise entered the council-chamber he was told that the king would see him in his closet, to reach which one had to pass through the guard-room below. The door was barred behind him that he might not return, when the trusty guards of the "Forty-fifth," under Dalahaide, already hidden behind the wall-tapestry, sprang upon the Balafré and forced him back upon the closed door through which he had just passed. Guise fell stabbed in the breast by Malines, and "lay long uncovered until an old carpet was found in which to wrap his corpse."

Below, in her own apartments, lay the queen-mother, dying, but listening eagerly for the rush of footsteps overhead, hoping and praying that Henri — the hitherto effeminate Henri who played with his sword as he would with a battledore, and who painted himself like a woman, and put rings in his ears — would not prejudice himself at this time in the eyes of

Rome by slaying the leader of the Church party.

Guise died as Henri said he would die, with the words on his lips: "*A moi, mes amis! — trahison! — à moi, Guise, — je me meurs,*" but the revenge of the Church party came when, at St. Cloud, the monk, Jacques Clément, poignarded the last of the Valois, and put the then heretical Henri de Navarre on the throne of France.

Within the southernmost confines of the château is the Tour de Foix, so called for the old faubourg near by. The upper story and roof of this curious round tower was the work of Catherine de Medici, who installed there her astrologer and maker of philtres, Cosmo Ruggieri.

Ruggieri was a most versatile person; he was astrologer, alchemist, and philosopher alike, besides being many other kinds of a rogue, all of which was very useful to the Medici now that she had come to power.

Catherine built an outside stairway up to the platform of this tower, and a great, flat, stone table was placed there to form a foundation for Ruggieri's cabalistic instruments. Even this stone table itself was an uncanny affair, if we are to believe the old chronicles. It rang out in a clear sharp note whenever struck with some hard body, and on its surface was graven a line which led the eye directly toward the golden *fleur-de-lys* on the cupola of Chambord's château, some three leagues distant on the other side of the Loire. What all this symbolism actually meant nobody except Catherine and her astrologer knew; at least, the details do not appear to have come down to enlighten posterity. Over the doorway of the observatory were graven the words, "*Vraniæ Sacrum,*" *i. e.*, consecrated to Uranius.

Wherever Catherine chose to reside, whether in Touraine or at Paris, her astrologer and his "*observatoire*" formed a part of her train. She had brought Cosmo from Italy, and never for a moment did he leave her. He was a sort of a private demon on whom Catherine could shoulder her poisonings and her stabs, and, as before said, he was an exceedingly busy functionary of the court.

That part of the structure built by Mansart for Gaston d'Orleans appears strange, solemn, and superfluous in connection with the sumptuousness of the earlier portions. With what poverty the architectural art of the seventeenth century expressed itself! What an inferiority came with the passing of the six-

teenth century and the advent of the following!
One finds a certain grandeur in the outlines of
this last wing, with its majestic cupola over
the entrance pavilion, but the general effect
of the decorations is one of a great paucity of
invention when compared to the more brilliant
Renaissance forerunners on the opposite side
of the courtyard.

It was under the régime of Gaston d'Orleans
that the gardens of the Château de Blois came
to their greatest excellence and beauty. In
1653 Abel Brunyer, the first physician of Gaston's suite, published a catalogue of the fruits
and flowers to be found here in these gardens,
of which he was also director. More than five
hundred varieties were included, three-quarters of which belonged to the flora of France.

Among the delicacies and novelties of the
time to be found here was the Prunier de Reine
Claude, from which those delicious green plums
known to all the world to-day as "Reine
Claudes" were propagated, also another variety which came from the Prunier de Monsieur,
somewhat similar in taste but of a deep purple
colour. The *pomme de terre* was tenderly
cared for and grown as a great novelty and
delicacy long before its introduction to general
cultivation by Parmentier. The tomato was

imported from Mexico, and even tobacco was grown; from which it may be judged that Gaston did not intend to lack the good things of life.

All these facts are recounted in Brunyer's "Hortus Regius Blesensis," and, in addition, one Morrison, an expatriate Scotch doctor, who had attached himself to Gaston, also wrote a competing work which was published in London in 1669 under the title of "Preludia Botanica," and which dealt at great length with the already celebrated gardens of the Château de Blois.

Morrison placed at the head of his work a Latin verse which came in time to be graven over the gateway of the gardens. This — as well as pretty much all record of it — has disappeared, but a repetition of the lines will serve to show with what admiration this paradise was held:

> "Hinc, nulli biferi miranda rosaria Pesti,
> Nec mala Hesperidum, vigili servata dracone.
> Si paradisiacis quicquam (sine crimine) campis
> Conferri possit, Blaesis mirabile specta.
> Magnifici Gastonis opus! Qui terra capaci . . .
> . . . . . . . . . .
> JACOBUS METELANUS SCOTUS."

Not merely in history has the famous château at Blois played its part. Writers of fiction have more than once used it as an accessory or the principal scenic background of their sword and cloak novels; none more effectively than Dumas in the D'Artagnan series.

The opening lines of " Le Vicomte de Bragelonne " are laid here. " It should have been a source of pride to the city of Blois," says Dumas, " that Gaston of Orleans had chosen it as his residence, and held his court in the ancient château of the States."

Here, too, in the second volume of the D'Artagnan romances, is the scene of that most affecting meeting between his Majesty Charles II., King of England, and Louis XIV.

Altogether one lives here in the very spirit of the pages of Dumas. Not only Blois, but Langeais, Chambord, Cheverny, Amboise, and many other châteaux figure in the novels with an astonishing frequency, and, whatever the critics may say of the author's slips of pen and memory, Dumas has given us a wonderfully faithful picture of the life of the times.

In 1793 all the symbols and emblems of royalty were removed from the château and destroyed. The celebrated bust of Gaston, the chief artistic attribute of that part of the edifice built by him, was decapitated, and the statue of Louis XII. over the entrance gateway was overturned and broken up. Afterward the château became the property of the "domaine" and was turned into a mere barracks. The Pavillon of Queen Anne became a "*magasin des subsistances militaires,* the Tour de l'Observatoire, a powder-magazine, and all the indignities imaginable were heaped upon the château.

In 1814 Blois became the last capital of Napoleon's empire, and the château walls sheltered the prisoners captured by the imperial army.

Blois's most luxurious church edifice was the old abbey church of St. Sauveur, which was built from 1138 to 1210. It lost the royal favour in 1697, when Louis XIV. made Blois a city of bishops as well as of counts, and transferred the chapter of St. Sauveur's to the bastard Gothic edifice first known as St. Solenne, but which soon took on the name of St. Louis. In spite of the claims of the old church, this cold, unfeeling, and ugly mixture of tomblike Renaissance became, and still remains, the bishop's church of Blois.

One must not neglect or forget the magnificent bridge which crosses the Loire at Blois. A work of 1717-24, it bears the Rue Denis Papin across its eleven solidly built masonry piers. Above the central arch is erected a memorial pyramid and tablet which states the fact that it was one of the first works of the reign of Louis XV.

Blois altogether, then, offers a multitudinous array of attractions for the tourist who makes his first entrance to the châteaux country through its doors. The town itself has not the appeal of Tours, of Angers, or of Nantes; but, for all that, its abundance of historic lore, the admirable preservation of its chief monument, and the general picturesqueness of its site and the country round about make up for many other qualities that may be lacking.

The Sologne, lying between Blois, Vierzon, and Châteauneuf-sur-Loire, is a great region of lakelets, sandy soil, and replanted Corsican pines, which to-day has taken on a new lease of life and a prosperity which was unknown in the days when the Comtes de Blois first erected that *maison de plaisance* on its western border which was afterward to aggrandize itself into the later Château de Chambord. The soil has been drained and the vine planted to a hitherto undreamed of extent, until to-day, if the land does not exactly blossom like the rose, it at least somewhat approaches it.

The *chaumières* of the Sologne have disappeared to a large extent, and their mud walls and thatched roofs are not as frequent a detail of the landscape as formerly, but even now there is a distinct individuality awaiting the artist who will go down among these vineyard workers of the Sologne and paint them and their surroundings as other parts have been painted and popularized. It will be hot work in the summer months, and lonesome work at all times, but there is a new note to be sounded if one but has the ear for it, and it is to be heard right here in this tract directly on the beaten track from north to south, and yet so little known.

The peasant of the Sologne formerly ate his *soupe au poireau* and a morsel of *fromage maigre* and was as content and happy as if his were a more luxurious board, as it in reality became when a stranger demanded hospitality. Then out from the *armoire* — that ever present adjunct of a French peasant's home, whether it be in Normandy, Touraine, or the Midi — came a bottle of *vin blanc,* bought in the wine-shops of Romorantin or Vierzon on some of his periodical trips to town.

To-day all is changing, and the peasant of the Sologne nourishes himself better and trims his beard and wears a round white collar on fête-days. He is proud of his well-kept appearance, but his neighbours to the north and the south will tell you that all this hides a deep malice, which is hard to believe, in spite of the well recognized saying, "*Sot comme un Solognat.*" The women have a physiognomy more passive; when young they are fresh and lip-lively, but as they grow older their charms pass quickly.

The Sologne in most respects has changed greatly since the days of Arthur Young. Then this classic land was reviled and vehement imprecations were launched upon the proprietors of its soil, — "those brilliant and ambitious gentlemen who figure so largely in the ceremonies of Versailles. To-day all is changed, and the gentleman farmer is something more than a *bourgeois parisien* who hunts and rides and apes "*le sport*" of the English country squire.

The jack-rabbit and the hare are the pests of the Sologne now that its sandy soil has been conquered, but they are quite successfully kept down in numbers, and the insects which formerly ravaged the vines are likewise less offensive than they used to be, so the Sologne may truly be said to have been transformed.

To-day, as in the days of the royal hunt, when Chambord was but a shooting-box of the

Counts of Blois, the Sologne is rife with small game, and even deer and an occasional *sanglier*.

"*La chasse*" in France is no mean thing to-day, and the Sologne, La Beauce, and the great national forests of Lyons and Rambouillet draw — on the opening of the season, somewhere between the 28th of August and the 2d of September of each year — their hundreds of thousands of Nimrods and disciples of St. Hubert. The bearer of the gun in France is indeed a most ardent sportsman, and in no European country can one buy in the open market a greater variety of small game, — all the product of those who pay their twenty francs for the privilege of bagging rabbits, hares, partridges, and the like. The hunters of France enjoy one superstition, however, and that is that to accidentally bag a crow on the first shot means a certain and sudden death before the day is over.

La Motte-Beuvron is celebrated in the annals of the Sologne; it is, in fact, the metropolis of the region, and the centre from which radiated the influences which conquered the soil and made of it a prosperous land, where formerly it was but a sandy, arid desert. La Motte-Beuvron is a long-drawn-out *bourgade*, like some of the populous centres of the great plain of Hungary, and there is no great prosperity or " up-to-dateness " to be observed, in spite of its constantly increasing importance, for La Motte-Beuvron and the country round about is one of the localities of France which is apparently not falling off in its population.

La Motte has a most imposing Hôtel de Ville, a heavy edifice of brick built by Napoleon III. — who has never been accused of having had the artistic appreciation of his greater ancestor — after the model of the Arsenal at Venice.

This is all La Motte has to warrant remark unless one is led to investigate the successful agricultural experiment which is still being carried out hereabouts. La Motte's hôtels and cafés are but ordinary, and there is no counter attraction of boulevard or park to place the town among those lovable places which travellers occasionally come upon unawares.

To realize the Sologne at its best and in its most changed aspect, one should follow the roadway from La Motte to Blois. He may either go by tramway *à vapeur,* or by his own means of communication. In either case he will then know why the prosperity of the Sologne and the contentment of the Solognat is assured.

Romorantin, still characteristic of the Sologne and its historic capital, is famous for its asparagus and its paternal château of François Premier, where that prince received the scar upon his face, at a tourney, which compelled him ever after to wear a beard.

To-day the Sous-Préfecture, the Courts and their prisoners, the Gendarmerie, and the Theatre are housed under the walls that once

*Native Types in the Sologne*

formed the château royal of Jean d'Angoulême; within whose apartments the gallant François was brought up.

The Sologne, like most of the other of the *petits pays* of France, is prolific in superstitions and traditionary customs, and here for some reason they deal largely of the marriage state. When the *paysan solognais* marries, he takes good care to press the marriage-ring well up to the third joint of his spouse's finger, " else she will be the master of the house," which is about as well as the thing can be expressed in English. It seems a simple precaution, and any one so minded might well do the same under similar circumstances, provided he thinks the proceeding efficacious.

Again, during the marriage ceremony itself, each of the parties most interested bears a lighted wax taper, with the belief that whichever first burns out, so will its bearer die first. It's a gruesome thought, perhaps, but it gives one an inkling of who stands the best chance of inheriting the other's goods, which is what matches are sometimes made for.

The marriage ceremony in the Sologne is a great and very public function. Intimates, friends, acquaintances, and any of the neighbouring populace who may not otherwise be occupied, attend, and eat, drink, and ultimately get merry. But they have a sort of process of each paying his or her own way; at least a collection is taken up to pay for the entertainment, for the Sologne peasant would otherwise start his married life in a state of bankruptcy from which it would take him a long time to recover.

The collection is made with considerable

*éclat* and has all the elements of picturesqueness that one usually associates with the wedding processions that one sees on the comic-opera stage. A sort of nuptial bouquet — a great bunch of field flowers — is handed round from one guest to another, and for a sniff of their fragrance and a participation in the collation which is to come, they make an offering, dropping much or little into a golden (not gold) goblet which is passed around by the bride herself.

In the Sologne there is (or was, for the writer has never seen it) another singular custom of the marriage service — not really a part of the churchly office, but a sort of practical indorsement of the actuality of it all.

The bride and groom are both pricked with a needle until the blood runs, to demonstrate that neither the man nor the woman is insensible or dreaming as to the purport of the ceremony about to take place.

As every French marriage is at the Mairie, as well as being held in church, this double ceremony (and the blood-letting as well) must make a very hard and fast agreement. Perhaps it might be tried elsewhere with advantage.

Montrichard, on the Cher, is on the borderland between the Blaisois and Touraine. Its donjon announces itself from afar as a magnificent feudal ruin. The town is moreover most curious and original, the great rectangular donjon rising high into the sky above a series of cliff-dwellers' chalk-cut homes, in truly weird fashion.

There is nothing so very remarkable about cliff-dwellers in the Loire country, and their aspect, manners, and customs do not differ greatly from those of their neighbours, who live below them.

Curiously enough these rock-cut dwellings appear dry and healthful, and are not in the least insalubrious, though where a *cave* has been devoted only to the storage of wine in vats, barrels, and bottles the case is somewhat different.

Montrichard itself, outside of these scores of homes burrowed out of the cliff, is most picturesque, with stone-pignoned gables and dormer-windows and window-frames cut or worked in wood or stone into a thousand amusing shapes.

Montrichard, with Chinon, takes the lead in interesting old houses in these parts; in fact, they quite rival the ruinous lean-to houses of Rouen and Lisieux in Normandy, which is say-

*Donjon of Montrichard*

ing a good deal for their picturesque qualities.

One-third of Montrichard's population live underground or in houses built up against the hillsides. Even the lovely old parish church backs against the rock.

Everywhere are stairways and *petits chemins* leading upward or downward, with little façades, windows, or doorways coming upon one in most unexpected and mysterious fashion at every turn.

The magnificent donjon is a relic of the work of that great fortress-builder, Foulques Nerra, Comte d'Anjou, who dotted the land wherever he trod with these masterpieces of their kind, most of them great rectangular structures like the donjons of Britain, but quite unlike the structures of their class mostly seen in France.

Richard Cœur de Lion occupied the fortress in 1108, but was obliged to succumb to his rival in power, Philippe-Auguste, who in time made a breach in its walls and captured it. Thereafter it became an outpost of his own, from whence he could menace the Comte d'Anjou.

# CHAPTER IV.

### CHAMBORD

CHAMBORD is four leagues from Blois, from which point it is usually approached. To reach it one crosses the Sologne, not the arid waste it has been pictured, but a desert which has been made to blossom as the rose.

A glance of the eye, given anywhere along the road from Blois to Chambord, will show a vineyard of a thousand, two thousand, or even more acres, where, from out of a soil that was once supposed to be the poorest in all wine-growing France, may be garnered a crop equalling a hundred dozen of bottles of good rich wine to the acre.

This wine of the Sologne is not one of the famous wines of France, to be sure, but what one gets in these parts is pure and astonishingly palatable; moreover, one can drink large potions of it — as do the natives — without being affected in either his head or his pocket-book.

From late September to early December there is a constant harvest going on in the vineyards, whose labourers, if not as picturesque and joyous as we are wont to see them on the comic-opera stage, are at least wonderfully clever and industrious, for they make a good wine crop out of a soil which previously gave a living only to charcoal-burners and goat-keepers.

François was indeed a rare devotee of the building mania when he laid out the wood which surrounds Chambord and which ultimately grew to some splendour. The nineteenth century saw this great wood cut and sold in huge quantities, so that to-day it is rather a scanty copse through which one drives on the way from Blois.

The country round about is by no means impoverished, — far from it. It is simply unworked to its fullest extent as yet. As it is plentifully surrounded by water it makes an ideal land for the growing of asparagus, strawberries, and grapes, and so it has come to be one of the most prosperous and contented regions in all the Loire valley.

The great white Château de Chambord, with its turrets and its magnificent lantern, looms large from whatever direction it is approached, though mostly it is framed by the somewhat stunted pines which make up the pleasant forest. The vistas which one sees when coming toward Chambord, through the drives and alleys of its park, with the château itself brilliant in the distance, are charming and fairy-like indeed. Straight as an arrow these roadways run, and he who traverses one of those centring at the château will see a tiny white fleck in the sunlight a half a dozen kilometres away, which, when it finally is reached, will be admitted to be the greatest triumph of the art-loving monarch.

François Premier was foremost in every artistic expression in France, and the court, as may be expected, were only too eager to follow the expensive tastes of their monarch, — when they could get the means, and when they could not, often enough François supplied the wherewithal.

François himself dressed in the richest of Italian velvets, the more brilliant the better, with a preponderant tendency toward pink and sky blue.

A dozen years after François came to the throne, a dozen years after the pleasant life of Amboise, when mother, daughter, and son lived together on the banks of the Loire in that

"Trinity of love," the monarch and his wife, Queen Claude of France, the daughter of Louis XII. and Anne of Brittany, came to live at Chambord on the edge of the sandy Sologne waste.

Here, too, came Marguerite d'Alençon, the ever faithful and devoted sister of François, the duke, her husband, and all the gay members of the court. The hunt was the order of the day, for the forest tract of the Sologne, scanty though it was in growth, abounded in small game.

Chambord at this time had not risen to the grand and ornate proportions which we see to-day, but set snugly on the low, swampy banks of the tiny river Cosson, a dull, gloomy mediæval fortress, whose only aspect of gaiety was that brought by the pleasure-loving court when it assembled there. In size it was ample to accommodate the court, but François's artistic temperament already anticipated many and great changes. The Loire was to be turned from its course and the future pompous palace was to have its feet bathed in the limpid Loire water rather than in the stagnant pools of the morass which then surrounded it.

As a triumph of the royal château-builder's art, Chambord is far and away ahead of Fontainebleau or Versailles, both of which were built in a reign which ended two hundred years later than that which began with the erection of Chambord. As an example of the arts of François I. and his time compared with those of Louis XIV. and his, Chambord stands forth with glorious significance.

On the low banks of the Cosson, François achieved perhaps the greatest triumph that Renaissance architecture had yet known.

It was either Chambord, or the reconstruction by François of the edifice belonging to the Counts of Blois, which resulted in the refinement of the Renaissance style less than a quarter of a century after its introduction into France by Charles VIII., — if he really was responsible for its importation from Italy. François lacked nothing of daring, and built and embellished a structure which to-day, in spite of numerous shortcomings, stands as the supreme type of a great Renaissance domestic edifice of state. Every device of decoration and erratic suggestion seems to have been carried out, not only structurally, as in the great double spiral of its central stairway, but in its interpolated details and symbolism as well.

It was at this time, too, that François began to introduce the famous salamander into his devices and ciphers; that most significant emblem which one may yet see on wall and ceiling of Chambord surrounded by the motto: "*Je me nourris et je meurs dans le feu.*"

Chambord, first of all, gives one a very high opinion of François Premier, and of the splendours with which he was wont to surround himself. The apartments are large and numer-

*Arms of François Premier, at Chambord*

ous and are admirably planned and decorated, though, almost without exception, bare to-day of furniture or furnishings.

To quote the opinion of Blondel, the celebrated French architect: "The Château de Chambord, built under François I. and Henri II., from the designs of Primatice, was never achieved according to the original plan. Louis XIII. and Louis XIV. contributed a certain completeness, but the work was really pursued afterward according to the notions of one Sertio."

The masterpiece of its constructive elements is its wonderful doubly spiralled central staircase, which permits one to ascend or descend without passing another proceeding in the opposite direction at the same time. Whatever may have been the real significance of this great double spiral, it has been said that it played its not unimportant part in the intrigue and scandal of the time. It certainly is a wonder of its kind, more marvellous even than that spiral at Blois, attributed, with some doubt perhaps, to Leonardo da Vinci, and certainly far more beautiful than the clumsy round tower up which horses and carriages were once driven at Amboise.

At all events, it probably meant something more than mere constructive ability, and a staircase which allows one individual to mount and another to descend without knowing of the presence of the other may assuredly be classed with those other mediæval accessories, sliding panels, hidden doorways, and secret cabinets.

Beneath the dome which terminates the staircase in the Orleans wing are three caryatides representing — it is doubtfully stated — François Premier, La Duchesse d'Étampes, and Madame la Comtesse de Châteaubriand, — a trinity of boon companions in intrigue.

In reality Chambord presents the curiously contrived arrangement of one edifice within another, as a glance of the eye at the plan will show.

The fosse, the usual attribute of a great mediæval château — it may be a dry one or a wet one, in this case it was a wet one — has disappeared, though Brantôme writes that he saw great iron rings let into the walls to which were attached "*barques et grands bateaux,*" which had made their way from the Loire via the dribbling Cosson.

The Cosson still dribbles its life away to-day, its moisture having, to a great part, gone to irrigate the sandy Sologne, but formerly it was doubtless a much more ample stream.

From the park the ornate gables and dormer-windows loom high above the green-swarded banks of the Cosson. It was so in François's time, and it is so to-day; nothing has been added to break the spread of lawn, except an iron-framed wash-house with red tiles and a sheet-iron chimney-pot beside the little river, and a tin-roofed garage for automobiles connected with the little inn outside the gates.

The rest is as it was of yore, at least, the same as the old engravings of a couple of hundreds of years ago picture it, hence it is a great shame, since the needs of the tiny village could not have demanded it, that the foreground could not have been left as it originally was.

The town, or rather village, or even hamlet, of Chambord is about the most abbreviated thing of its kind existent. There is practically no village; there are a score or two of houses, an inn of the frankly tourist kind, which evidently does not cater to the natives, the aforesaid wash-house by the river bank, the dwellings of the gamekeepers, gardeners, and workmen on the estate, and a diminutive church rising above the trees not far away. These accessories practically complete the make-up of the little settlement of Chambord, on the borders of the Blaisois and Touraine.

Chambord has been called top-heavy, but it is hardly that. Probably the effect is caused by its low-lying situation, for, as has been intimated before, this most imposing of all of the Loire châteaux has the least desirable situation of any. There is a certain vagueness and foreignness about the sky-line that is almost

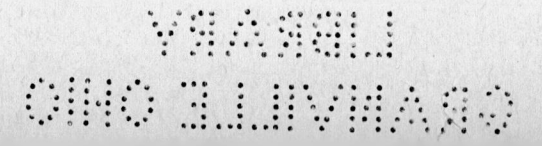

Eastern, though we recognize it as pure Renaissance. Perhaps it is the magnitude and lonesomeness of it all that makes it seem so strange, an effect that is heightened when one steps out upon its roof, with the turrets, towers, and cupolas still rising high above.

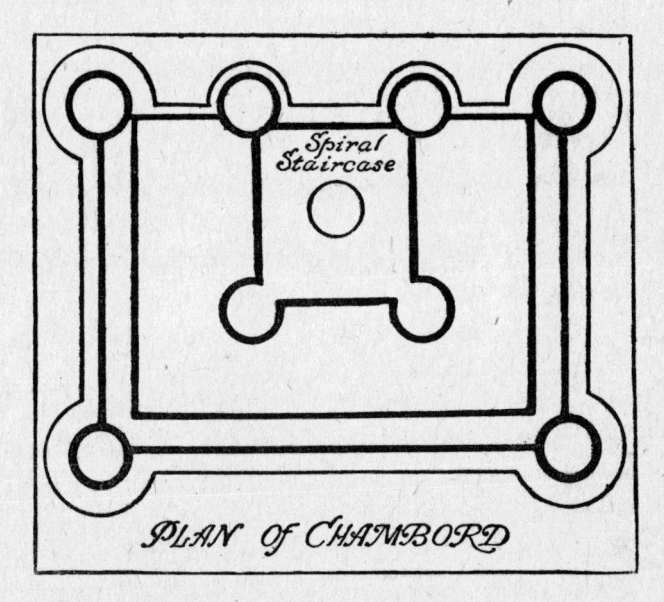

PLAN OF CHAMBORD

The ground-plan is equally magnificent, flanked at every corner by a great round tower, with another quartette of them at the angles of the interior court.

Most of the stonework of the fabric is brilliant and smooth, as if it were put up but yesterday, and, beyond the occasional falling of a tile from the wonderful array of chimney-pots, but little evidences are seen exteriorly of its having decayed in the least. On the tower which flanks the little door where one meets the *concierge* and enters, there are unmistakable marks of bullets and balls, which a revolutionary or some other fury left as mementoes of its passage.

Considering that Chambord was not a product of feudal times, these disfigurements seem out of place; still its peaceful motives could hardly have been expected to have lasted always.

The southern façade is not excelled by the elevation of any residential structure of any age, and its outlines are varied and pleasing enough to satisfy the most critical; if one pardons the little pepper-boxes on the north and south towers, and perforce one has to pardon them when he recalls the magnificence of the general disposition and sky-line of this marvellously imposing château of the Renaissance.

François Premier made Chambord his favourite residence, and in fact endowed Pierre Nepveu — who for this work alone will be considered one of the foremost architects of the

Château de Chambord

French Renaissance — with the inspiration for its erection in 1526.

A prodigious amount of sculpture by Jean Cousin, Pierre Bontemps, Jean Goujon, and Germain Pilon was interpolated above the doorways and windows, in the framing thereof, and above the great fireplaces. Inside and out, above and below, were vast areas to be covered, and François allowed his taste to have full sway.

The presumptuous François made much of this noble residence, perhaps because of his love of *la chasse,* for game abounded hereabouts, or perhaps because of his regard for the Comtesse Thoury, who occupied a neighbouring château.

For some time before his death, François still lingered on at Chambord. Marguerite and her brother, both now considerably aged since the happier times of their childhood in Touraine, always had an indissoluble fondness for Chambord. Marguerite had now become Queen of Navarre, but her beauty had been dimmed with the march of time, and she no longer was able to comfort and amuse her kingly brother as of yore. His old pleasures and topics of conversation irritated him, and he had even tired of poetry, art, and political affairs.

Above all, he shamefully and shamelessly abused women, at once the prop and the undermining influence of his kingly power in days gone by. There is an existing record to the effect that he wrote some "window-pane" verse on the window of his private apartment to the following effect:

> "Souvent femme varie;
> Mal habile quis'y fie!"

If this be not apocryphal, the incident must have taken place long years before that celebrated "window-pane" verse of Shenstone's, and François is proven again a forerunner, as he was in many other things.

Without doubt the Revolution did away with this square of glass, which — according to Piganiol de la Force — existed in the middle of the eighteenth century. Perhaps François's own jealous humour prompted him to write these cynical lines, and then again perhaps it is merely one of those fables which breathe the breath of life in some unaccountable manner, no one having been present at its birth, and hearsay and tradition accounting for it all.

François, truly, was failing, and he and his sister discussed but sorrowful subjects: the death of his favourite son, Charles, the inheritor of the throne, at Abbeville, where he became infected with the plague, and also the death of him whom he called "his old friend," Henry VIII. of England, a monarch whose amours were as numerous and celebrated as his own.

Henri II. preferred the attractions of Anet to Chambord, while Catherine de Medici and Charles IX. cared more for Blois, Chaumont, and Chenonceaux. Louis XIII. and Louis XIV. only considered it as a rendezvous for the chase, and the latter's successor, Louis XV., gave it to the illustrious Maurice de Saxe, the victor of Fontenoy, who spent his old age here, amid fêtes, pleasures, and military parades. Near by are the barracks, built for the accommodation of the regiment of horse formed by the maréchal and devoted to his special guardianship and pleasure, and paid for by the king, who in turn repaid himself — with interest — from the public treasury. The exercising of this "little army" was one of the chief amusements of the illustrious old soldier.

"A de feints combats
Lui-même en se jouant conduit les vieux soldats" —

wrote the Abbé de Lille in contemporary times.

King Stanislas of Poland lived here from

1725 to 1733, and later it was given to Maréchal Berthier, by whose widow it was sold in 1821.

It was bought by national subscription for a million and a half of francs and given to the Duc de Bordeaux, who immediately commenced its restoration, for it had been horribly mutilated by Maréchal de Saxe, and the surrounding wood had been practically denuded under the Berthier occupancy.

The Duc de Bordeaux died in 1883, and his heirs, the Duc de Parme and the Comte de Bardi, are now said to spend a quarter of a million annually in the maintenance of the estate, the income of which approximates only half that sum.

There are thirteen great staircases in the edifice, and a room for every day in the year. On the ground floor is the Salle des Gardes, from which one mounts by the great spiral to another similar apartment with a barrel-vaulted roof, which in a former day was converted into a theatre, where in 1669-70 were held the first representations of " Pourceaugnac " and " Le Bourgeois Gentilhomme," and where Molière himself frequently appeared.

The second floor is know as the " *grandes terrasses* " and surrounds the base of the great central lantern so admired from the exterior. On this floor, to the eastward, were the apartments of François Premier. The chapel was constructed by Henri II., but the tribune is of the era of Louis XIV. This tribune is decorated with a fine tapestry, made by Madame Royale while imprisoned in the Temple. At the base of the altar is also a tapestry made and presented to the Comte de Chambord by the women of the Limousin.

The apartments of Louis XIV. contain portraits of Madame de Maintenon and Madame de Lafayette, a great painting of the "Bataille de Fontenoy," and another of the Comte de Chambord on horseback.

## CHAPTER V.

### CHEVERNY, BEAUREGARD, AND CHAUMONT

From Chambord and its overpowering massiveness one makes his way to Chaumont, on the banks of the Loire below Blois, by easy stages across the plain of the Sologne.

One leaves the precincts of Chambord by the back entrance, as one might call it, through six kilometres of forest road, like that by which one enters, and soon passes the little townlet of Bracieux.

One gets glimpses of more or less modern residential châteaux once and again off the main road, but no remarkably interesting structures of any sort are met with until one reaches Cheverny. Just before Cheverny one passes Cour-Cheverny, with a curious old church and a quaint-looking little inn beside it.

Cheverny itself is, however, the real attraction, two kilometres away. Here the château is opened by its private owners from April to

*Château de Cheverny*

October of each year, and, while not such a grand establishment as many of its contemporaries round about, it is in every way a perfect residential edifice of the seventeenth century, when the flowery and ornate Renaissance had given way to something more severely classical, and, truth to tell, far less pleasing in an artistic sense.

Cheverny belongs to-day to the Marquis de Vibraye, one of those undying titles of the French nobility which thrive even in republican France and uphold the best traditions of the *noblesse* of other days.

The château was built much later than most of the neighbouring châteaux, in 1634, by the Comte de Cheverny, Philippe Hurault. It sits green-swarded in the midst of a beautifully wooded park, and the great avenue which faces the principal entrance extends for seven kilometres, a distance not excelled, if equalled, by any private roadway elsewhere.

In its constructive features the château is more or less of rectangular outlines. The pavilions at each corner have their openings *à la impériale,* with the domes, or lanterns, so customary during the height of the style under Louis XIV. An architect, Boyer by name, who came from Blois, where surely he had the opportunity of having been well acquainted with a more beautiful style, was responsible for the design of the edifice at Cheverny.

The interior decorations in Cordovan leather, the fine chimneypieces, and the many elaborate historical pictures and wall paintings, by Mosnier, Clouet, and Mignard, are all of the best of their period; while the apartments themselves are exceedingly ample, notably the Appartement du Roi, furnished as it was in the days of "Vert Galant," the Salle des Gardes, the library and an elaborately traceried staircase. In the chapel is an altar-table which came from the Église St. Calais, in the château at Blois.

Just outside the gates is a remarkable crotchety old stone church, with a dwindling, toppling spire. It is poor and impoverished when compared with most French churches, and has a most astonishing timbered veranda, with a straining, creaking roof running around its two unobstructed walls. The open rafters are filled with all sorts of rubbish, and the local fire brigade keeps its hose and ladders there. A most suitable old rookery it is in which to start a first-class conflagration.

Within are a few funeral marbles of the Hurault family, and the daily offices are con-

# Cheverny, Beauregard, Chaumont 113

*Cheverny - sur - Loire*

ducted with a pomp most unexpected. Altogether it forms, as to its fabric and its functions, as strong a contrast of activity and decay as one is likely to see in a long journey.

The town itself is a sleepy, unprogressive place, where automobilists may not even buy *essence à pétrole,* and, though boasting — if the indolent old town really does boast — a couple of thousand souls, one still has to journey to Cour-Cheverny to send a telegraphic despatch or buy a daily paper.

Between Cheverny and Blois is the Forêt de Russy, which will awaken memories of the boar-hunts of François I., which, along with art in all its enlightening aspects, appears to have been one of the chief pleasures of that monarch. Perhaps one ought to include also the love of fair women, but with them he was not so constant.

On the road to Blois, also, one passes the Château de Beauregard; that is, one usually passes it, but he shouldn't. It is built, practically, within the forest, on the banks of the little river Beauvron. An iron *grille* gives entrance to a beautiful park, and within is the château, its very name indicating the favour with which it was held by its royal owner. It was in 1520 that François I. established it as a *rendezvous de chasse*. Under his son, Henri II., it was reconstructed, in part; entirely remodelled in the seventeenth century; and "modernized" — whatever that may mean — in 1809, and again, more lately, restored by the Duc de Dino. It belongs to-day to the Comte de Cholet, who has tried his hand at "restoration" as well.

The history of this old château is thus seen to have been most varied, and it is pretty sure to have lost a good deal of its original character in the transforming process.

The interior is more attractive than is the exterior. There is a grand gallery of portraits of historical celebrities, more than 350, executed between 1617 and 1638 by Paul Ardier, Counsellor of State, who thus combined the accomplishment of the artist with the sagacity of the statesman.

The ceilings of the great rooms are mostly elaborate works in enamel and carved oak, and there is a tiled floor (*carrelage*) in the portrait gallery, in blue faïence, representing an army in the order of battle, which must have delighted the hearts of the youthful progeny who may have been brought up within the walls of the château. This pavement is moreover an excellent example of the craftsmanship of tile-making.

One gains admission to the château freely from the *concierge,* who in due course expects her *pourboire,* and sees that she gets it. But what would you, inquisitive traveller? You have come here to see the sights, and Beauregard is well worth the price of admission, which is anything you like to give, certainly not less than a franc.

One may return to Blois through the forest, or may continue his way down the river to Chaumont on the left bank.

At Chaumont the Loire broadens to nearly double the width at Blois, its pebbles and sandbars breaking the mirror-like surface into innumerable pools and *étangs.* There is a bridge which connects Chaumont with the railway at Onzain and the great national highway from Tours to Blois. The bridge, however, is so hideous a thing that one had rather go miles out of his way than accept its hospitality. It is simply one of those unsympathetic wire-rope affairs with which the face of the globe is being covered, as engineering skill progresses and the art instinct dies out.

The Château de Chaumont is charmingly situated, albeit it is not very accessible to

*Chaumont*

strangers after one gets there, as it is open to the public only on Thursdays, from July to December. It is exactly what one expects to find, — a fine riverside establishment of its epoch, and in architectural style combining the well-recognized features of late Gothic and the early Renaissance. It is not moss-grown or decrepit in any way, which fact, considering its years, is perhaps remarkable.

The park of the château is only of moderate extent, but the structure itself is, comparatively, of much larger proportions. The ideal view of the structure is obtained from midway on that ungainly bridge which spans the Loire at this point. Here, in the gold and purple of an autumn evening, with the placid and far-reaching Loire, its pools and its bars of sand and pebble before one, it is a scene which is as near idyllic as one is likely to see.

The town itself is not attractive; one long, narrow lane-like street, lined on each side by habitations neither imposing nor of a tumble-down picturesqueness, borders the Loire. There is nothing very picturesque, either, about the homes of the vineyard workers round about. Below and above the town the great highroad runs flat and straight between Tours and Blois on either side of the river, and automobilists and cyclists now roll along where the state carriages of the court used to roll when François Premier and his sons journeyed from one gay country house to another.

It is to be inferred that the aspect of things at Chaumont has not changed much since that day,—always saving that spider-net wire bridge. The population of the town has doubtless grown somewhat, even though small towns in France sometimes do not increase their population in centuries; but the topographical

*Signature of Diane de Poitiers*

aspect of the long-drawn-out village, backed by green hills on one side and the Loire on the other, is much as it always has been.

The château at Chaumont had its origin as far back as the tenth century, and its proprietors were successively local seigneurs, Counts of Blois, the family of Amboise, and Diane de Poitiers, who received it from Catherine in exchange for Chenonceaux. This was not a fair exchange, and Diane was, to some extent, justified in her complaints.

Chaumont was for a time in the possession

of Scipion Sardini, one of the Italian partisans of the Medici, " whose arms bore *trois sardines d'argent,*" and who had married Isabelle de la Tour, " *la Demoiselle de Limieul* " of unsavoury reputation.

The " *Demoiselle de Limieul* " was related, too, to Catherine, and was celebrated in the gallantries of the time in no enviable fashion. She was a member of that band of demoiselles whose business it was — by one fascination or another — to worm political secrets from the nobles of the court. One horrible scandal connected the unfortunate lady with the Prince de Condé, but it need not be repeated here. The Huguenots ridiculed it in those memorable verses beginning thus:

> " Puella illa nobilis
> Quæ erat tam amabilis."

After the reign of Sardini and of his direct successors, the house of Bullion, Chaumont passed through many hands. Madame de Staël arrived at the château in the early years of the nineteenth century, when she had received the order to separate herself from Paris, " by at least forty leagues." She had made the circle of the outlying towns, hovering about Paris as a moth about a candle-flame; Rouen, Auxerre, Blois, Saumur, all had entertained her, but now she came to establish herself in this Loire citadel. As the story goes, journeying from Saumur to Tours, by post-chaise, on the opposite side of the river, she saw the imposing mass of Chaumont rising high above the river-bed, and by her good graces and winning ways installed herself in the affections of the then proprietor, M. Leray, and continued her residence "and made her court here for many years."

Chaumont is to-day the property of the Princesse de Broglie, who has sought to restore it, where needful, even to reëstablishing the ancient fosse or moat. This last, perhaps, is not needful; still, a moated château, or even a moated grange has a fascination for the sentimentally inclined.

At the drawbridge, as one enters Chaumont to-day, one sees the graven initials of Louis XII. and Anne de Bretagne, the arms of Georges d'Amboise, surmounted by his cardinal's hat, and those of Charles de Chaumont, as well as other cabalistic signs: one a representation of a mountain (apparently) with a crater-like summit from which flames are breaking forth, while hovering about, back to back, are two C's: ↄC. The Renaissance artists greatly affected the rebus, and this perhaps has some reference to the etymology of the name Chaumont, which has been variously given as coming from *Chaud Mont, Calvus Mont,* and *Chauve Mont.*

Georges d'Amboise, the first of the name, was born at Chaumont in 1460, the eighth son of a family of seventeen children. It was a far cry, as distances went in those days, from the shores of the shallow, limpid Loire to those of the forceful, turgent Seine at Rouen, where in the great Cathedral of Notre Dame, this first Georges of Amboise, having become an archbishop and a cardinal, was laid to rest beneath that magnificent canopied tomb before which visitors to the Norman capital stand in wonder. The mausoleum bears this epitaph, which in some small measure describes the activities of the man.

> "Pastor eram cleri, populi pater ; aurea sese
> Lilia subdebant, quercus et ipsa mihi.
>
> "Martuus en jaceo, morte extinguunter honores,
> Et virtus, mortis nescia, mort viret."

His was not by any means a life of placidity and optimism, and he had the air and reputation of doing things. There is a saying, still current in Touraine: *"Laissez faire à Georges."*

The second of the same name, also an Archbishop of Rouen and a cardinal, succeeded his uncle in the see. He also is buried beneath the same canopy as his predecessor at Rouen.

The main portal of the château leads to a fine quadrilateral court with an open gallery overlooking the Loire, which must have been a magnificent playground for the nobility of a former day. The interior embellishments are fine, some of the more noteworthy features being a grand staircase of the style of Louis XII.; the Salle des Gardes, with a painted ceiling showing the arms of Chaumont and Amboise; the Salle du Conseil, with some fine tapestries and a remarkable tiled floor, depicting scenes of the chase; the Chambre de Catherine de Medici (she possessed Chaumont for nine years), containing some of the gifts presented to her upon her wedding with Henri II.; and the curious Chambre de Ruggieri, the astrologer whom Catherine brought from her Italian home, and who was always near her, and kept her supplied with charms and omens, good and bad, and also her poisons.

Ruggieri's observatory was above his apartment. It was at Chaumont that the astrologer overstepped himself, and would have used his magic against Charles IX. He did go so far as to make an image and inflict certain indignities upon it, with the belief that the same would befall the monarch himself. Ruggieri went to the galleys for this, but the scheming Catherine soon had him out again, and at work with his poisons and philtres.

Finally there is the Chambre de Diane de Poitiers, Catherine's more than successful rival, with a bed (modern, it is said) and a series of sixteenth-century tapestries, with various other pieces of contemporary furniture. A portrait of Diane which decorates the apartment is supposed to be one of the three authentic portraits of the fair huntress. The chapel has a fine tiled pavement and some excellent glass.

Chaumont is eighteen kilometres from Blois and the same distance from Amboise. It has not the splendour of Chambord, but it has a greater antiquity, and an incomparably finer situation, which displays its coiffed towers and their *mâchicoulis* and cornices in a manner not otherwise possible. It is one of those picture châteaux which tell a silent story quite independent of guide-book or historical narrative.

It was M. Donatien Le Ray de Chaumont, the superintendent of the forests of Berry and the Blaisois, under Louis XVI., who gave hospitality to Benjamin Franklin, and turned over to the first American ambassador to France the occupancy of his house at Passy, where Franklin lived for nine consecutive years.

Of this same M. de Chaumont Americans cannot have too high a regard, for his timely and judicious hospitality has associated his name, only less permanently than Franklin's, with the early fortunes of the American republic.

Besides his other offices, M. de Chaumont was the intendant of the Hôtel des Invalides, at Paris, holding confidential relations with the ministry of the young king, and was in the immediate enjoyment of a fortune which amounted to two and a half million of francs, besides owning, in addition to Chaumont on the Loire, another château in the Blaisois. This château he afterward tendered to John Adams, who declined the offer in a letter, written at Passy-sur-Seine, February 25, 1779, in the following words: " . . . To a mind as much addicted to retirement as mine, the situation you propose would be delicious indeed, provided my country were at peace and my family with me; but, separated from my family and with a heart bleeding with the wounds of its country, I should be the most miserable being on earth. . . ."

The potteries, which now form the stables

of the château at Chaumont, are somewhat reminiscent of Franklin. M. de Chaumont had established a pottery here, where he had found a clay which had encouraged him to hope that he could compete with the English manufacturers of the time. Here the Italian Nini, who was invited to Chaumont, made medallions much sought for by collectors, among others one of Franklin, which was so much admired as a work of art, and became so much in demand that in later years replicas were made and are well known to amateurs.

The family of Le Ray de Chaumont were extensively known in America, where they became large landholders in New York State in the early nineteenth century, and the head of the family seems to have been an amiable and popular landlord. The towns of Rayville and Chaumont in New York State still perpetuate his name.

The two male members of the family secured American wives; Le Ray himself married a Miss Coxe, and their son a Miss Jahel, both of New York.

From an anonymous letter to the New York *Evening Post* of November 19, 1885, one quotes the following:

"It was in Blois that I first rummaged

among these shops, whose attractions are almost a rival to those of the castle, though this is certainly one of the most interesting in France. The traveller will remember the long flight of stone steps which climbs the steep hill in the centre of the town. Near the foot of this hill there is a well-furnished book-shop; its windows display old editions and rich bindings, and tempt one to enter and inquire for antiquities. Here I found a quantity of old notarial documents and diplomas of college or university, all more or less recently cleared out from some town hall, or unearthed from neighbouring castle, and sold by a careless owner, as no longer valuable to him. This was the case with most of the parchments I found at Blois; they had been acquired within a few years from the castle of Madon, and from a former proprietor of the neighbouring castle of Chaumont (the *calvus mons* of mediæval time), and most of them pertained to the affairs of the *seigneurie de Chaumont*. Contracts, executions, sales of vineyards and houses, legal decisions, *actes de vente,* loans on mortgages, the marriage contract of a M. Lubin, — these were the chief documents that I found and purchased.''

The traveller may not expect to come upon

duplicates of these treasures again, but the incident only points to the fact that much documentary history still lies more or less deeply buried.

# CHAPTER VI.

### TOURAINE: THE GARDEN SPOT OF FRANCE

> "C'est une grande dame, une princesse altière,
>   Chacun de ses châteaux, marqué du sceau royal,
>   Lui fait une toilette en dentelle de pierre
>   Et son splendide fleuve un miroir de cristal."

It is difficult to write appreciatively of Touraine without echoing the words of some one who has gone before, and it is likely that those who come after will find the task no easier.

Truly, as a seventeenth-century geographer has said: "Here is the most delicious and the most agreeable province of the kingdom. It has been named the garden of France because of the softness of its climate, the affability of its people, and the ease of its life."

The poets who have sung the praises of Touraine are many, Ronsard, Remy Belleau, Du Bellay, and for prose authors we have at the head, Rabelais, La Fontaine, Balzac, and Alfred de Vigny. Merely to enumerate them all would

# Touraine: Garden Spot of France

be impossible, but they furnish a fund of quotable material for the traveller when he is writing home, and are equally useful to the maker of guide-books.

One false note on Touraine, only, has ever rung out in the world of literature, and that was from Stendahl, who said: "*La Belle Touraine n'existe pas!*" The pages of Alfred de Vigny and Balzac answer this emphatically, and to the contrary, and every returning traveller apparently sides with them and not with Stendahl.

How can one not love its prairies, gently sloping to the caressing Loire, its rolling hills and dainty ravines? The broad blue Loire is always vague and tranquil here, at least one seems always to see it so, but the beauty of Touraine is, after all, a quiet beauty which must be seen to be appreciated, and lived with to be loved.

It is a land of most singular attractions, neither too hot nor too cold, too dry nor too damp, with a sufficiency of rain, and an abundance of sunshine. Its market-gardens are prolific in their product, its orchards overflowing with plenitude, and its vineyards generous in their harvest.

Touraine is truly the region where one may

read history without books, with the very pages of nature punctuated and adorned with the marvels of the French Renaissance. Louis XI. gave the first impetus to the alliance of the great domestic edifice — which we have come to distinguish as the residential château — with the throne, and the idea was amplified by Charles VIII. and glorified by François Premier.

In the brilliant, if dissolute, times of the early sixteenth century François Premier and his court travelled down through this same Touraine to Loches and to Amboise, where François's late gaoler, Charles Quint, was to be received and entertained. It was after François had returned from his involuntary exile in Spain, and while he was still in residence at the Louvre, that the plans for the journey were made. To the Duchesse d'Étampes François said, — the duchess who was already more than a rival of both Diane and the Comtesse de Châteaubriant, — "I must tear myself away from you to-morrow. I shall await my brother Charles at Amboise on the Loire."

"Shall you not revenge yourself upon him, for his cruel treatment of you?" said the wily favourite of the time. "If he, like a fool, comes to Touraine, will you not make him revoke the treaty of Madrid or shut him up in one of Louis XI.'s oubliettes?"

"I will persuade him, if possible," said François, "but I shall never force him."

In due time François did receive his brother king at Amboise and it was amid great ceremony and splendour. His guest could not, or would not, mount steps, so that great inclined plane, up which a state coach and its horses might go, was built. Probably there was a good reason for the emperor's peculiarity, for that worthy or unworthy monarch finally died of gout in the monastery of San Juste.

The meeting here at Amboise was a grand and ceremonious affair and the Spanish monarch soon came to recognize a possible enemy in the royal favourite, Anne de Pisselieu. The emperor's eyes, however, melted with admiration, and he told her that only in France could one see such a perfection of elegance and beauty, with the result that — as is popularly adduced — the susceptible, ambitious, and unfaithful duchess betrayed François more than once in the affairs attendant upon the subsequent wars between France, England, and Spain.

From Touraine, in the sixteenth century,

*[margin note: This was the first chateaux that I visited.]*

spread that influence which left its impress even on the capital of the kingdom itself, not only in respect to architectural art, but in manners and customs as well.

Whatever may be the real value of the Renaissance as an artistic expression, the discussion of it shall have no place here, beyond the qualifying statement that what we have come to know as the French Renaissance — which undeniably grew up from a transplanted Italian germ — proved highly tempting to the mediæval builder for all manner of edifices, whereas it were better if it had been confined to civic and domestic establishments and left the church pure in its full-blown Gothic forms.

Curiously enough, here in Touraine, this is just what did happen. The Renaissance influence crept into church-building here and there — and it is but a short step from the "*gothique rayonnant*" to what are recognized as well-defined Renaissance features; but it is more particularly in respect to the great châteaux, and even smaller dwellings, that the superimposed Italian details were used. A notable illustration of this is seen in the Cathedral of St. Gatien at Tours. It is very beautiful and has some admirable Gothic features, but there are occasional constructive details, as well as those for decorative effect alone, which are decidedly not good Gothic; but, as they are, likewise, not Renaissance, they hence cannot be laid to its door, but rather to the architect's eccentricity.

In the smaller wayside churches, such as one sees at Cormery, at Cheverny, and at Cour-Cheverny, there is scarcely a sign of Renaissance, while their neighbouring châteaux are nothing else, both in construction and in decoration.

The Château de Langeais is, for the most part, excellent Gothic, and so is the church near by. Loches has distinct and pure Gothic details both in its church and its château, quite apart from the Hôtel de Ville and that portion of the château now used as the Sous-Préfecture, which are manifestly Renaissance; hence here in Touraine steps were apparently taken to keep the style strictly non-ecclesiastical.

A glance of the eye at the topography of this fair province stamps it at once as something quite different from any other traversed by the Loire. Two of the great " routes nationales " cross it, the one via Orleans, leading to Nantes, and the other via Chartres, going to Bordeaux. It is crossed and recrossed by innumerable " routes secondaires," " départementales," "vicinales" and "particulières," second to none of their respective classes in other countries, for assuredly the roads of France are the best in the world. Many of these great ways of communication replaced the ancient Roman roads, which were the pioneers of the magnificent roadways of the France of to-day.

Almost invariably Touraine is flat or rolling, its highest elevation above the sea being but a hundred and forty-six metres, scarce four hundred and fifty feet, a fact which accounts also for the gentle flow of the Loire through these parts.

All the fruits of the southland are found here, the olive alone excepted. Mortality, it is said, and proved by figures, is lower than in any other part of France, and for this reason many dwellers in the large cities, if they may not all have a mediæval château, have at least a villa, far away from "the madding crowd," and yet within four hours' travel of the capital itself.

Touraine, properly speaking, has no natural frontiers, as it is not enclosed by rivers or mountains. It is, however, divided by the Loire into two distinct regions, the Méridionale and the Septentrionale; but the dress, the physiognomy, the language, and the predilec-

*The Loire in Touraine*

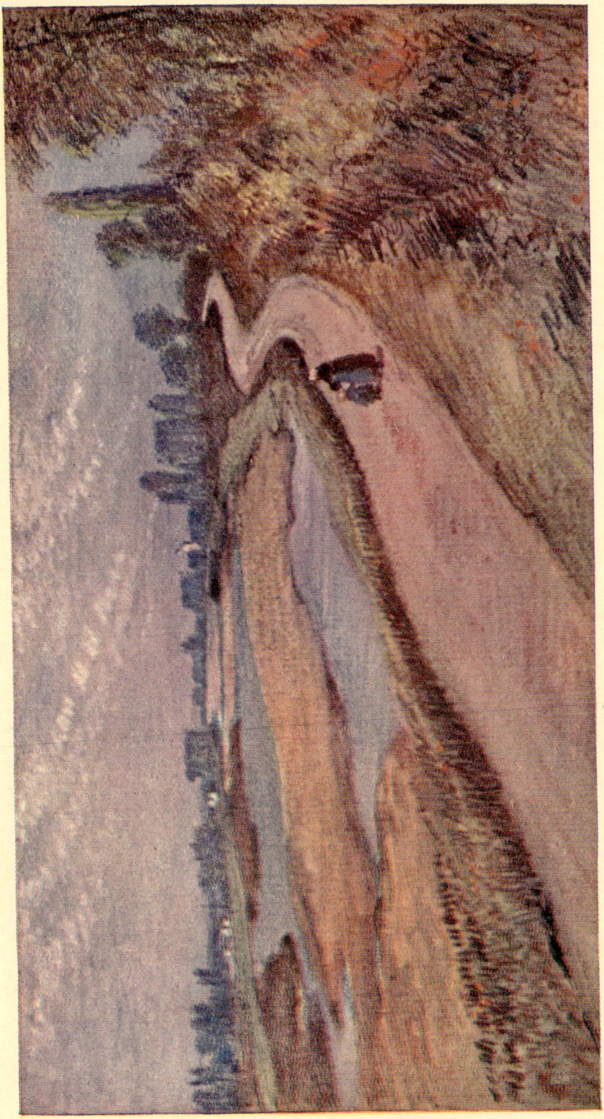

tions of the people are everywhere the same, though the two sections differ somewhat in temperament. In the south, the Tourangeau is timid and obliging, but more or less engrossed in his affairs; in the north, he is proud, egotistical, and a little arrogant, but, above all, he likes his ease and comfort, something after the manner of " mynheer " of Holland.

These are the characteristics which are enumerated by Stanislas Bellanger of Tours, in " La Touraine Ancienne et Moderne," and they are traceable to-day, in every particular, to one who knows well the by-paths of the region.

Formerly the peasant was, in his own words, " *sous la main de M. le comte,*" but, with the coming of the eighteenth century, all this was changed, and the conditions which, in England, succeeded feudalism, are unknown in Touraine, as indeed throughout France.

The two great divisions which nature had made of Touraine were further cut up into five *petits pays;* les Varennes, le Veron, la Champeigne, la Brenne, and les Gâtines; names which exist on some maps to-day, but which have lost, in a great measure, their former distinction.

There is a good deal to be said in favour of the physical and moral characteristics of the inhabitants of Touraine. Just as the descendants of the Phoceans, the original settlers of Marseilles, differ from the natives of other parts of France, so, too, do the Tourangeaux differ from the inhabitants of other provinces. The people of Touraine are a mixture of Romans, Visigoths, Saracens, Alains, Normans and Bretons, Anglais and Gaulois; but all have gradually been influenced by local conditions, so that the native of Touraine has become a distinct variety all by himself. The deliciousness of the "garden of France" has altered him so that he stands to-day as more distinctly French than the citizen of Paris itself.

Touraine, too, has the reputation of being that part of France where is spoken the purest French. This, perhaps, is as true of the Blaisois, for the local bookseller at Blois will tell one with the most dulcet and understandable enunciation that it is at Blois that one hears the best accent. At any rate, it is something found within a charmed circle, of perhaps a hundred miles in diameter, that does not find its exact counterpart elsewhere. As Seville stands for the Spanish tongue, Florence for the Italian, and Dresden for the German, so Tours stands for the French.

The history of the Loire in Touraine, as is the case at Le Puy, at Nevers, at Sancerre, or at Orleans, is abundant and vivid, and the monuments which line its banks are numerous and varied, from the fortress-château of Amboise to the Cathedral of St. Gatien at Tours with its magnificent bejewelled façade. The ruined towers of the castle of Cinq-Mars, with its still more ancient Roman "pile," and the feudal châteaux of the countryside are all eloquent, even to-day, in their appeal to all lovers of history and romance.

There are some verses, little known, in praise of the Loire, as it comes through Touraine, written by Houdon des Landes, who lived near Tours in the eighteenth century. The following selection expresses their quality well and is certainly worthy to rank with the best that Balzac wrote in praise of his beloved Touraine.

> "La Loire enorgueillit ses antiques cités,
> Et couronne ses bords de coteaux enchantés;
> Dans ses vallons heureux, sur ses rives aimées,
> Les prés ont déployé leurs robes parfumées;
> Le saule humide et souple y lance ses rameaux.
> Ses coteaux sont peuplés, et le rocher docile
> A l'homme qui le creuse offre un champêtre asile.

> De notre vieille Gaule, ô fleuve paternel !
> Fleuve des doux climats ! la Vallière et Sorel
> Sur tes bords fortunés naquirent, et la gloire
> A l'une dût l'amour, à l'autre la victoire."

Again and again Balzac's words echo in one's ears from his "Scène de la Vie de Province." The following quotations are typical of the whole:

"The softness of the air, the beauty of the climate, all tend to a certain ease of existence and simplicity of manner which encourages an appreciation of the arts."

"Touraine is a land to foster the ambition of a Napoleon and the sentiment of a Byron."

Another writer, A. Beaufort, a publicist of the nineteenth century, wrote:

"The Tourangeaux resemble the good Adam in the garden of Eden. They drink, they eat, they sleep and dream, and care not what their neighbour may be doing."

Touraine was indeed, at one time, a veritable Eden, though guarded by fortresses, *hallebardes,* and arquebuses, but not the less an Eden for all that. In addition it was a land where, in the middle ages, the seigneurs made history, almost without a parallel in France or elsewhere.

Touraine, truly enough, was the centre of the

old French monarchy in the perfection of its pomp and state; but it is also true that Touraine knew little of the serious affairs of kings, though some all-important results came from events happening within its borders.

Paris was the law-making centre in the sixteenth century, and Touraine knew only the domestic life and pleasures of royalty. Etiquette, form, and ceremony were all relaxed, or at least greatly modified, and the court spent in the country what it had levied in the capital.

Curiously enough, the monarchs were omnipotent and influential here, though immediately they quartered themselves in Paris their powers waned considerably; indeed, they seemed to lose their influence upon ministers and vassals alike.

Louis XIII., it is true, tried to believe that Paris was France, — like the Anglo-Saxon tourists who descend upon it in such great numbers to-day, — and built Versailles; but there was never much real glory about its cold and pompous walls.

The fortunes of the old châteaux of Touraine have been most varied. Chambord is vast and bare, elegant and pompous; Blois, just across the border, is a tourist sight of the first rank whose salamanders and porcupines have been well cared for by the paternal French government. Chaumont, Chenonceaux, Langeais, Azay-le-Rideau, and half a dozen others are still inhabited, and are gay with the life of twentieth-century luxury; Amboise is a possession of the Orleans family; Loches is, in part, given over to the uses of a sous-préfecture; and Chinon's châteaux are but half-demolished ruins. Besides these there are numerous smaller residential châteaux of the nobility scattered here and there in the Loire watershed.

There have been writers who have sought to commiserate with "the poor peasant of Touraine," as they have been pleased to think of him, and have deplored the fact that his sole possession was a small piece of ground which he and his household cultivated, and that he lived in a little whitewashed house, built with his own hands, or those of his ancestors. Though the peasant of Touraine, as well as of other parts of the countryside, works for an absurdly small sum, and for considerably less than his brother nearer Paris, he sells his produce at the nearest market-town for a fair price, and preserves a spirit of independence which is as valuable as are some of the things which are thrust upon him in some other lands under the guise of benevolent charity, really patronage of a most demeaning and un-moral sort. At night the Touraine peasant returns to his own hearthstone conscious that he is a man like all of his fellows, and is not a mere atom ground between the upper and nether millstones of the landlord and the squire. He cooks his "*bouillie*" over three small sticks and retires to rest with the fond hope that on the next market-day following the prices of eggs, chickens, cauliflowers, or tomatoes may be higher. He is the stuff that successful citizens are made of, and is not to be pitied in the least, even though it is only the hundredth man of his community who ever does rise to more wealth than a mere competency.

Touraine, rightly enough, has been called the garden of France, but it is more than that, much more; it is a warm, soft land where all products of the soil take on almost a subtropical luxuriance. Besides the great valley of the Loire, there are the valleys of the tributaries which run into it, in Touraine and the immediate neighbourhood, all of which are fertile as only a river-bottom can be. It is true that there are numerous formerly arid and sandy plateaux, quite unlike the abundant plains of La Beauce, though to-day, by care and skill, they have been made to rival the rest of the region in productiveness.

The Département d'Indre et Loire is the richest agricultural region in all France so far as the variety and abundance of its product goes, rivalling in every way the opulence of the Burgundian hillsides. Above all, Touraine stands at the head of the vine-culture of all the Loire valley, the *territoire vinicole* lapping over into Anjou, where are produced the celebrated *vins blancs* of Saumur.

The vineyard workers of Touraine, in the neighbourhood of Loches, have clung closely to ancient customs, almost, one may say, to the destruction of the industry, though of late new methods have set in, and, since the blight now some years gone by, a new prosperity has come.

The day worker, who cares for the vines and superintends the picking of the grapes by the womenfolk and the children, works for two francs fifty centimes per day; but he invariably carries with him to the scene of his labours a couple of cutlets from a young and juicy *brebis,* or even a *poulet rôti,* so one may judge from this that his pay is ample for his needs in this land of plenty.

In the morning he takes his bowl of soup and a cup of white wine, and of course huge hunks

The Vintage in Touraine

of bread, and finally coffee, and on each Sunday he has his *rôti à la maison*. All this demonstrates the fact that the French peasant is more of a meat eater in these parts than he is commonly thought to be.

Touraine has no peculiar beauties to offer the visitor; there is nothing *outré* about it to interest one; but, rather, it wins by sheer charm alone, or perhaps a combination of charms and excellencies makes it so truly a delectable land.

The Tourangeaux themselves will tell you, when speaking of Rabelais and Balzac, that it is the land of " *haute graisse, féconde et spirituelle.*" It is all this, and, besides its spirituelle components, it will supply some very real and substantial comforts. It is the Eden of the gourmandiser of such delicacies as *truffes, rilettes,* and above all, *pruneaux,* which you get in one form or another at nearly every meal. Most of the good things of life await one here in abundance, with kitchen-gardens and vineyards at every one's back door. Truly Touraine is a land of good living.

Life runs its course in Touraine, " *facile et bonne,*" without any extremes of joy or sorrow, without chimerical desires or infinite despair, and the agreeable sensations of life predominate, — the first essential to real happiness.

Some one has said, and certainly not without reason, that every Frenchman has a touch of Rabelais and of Voltaire in his make-up. This is probably true, for France has never been swept by a wave of puritanism such as has been manifest in most other countries, and *le gros rire* is still the national philosophy.

In a former day a hearty laugh, or at least an amused cynicism, diverted the mind of the martyr from threatened torture and even violent death. Brinvilliers laughed at those who were to torture her to death, and De la Barre and Danton cracked jokes and improvised puns upon the very edge of their untimely graves.

Touraine has the reputation of being a wonderfully productive field for the book collector, though with books, like many other treasures of a past time, the day has passed when one may " pick up " for two sous a MS. worth as many thousands of francs; but still bargains are even now found, and if one wants great calf-covered tomes, filled with fine old engravings, bearing on the local history of the *pays*, he can generally find them at all prices here in old Touraine.

There was a more or less apocryphal story

told us and the landlady of our inn concerning a find which a guest had come upon in a little roadside hamlet at which he chanced to stop. He was one of those omnipresent *commis voyageurs* who thread the French provinces up and down, as no other country in the world is "travelled" or "drummed." He was the representative for a brandy shipper, one of those substantial houses of the cognac region whose product is mostly sold only in France; but this fact need not necessarily put the individual very far down in the social scale. Indeed, he was a most amiable and cultivated person.

Our fellow traveller had come to a village where all the available accommodations of the solitary inn were already engaged; therefore he was obliged to put up with a room in the town, which the landlord hunted out for him. Repairing to his room without any thought save that of sleep, the traveller woke the next morning to find the sun streaming through the opaqueness of a brilliantly coloured window. Not stained glass here, surely, thought the stranger, for his lodging was a most humble one. It proved to be not glass at all; merely four great vellum leaves, taken from some ancient tome and stuck into the window-framing where the glass ought to have been. Daylight was filtering dimly through the rich colouring, and it took but a moment to become convinced that the sheets were something rare and valuable. He learned that the pages were from an old Latin MS., and that the occupant of the little dwelling had used "*the paper*" in the place of the glass which had long since disappeared. The vellum and its illuminations had stood the weather well, though somewhat dimmed in comparison with the brilliancy of the remaining folios, which were found below-stairs. There were in all some eighty pages, which were purchased for a modest forty sous, and everybody satisfied.

The volume had originally been found by the father of the old dame who then had possession of it in an old château in revolutionary times. Whether her honoured parent was a pillager or a protector did not come out, but for all these years the possession of this fine work meant no more to this Tourangelle than a supply of "paper" for stopping up broken window-panes.

"She parted readily enough with the remaining leaves," said our Frenchman, "but nothing would induce her to remove those which filled the window." "No, we have no more

# Touraine: Garden Spot of France

glass, and these have answered quite well for a long time now," she said. And such is the simplicity of the French provincial, even to-day — *sometimes.*

# CHAPTER VII.

### AMBOISE

As one approaches Amboise, he leaves the comparatively insalubrious plain of the Sologne and the Blaisois and enters Touraine.

Amboise! What history has been made there; what a wealth of action its memories recall, and what splendour, gaiety, and sadness its walls have held! An entire book might be written about the scenes which took place under its roof.

To-day most travellers are content to rush over its apartments, gaze at its great round tower, view the Loire, which is here quite at its best, from the battlements, and, after a brief admiration of the wonderfully sculptured portal of its chapel, make their way to Chenonceaux, or to the gay little metropolis of Tours.

No matter whither one turns his steps from Amboise, he will not soon forget this great fortress-château and the memories of the *petite bande* of blondes and brunettes who followed in the wake of François Premier.

*Château d'Amboise*

Here, and at Blois, the recollections of this little band are strong in the minds of students of romance and history. Some one has said that along the corridors of Amboise one still may meet the wraiths of those who in former days went airily from one pleasure to another, but this of course depends upon the mood and sentiment of the visitor.

Amboise has a very good imitation of the climate of the south, and the glitter of the Loire at midday in June is about as torrid a picture as one can paint in a northern clime. It is not that it is so very hot in degree, but that the lack of shade-trees along its quays gives Amboise a shimmering resemblance to a much warmer place than it really is. The Loire is none too ample here, and frets its way, as it does through most of its lower course, through banks of sand and pebbles in a more or less vain effort to look cool.

Amboise is old, for, under the name of Ambatia, it existed in the fourth century, at which epoch St. Martin, the patron of Tours, threw down a pagan pyramidal temple here and established Christianity; and Clovis and Alaric held their celebrated meeting on the Ile St. Jean in 496. It was not long after this, according to the ancient writers, that some sort of a fortified château took form here. Louis-le-Bègue gave Amboise to the Counts of Anjou, and Hughes united the two independent seigneuries of the château and the bourg. After the Counts of Anjou succeeded the Counts of Berry, Charles VII., by appropriation, confiscation, seizure, or whatever you please to call it, — history is vague as to the real motive, — united Amboise to the possessions of the Crown in 1434. Louis XI. lived for a time at this strong fortress-château, before he turned his affections so devotedly to Plessis-les-Tours. Charles VIII. was born and died here, and it was he who added the Renaissance details, or at least the first of them, upon his return from Italy. Indeed, it is to him and to the nobles who followed in his train during his Italian travels that the introduction of the Renaissance into France is commonly attributed.

It was at Amboise that Charles VIII., forgetful of the miseries of his Italian campaign, set about affairs of state with a renewed will and vigour. He was personally superintending some alterations in the old castle walls, and instructing the workmen whom he brought from Italy with him as to just how far they might introduce those details which the world has come to know as Renaissance, when, in passing beneath a low overhanging beam, he struck his head so violently that he expired almost immediately (April 17, 1498).

Louis XII., the superstitious, lived here for some time, and here occurred some of the most important events in the life of the great François, the real popularizer of the new architectural Renaissance.

It was in the old castle of Amboise, the early home of Louis XII., that his appointed successor, his son-in-law and second cousin, François, was brought up. Here he was educated by his mother, Louise de Savoie, Duchesse d'Angoulême, together with that bright and shining light, that Marguerite who was known as the "Pearl of the Valois," poetess, artist, and court intriguer. Here the household formed what in the early days François himself was pleased to call a "trinity of love."

Throughout the structure may yet be seen the suggestions of François's artistic instincts, traced in the window-framings of the façade, in the interior decorations of the long gallery, and on the terrace hanging high above the Loire.

In the park and in the surrounding forest François and his sister Marguerite passed many happy days of their childhood. Marguerite, who had already become known as the "tenth muse," had already thought out her "Heptameron," whilst François tried his prentice hand at love-rhyming, an expression of sentiment which at a later period took the form of avowals in person to his favourites.

One recalls those stanzas to the memory of Agnes Sorel, beginning:

> "Gentille Agnès plus de loz tu mérite,
> La cause était de France recouvrir;
> Que ce que peut dedans un cloître ouvrir
> Close nonnaine? ou bien dévot hermite?"

François was more than a lover of the beautiful. His appreciation of architectural art amounted almost to a passion, and one might well claim him as a member of the architectural guild, although, in truth, he was nothing more than a generous patron of the craftsmen of his day.

François was the real father of the French Renaissance, the more splendid flower which grew from the Italian stalk. He had no liking for the Van Eycks and Holbeins of the Dutch school, reserving his favour for the frankly languid masters from the south. He brought from Italy Cellini, Primaticcio, and the great Leonardo, who it is said had a hand in that wonderful shell-like spiral stairway in the château at Blois.

By just what means Da Vinci was inveigled from Italy will probably never be known. The art-loving François visited Milan, and among its curiosities was shown the even then celebrated "Last Supper" of Leonardo. The next we know is that, "*François repasse les Alpes ayant avec lui Mon Sieur Lyonard, son peintre.*" Leonardo was given a pension of seven *ecus de France* per year and a residence near Amboise. Vasari recounts very precisely how Leonardo expired in the arms of his kingly patron at Amboise, but on the other hand, the court chronicles have said that François was at St. Germain on that day. Be this as it may, the intimacy was a close one, and we may be sure that François felt keenly the demise of this most celebrated painter of his court.

It was during those early idyllic days at Amboise that the character of François was formed, and the marvel is that the noble and endearing qualities did not exceed the baser ones. To be sure his after lot was hard, and his real and fancied troubles many, and they were not made the less easy to bear because of his numerous female advisers.

In his youth at Amboise his passions still

slumbered, but when they did awaken, they burst forth with an unquenchable fury. Meantime he was working off any excess of imagination by boar-hunts and falconry in the neighbouring forest of Chanteloup, and had more than one hand-to-hand affray with resentful citizens of the town, when he encroached upon what they considered their traditional preserves. So he grew to man's estate, but the life that he lived in his youth under the kingly roof of the château at Amboise gave him the benefits of all the loyalty which his fellows knew, and it helped him carry out the ideas which were bequeathed to him by his uncle.

It was at a sitting of the court at Amboise, when François was still under his mother's wing, — at the age of twenty only, — that the Bourbon affair finally came to its head. Many notables were mixed up in it as partisans of the ungrateful and ambitious Bourbon, Charles de Montpensier, Connétable de France. It was an office only next in power to that of the sovereign himself, and one which had been allowed to die out in the reign of Louis XI. The final outcome of it all was that François became a prisoner at Pavia, through the treachery of the Connétable and his followers, who went over *en masse* to François's rival, Charles V., who, as Charles II., was King of Spain.

Of the subsequent meeting with the Emperor Charles on French soil, François said to the Duchesse d'Étampes: "It is with regret that I leave you to meet the emperor at Amboise on the Loire." And he added: "You will follow me with the queen." His queen at this time was poor Eleanor of Portugal, herself a Spanish princess, Claude of France, his first wife, having died. "These two," says Brantôme, "were the only virtuous women of his household."

The Emperor Charles was visibly affected by the meeting, though, it is true, he had no love for his old enemy, François. Perhaps it was on account of the duchess, for whom François had put aside Diane. At any rate, the emperor was gallant enough to say to her: "It is only in France that I have seen such a perfection of elegance and beauty. My brother, your king, should be the envy of all the sovereigns of Europe. Had I such a captive at my palace in Madrid, there were no ransom that I would accept for her."

François cared not for the lonely Spanish princess whom he had made his queen; but he was somewhat susceptible to the charms of his daughter-in-law, Catherine de Medici, the wife of his son Henri, who, when at Amboise, was his ever ready companion in the chase.

François was inordinately fond of the hunt, and made of it a most strenuous pastime, full of danger and of hard riding in search of the boar and the wolf, which abounded in the thick underwood in the neighbourhood. One wonders where they, or, rather, their descendants, have disappeared, since nought in these days but a frightened hare, a partridge, or perhaps a timid deer ever crosses one's path, as he makes his way by the smooth roads which cross and recross the forest behind Amboise.

When François II. was sixteen he became the nominal king of France. To Amboise he and his young bride came, having been brought thither from Blois, for fear of the Huguenot rising. The court settled itself forthwith at Amboise, where the majestic feudal castle piled itself high up above the broad, limpid Loire, feeling comparatively secure within the protection of its walls. Here the Loire had widened to the pretensions of a lake, the river being spanned by a bridge, which crossed it by the help of the island, as it does to-day.

Over this old stone bridge the court approached the castle, the retinue brilliant with all the trappings of a luxurious age, archers, pages, and men-at-arms. The king and his new-found bride, the winsome Mary Stuart, rode well in the van. In their train were Catherine, the "queen-mother" of three kings, the Cardinal de Lorraine, the Duc de Guise, the Duc de Nemours, and a vast multitude of gay retainers, who were moved about from place to place like pawns upon the chess-board, and with about as much consideration.

The gentle Mary Stuart, born in 1542, at Linlithgow, in stern Caledonia, of a French mother, — Marie de Lorraine, — was doomed to misfortune, for her father, the noble James V., prophesied upon his death-bed that the dynasty would end with his daughter.

At the tender age of five Mary was sent to France and placed in a convent. Her education was afterward continued at court under the direction of her uncle, the Cardinal de Lorraine. By ten she had become well versed in French, Latin, and Italian, and at one time, according to Brantôme, she gave a discourse on literature and the liberal arts — so flourishing at the time — before the king and his court. Ronsard was her tutor in versification, which became one of her favourite pursuits.

Mary Stuart's charms were many. She was

tall and finely formed, with auburn hair shining like an aureole above her intellectual forehead, and with a skin of such dazzling whiteness — a trite saying, but one which is used by Brantôme — "that it outrivalled the whiteness of her veil."

In the spring of 1558, when she was but sixteen, Mary Stuart was married to the Dauphin, the weak, sickly François II., himself but a youth. He was, however, sincerely and deeply fond of his young wife.

Unexpectedly, through the death of Henri II. at the hands of Montgomery at that ever debatable tournament, François II. ascended the throne of France, and Mary Stuart saw herself exalted to the dizzy height which she had not so soon expected. She became the queen of two kingdoms, and, had the future been more propitious, the whole map of Europe might have been changed.

Disease had marked the unstable François for its own, and within a year he passed from the throne to the grave, leaving his young queen a widow and an orphan.

Shortly afterward "*la reine blanche*" returned to her native Scotland, bidding France that long, last, sad adieu so often quoted:

> " Farewell, beloved France, to thee!
>   Best native land,
>   The cherished strand
> That nursed my tender infancy!
> Farewell my childhood's happy day!
> The bark, which bears me thus away,
>   Bears but the poorer moiety hence,
> The nobler half remains with thee,
>   I leave it to thy confidence,
> But to remind thee still of me! "

The young sovereigns had had a most stately suite of apartments prepared for them at Amboise, the lofty windows reaching from floor to ceiling and overlooking the river and the vast terrace where was so soon to be enacted that bloody drama to which they were to be made unwilling witnesses.

This gallery was wainscoted with old oak and hung with rich leathers, and the lofty ceiling was emblazoned with heraldic emblems and monograms, as was the fashion of the day. Brocades and tapestries, set in great gold frames, lined the walls, and, in a boudoir or retiring-room beyond, still definitely to be recognized, was a remarkable series of embroidered wall decorations, a tapestry of flowers and fruits with an arabesque border of white and gold, truly a queenly apartment, and one that well became the luxurious and dainty

Mary, who came from Scotland to marry the youthful François.

Mary Stuart knew little at the time as to why they had so suddenly removed from Blois, but François soon told her, something after this wise: "Our mother," said he, "is deeply concerned with affairs of state. There is some conspiracy against her and your uncles, the Guises."

"Tell me," she demanded, "concerning this dreadful conspiracy."

"Were you not suspicious," he asked, querulously, "when we left for Amboise so suddenly?"

"*Ah, non, mon François,* methought that we came here to hold a jousting tourney and to hunt in the forest. . . ."

"Well, at any rate, we are secure here from Turk, or Jew, or Huguenot, my queen," replied the king.

Within a short space a council was called in the great hall of Amboise, which the Huguenot chiefs, Condé, Coligny, the Cardinal de Chatillon, — who appears to have been a sort of a religious renegade, — were requested to attend. A conciliatory edict was to be prepared, and signed by the king, as a measure for gaining time and learning further the plans of the conspirators.

This edict ultimately was signed, but it was in force but a short time and was a subterfuge which the youthful king deep in his heart — and he publicly avowed the fact — deeply resented. Furthermore it did practically nothing toward quelling the conspiracy.

Through the plains of Touraine and over the hills from Anjou the conspirators came in straggling bands, to rendezvous for a great *coup de main* at Amboise. They halted at farms and hid in vineyards, but the royalists were on the watch and one after another the wandering bands were captured and held for a bloody public massacre when the time should become ripe. In all, two thousand or more were captured, including Jean Barri de la Renaudie. This man was the leader, but he was merely a bold adventurer, seeking his own advantage, and caring little what cause employed his peculiar talents. This was his last affair, however, for his corpse soon hung in chains from Amboise's bridge. Condé, Coligny, and the other Calvinists soon learned that the edict was not worth the paper on which it was written.

After the two thousand had been dispersed

or captured the "queen-mother" threw off the mask. She led the trembling child-king and queen toward the southern terrace, where, close beneath the windows of the château, was built a scaffold, covered with black cloth, before which stood the executioner clothed in scarlet. The prisoners were ranged by hundreds along the outer rampart, guarded by archers and musketeers. The windows of the royal apartment were open and here the company placed themselves to witness the butchery to follow.

Speechless with horror sat the young king and queen, until finally, as another batch of mutilated corpses were thrown into the river below, the young queen swooned.

"My mother," said François, "I, too, am overcome by this horrible sight. I crave your Highness's permission to retire; the blood of my subjects, even of my enemies, is too horrible to contemplate."

"My son," said the bloodthirsty Catherine, "I command you to stay. Duc de Guise, support your niece, the Queen of France. Teach her her duty as a sovereign. She must learn how to govern those hardy Scots of hers."

It was on the very terraced platform on which one walks to-day that, between two ranks of *hallebardiers* and arquebusiers, moved that long line of bareheaded and bowed men whose prayers went up to heaven while they awaited the fate of the gallows.

Either the cord or the sword-blade quickly accounted for the lives of this multitude, and their blood flowed in rivulets, while above in the gallery the willing and unwilling onlookers were gay with laughter or dumb with sadness.

When all this horrible murdering was over the Loire was literally a reeking mass of corpses, if we are to believe the records of the time. The chief conspirators were hung in chains from the castle walls, or from the bridge, and the balustrades which overhang the street, which to-day flanks the Loire beneath the castle walls, were filled with a ribald crew of jeering partisans who knew little and cared less for religion of any sort.

Some days after the execution of the Calvinists the "Protestant poet" and historian passed through the royal city with his *précepteur* and his father, and was shown the rows of heads planted upon pikes, which decorated the castle walls, and thereupon vowed, if not to avenge, at least to perpetuate the infamy in prose and verse, and this he did most effectually.

An odorous garden of roses, lilacs, honeysuckle, and hawthorn framed the joyous architecture of the château, then as now, in adorable fashion; but it could not purify the malodorous reputation which it had received until the domain was ceded by Louis XIV. to the Duc de Penthièvre and made a *duché-pairie*.

It would be possible to say much more, but this should suffice to stamp indelibly the fact that Touraine, in general, and the château of Amboise, in particular, cradled as much of the thought and action of the monarchy in the fifteenth and sixteenth centuries as did the capital itself. At any rate the memory of it all is so vivid, and the tangible monuments of the splendour and intrigue of the court of those days are so very numerous and magnificent, that one could not forget the parts they played — once having seen them — if he would.

After the assassination of the Duc de Guise at Blois, Amboise became a prison of state, where were confined the Cardinal de Bourbon and César de Vendôme (the sons of Henri IV. and Gabrielle d'Estrées), also Fouquet and Lauzun. In 1762 the château was given by Louis XV. to the Duc de Choiseul, and the great Napoleon turned it over to his ancient colleague, Roger Ducos, who apparently cared

*Sculpture from the Chapelle de St. Hubert*

# Amboise

little for its beauties or associations, for he mutilated it outrageously.

In later times the history of the château and its dependencies has been more prosaic. The Emir Abd-el-Kader was imprisoned here in 1852, and Louis Napoleon stayed for a time within its walls upon his return from the south. To-day it belongs to the family of Orleans, to whom it was given by the National Assembly in 1872, and has become a house of retreat for military veterans. This is due to the generosity of the Duc d'Aumale into whose hands it has since passed. The restoration which has been carried on has made of Amboise an ideal reproduction of what it once was, and in every way it is one of the most splendid and famous châteaux of its kind, though by no means as lovable as the residential châteaux of Chenonceaux or Langeais.

The Chapelle de St. Hubert, which was restored by Louis Philippe, is the chief artistic attraction of Amboise; a bijou of full-blown Gothic. It is a veritable architectural joy of the period of Charles VIII., to whom its erection was due. Its portal has an adorable bas-relief, representing "La Chasse de St. Hubert," and showing St. Hubert, St. Christopher, and St. Anthony, while above, in the tympanum, are effigies of the Virgin, of Charles VIII., and of Anne de Bretagne. The sculpture is, however, comparatively modern, but it embellishes a shrine worthy in every way, for there repose the bones of Leonardo da Vinci. Formerly Da Vinci's remains had rested in the chapel of the château itself, dedicated to St. Florentin.

Often the Chapelle de St. Hubert has been confounded with that described by Scott in "Quentin Durward," but it is manifestly not the same, as that was located in Tours or near there, and his very words describe the architecture as "of the rudest and meanest kind," which this is not. Over the arched doorway of the chapel at Tours there was, however, a "statue of St. Hubert with a bugle-horn around his neck and a leash of greyhounds at his feet," which may have been an early suggestion of the later work which was undertaken at Amboise.

All vocations came to have their protecting saints in the middle ages, and, since "*la chasse*" was the great recreation of so many, distinction was bestowed upon Hubert as being one of the most devout. The legend is sufficiently familiar not to need recounting here, and, anyway, the story is plainly told in this sculptured panel over the portal of the chapel at Amboise.

In this Chapel of St. Hubert was formerly held "that which was called a hunting-mass. The office was only used before the noble and powerful, who, while assisting at the solemnity, were usually impatient to commence their favourite sport."

The ancient Salle des Gardes of the château, with the windows giving on the balcony overlooking the river, became later the Logis du Roi. From this great chamber one passes on to the terrace near the foot of the Grosse Tour, called the Tour des Minimes. It is this tower which contains the "*escalier des voitures.*" The entrance is through an elegant portico leading to the upper stories. Above another portico, leading from the terrace to the garden, is to be seen the emblem of Louis XII., the porcupine, so common at Blois.

In the fosse, which still remains on the garden side, was the universally installed *jeu-de-paume,* a favourite amusement throughout the courts of Europe in the middle ages.

At the base of the château are clustered numerous old houses of the sixteenth century, but on the river-front these have been replaced with pretentious houses, cafés, automobile garages, and other modern buildings.

Near the Quai des Violettes are a series of subterranean chambers known as the Greniers de César, dating from the sixteenth century.

Even at this late day one can almost picture the great characters in the drama of other

*Cipher of Anne de Bretagne, Hôtel de Ville, Amboise*

times who stalked majestically through the apartments, and over the very flagstones of the courts and terraces which one treads to-day; Catherine de Medici with her ruffs and velvets; Henri de Guise with all his wiles; Condé the proud; the second François, youthful but wise; his girl queen, loving and sad; and myriads more of all ranks and of all shades of morality, — all resplendent in the velvets and gold of the costume of their time.

# Amboise

Near the château is the Clos Luce, a Gothic habitation in whose oratory died Leonardo da Vinci, on May 2, 1519.

Immediately back of the château is the Forêt d'Amboise, the scene of many gay hunting parties when the court was here or at Chenonceaux, which one reaches by traversing the forest route. On the edge of this forest is Chanteloup, remembered by most folk on account of its atrocious Chinese-like pagoda, built of the débris of the Château de la Bourdaisière, by the Duc de Choiseul, in memory of the attentions he received from the nobles and bourgeois of the ville upon the fall of his ministry and his disgrace at the hands of Louis XV. and La Du Barry. It is a curious form to be chosen when one had such beautiful examples of architectural art near by, only equalled, perhaps, in atrociousness by the "Royal Pavilion" of England's George IV.

La Bourdaisière, near Amboise, of which only the site remains, if not one of the chief tourist attractions of the château country, has at least a sentimental interest of abounding importance for all who recall the details of the life of "La Belle Gabrielle."

Here in Touraine Gabrielle d'Estrées was born in 1565. She was twenty-six years old when Henri IV. first saw her in the château of her father at Cœuvres. So charmed was he with her graces that he made her his *maîtresse* forthwith, though the old court-life chronicles of the day state that she already possessed something more than the admiration of Sebastian Zamet, the celebrated financier.

# CHAPTER VIII.

### CHENONCEAUX

"The castle of Chenonceaux is a fine place on the river Cher, in a fine and pleasant country."

FRANCOIS PREMIER.

"The castle of Chenonceaux is one of the best and most beautiful of our kingdom."

HENRI II.

THE average visitor will come prepared to worship and admire a château so praised by two luxury-loving Kings of France.

Chenonceaux is noted chiefly for its château, but the little village itself is charming. The houses of the village are not very new, nor very old, but the one long street is most attractive throughout its length, and the whole atmosphere of the place, from September to December, is odorous with the perfume of red-purple grapes. The vintage is not the equal of that of the Bordeaux region, perhaps, nor of Chinon, nor Saumur; but the *vin du pays* of the Cher and the Loire, around Tours, is not to be despised.

Most tourists come to Chenonceaux by train from Tours; others drive over from Amboise, and yet others come by bicycle or automobile. They are not as yet so numerous as might be expected, and accordingly here, as elsewhere in Touraine, every facility is given for visiting the château and its park.

If you do not hurry off at once to worship at the abode of the fascinating Diane, one of the brightest ornaments of the court of François Premier and his son Henri, you will enjoy your dinner at the Hôtel du Bon Laboureur, though most likely it will be a solitary one, and you will be put to bed in a great chamber overlooking the park, through which peep, in the moonlight, the turrets of the château, and you may hear the purling of the waters of the Cher as it flows below the walls.

Jean Jacques Rousseau, like François I., called Chenonceaux a beautiful place, and he was right; it is all of that and more. Here one comes into direct contact with an atmosphere which, if not feudal, or even mediæval, is at least that of several hundred years ago.

Chenonceaux is moored like a ship in the middle of the rapidly running Cher, a dozen miles or more above where that stream enters the Loire. As a matter of fact, the château practically bridges the river, which flows under its foundations and beneath its drawbridge on either side, besides filling the moat with water. The general effect is as if the building were set in the midst of the stream and formed a sort of island château. Round about is a gentle meadow and a great park, which give to this turreted architectural gem of Touraine a setting which is equalled by no other château.

What the château was in former days we can readily imagine, for nothing is changed as to the general disposition. Boats came to the water-gate, as they still might do if such boats still existed, in true, pictorial legendary fashion. To-day, the present occupant has placed a curiosity on the ornamental waters in the shape of a gondola. It is out of keeping with the grand fabric of the château, and it is a pity that it does not cast itself adrift some night. What has become of the gondolier, who was imported to keep the craft company, nobody seems to know. He is certainly not in evidence, or, if he is, has transformed himself into a groom or a *chauffeur*.

The Château of Chenonceaux is not a very ample structure; not so ample as most photographs would make it appear. It is not tiny, but still it has not the magnificent proportions of Blois, of Chambord, or even of Langeais. It was more a habitation than it was a fortress, a *maison de campagne,* as indeed it virtually became when the Connétable de Montmorency took possession of the structure in the name of the king, when its builder, Thomas Bohier, the none too astute minister of finances in Normandy, came to grief in his affairs.

François I. came frequently here for " *la chasse,*" and his memory is still kept alive by the Chambre François Premier. François held possession till his death, when his son made it over to the " admired of two generations," Diane de Poitiers.

Diane's memory will never leave Chenonceaux. To-day it is perpetuated in the Chambre de Diane de Poitiers; but the portrait by Leonardo da Vinci, which was supposed to best show her charms, has now disappeared from the " long gallery " at the château. This portrait was painted at the command of François, before Diane transferred her affections to his son.

No one knows when or how Diane de Poitiers first came to fascinate François, or how or why her power waned. At any rate, at the time François pardoned her father, the witless Comte de St. Vallier, for the treacherous part he played in the Bourbon conspiracy, he really believed her to be the " brightest ornament of a beauty-loving court."

Certainly, Diane was a powerful factor in the politics of her time, though François himself soon tired of her. Undaunted by this, she forthwith set her cap for his son Henri, the Duc d'Orleans, and won him, too. Of her beauty the present generation is able to judge for itself by reason of the three well-known and excellent portraits of contemporary times.

Diane's influence over the young Henri was absolute. At his death her power was, of course, at an end, and Chenonceaux, and all else possible, was taken from her by the orders of Catherine, the long-suffering wife, who had been put aside for the fascinations of the charming huntress.

It must have been some satisfaction, however, to Diane, to know that, in his fatal joust with Montgomery, Henri really broke his lance and met his death in her honour, for the records tell that he bore her colours on his lance, besides her initials set in gold and gems on his shield.

Catherine's eagerness to drive Diane from the court was so great, that no sooner had her spouse fallen — even though he did not actually die for some days — than she sent word to Diane, "who sat weeping alone," to instantly quit the court; to give up the crown jewels — which Henri had somewhat inconsiderately given her; and to "give up Chenonceaux in Touraine," Catherine's Naboth's vineyard, which she had so long admired and coveted. She had known it as a girl, when she often visited it in company with her father-in-law, the appreciative but dissolute François, and had ever longed to possess it for her own, before even her husband, now dead, had given it to "that old hag Diane de Poitiers, Duchesse de Valentinois."

Diane paid no heed to Catherine's command. She simply asked: "Is the king yet dead?"

"No, madame," said the messenger, "but his wound is mortal; he cannot live the day."

"Tell the queen, then," replied Diane, "that her reign is not yet come; that I am mistress still over her and the kingdom as long as the king breathes the breath of life."

Henri was more or less an equivocal character, devoted to Diane, and likewise fond —

one says it with caution — of his wife. He caused to be fashioned a monogram (seen at Chenonceaux) after this wise:

supposedly indicating his attachment for Diane and his wife alike. The various initials of the cipher are in no way involved. Diane returned the compliment by decorating an apartment for the king, at her Château of Anet, with the black and white of the Medici arms.

The Château of Chenonceaux, so greatly coveted by Catherine when she first came to France, and when it was in the possession of Diane, still remains in all the regal splendour of its past. It lies in the lovely valley of the Cher, far from the rush and turmoil of cities and even the continuous traffic of great thoroughfares, for it is on the road to nowhere unless one is journeying cross-country from the lower to the upper Loire. This very isolation resulted in its being one of the few monuments spared from the furies of the Revolution, and, " half-palace and half-château," it glistens with the purity of its former glory, as picturesque as ever, with turrets, spires, and rooftops all mellowed with the ages in a most entrancing manner.

Even to-day one enters the precincts of the château proper over a drawbridge which spans an arm of the Loire, or rather, a moat which leads directly from the parent stream. On the opposite side are the bridge piers supporting five arches, the work of Diane when she was the fair chatelaine of the domain. This ingenious thought proved to be a most useful and artistic addition to the château. It formed a flagged promenade, lovely in itself, and led to the southern bank of the Cher, whence one got charming vistas of the turrets and rooftops of the château through the trees and the leafy avenues which converged upon the structure.

When Catherine came she did not disdain to make the best use of Diane's innovation that suggested itself to her, which was simply to build the " Long Gallery " over the arches of this lovely bridge, and so make of it a veritable house over the water. A covering was made quite as beautiful as the rest of the structure, and thus the bridge formed a spacious wing of two stories. The first floor — known as the

*Château de Chenonceaux*

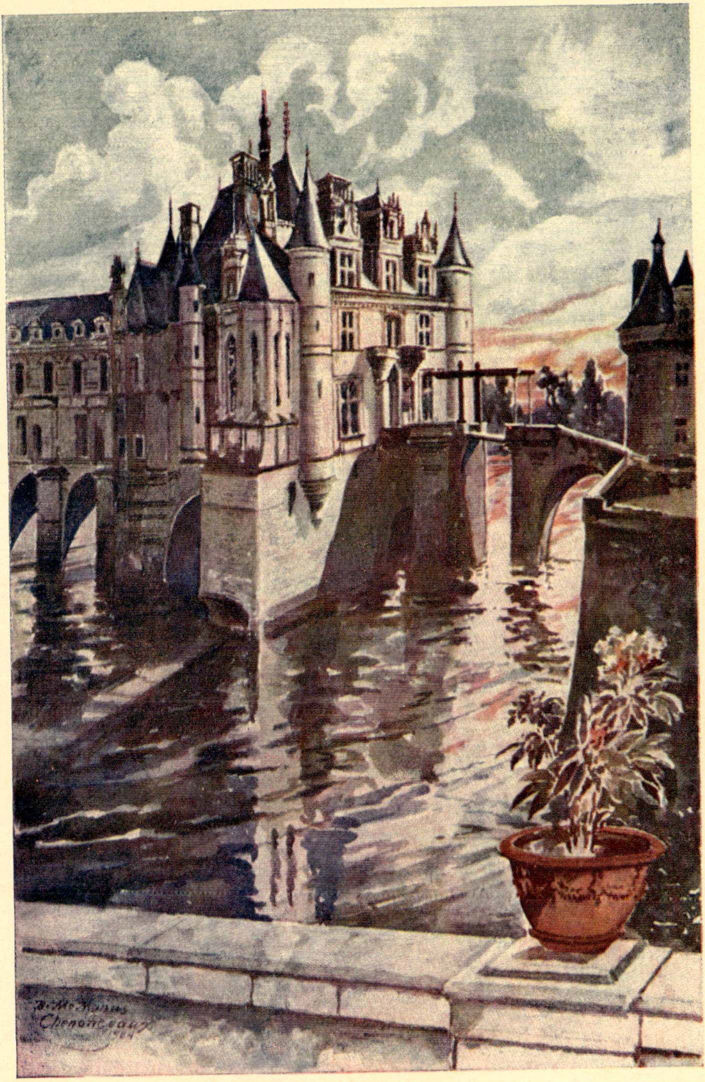
Chenonceaux

"Long Gallery"— was intended as a banqueting-hall, and possessed four great full-length windows on either side looking up and down stream, from which was seen — and is to-day

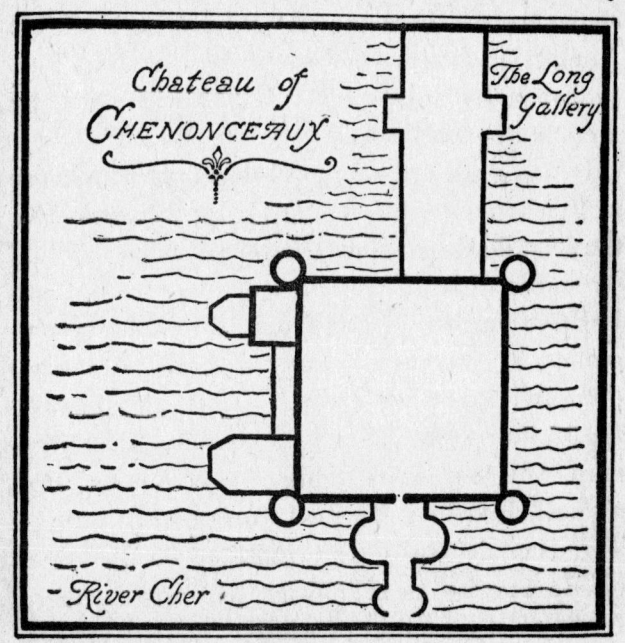

— an outlook as magnificently idyllic as is possible to conceive. Jean Goujon had designed for the ceiling one of those wonder-works for which he was famous, but if the complete plan was ever carried out, it has disappeared, for only a tiny sketch of the whole scheme remains to-day.

Catherine came in the early summer to take possession of her long-coveted domain. Being a skilful horsewoman, she came on horseback, accompanied by a "*petite bande*" of feminine charmers destined to wheedle political secrets from friends and enemies alike, — a real "*escadron volant de la reine*," as it was called by a contemporary.

It was a gallant company that assembled here at this time, — the young King Charles IX., the Duc de Guise, and "two cardinals mounted on mules," — Lorraine, a true Guise, and D'Este, newly arrived from Italy, and accompanied by the poet Tasso, wearing a "gabardine and a hood of satin." Catherine showed the Italian great favour, as was due a countryman, but there was another poet among them as well, Ronsard, the poet laureate of the time. The Duc de Guise had followed in the wake of Marguerite, unbeknownst to Catherine, who frowned down any possibility of an alliance between the houses of Valois and Lorraine.

A great fête and water-masque had been arranged by Catherine to take place on the Cher, with a banquet to follow in the Long Gallery in honour of her arrival at Chenonceaux.

When twilight had fallen, torches were ignited and myriads of lights blazed forth from the boats on the river and from the windows of the château. Music and song went forth into the night, and all was as gay and lovely as a Venetian night's entertainment. The hunting-horns echoed through the wooded banks, and through the arches above which the château was built passed great highly coloured barges, including a fleet of gondolas to remind the queen-mother of her Italian days, — the ancestors perhaps of the solitary gondola which to-day floats idly by the river-bank just before the grand entrance to the château. From *parterre* and *balustrade,* and from the clipped yews of the ornamental garden, fairy lamps burned forth and dwindled away into dim infinity, as the long lines of soft light gradually lost themselves in the forest. It was a grand affair and idyllic in its unworldliness. One may not see its like to-day, for electric lights and " rag-time " music, which mostly comprise the attractions of such *al fresco* pleasures, will hardly produce the same effect.

Among the great fêtes at Chenonceaux will always be recalled that given by the court upon the coming of the youthful François II. and Mary Stuart, after the horrible massacres at Amboise.

All the Renaissance skill of the time was employed in the erection of pompous accessories, triumphal arches, columns, obelisks, and altars. There were innumerable tablets also, bearing inscriptions in Latin and Greek, — which nobody read, — and a fountain which bore the following:

> "Au saint bal des dryades,
> A Phœbus, ce grand dieu,
> Aux humides nyades,
> J'ai consacré ce lieu."

Of Chenonceaux and its glories what more can be said than to quote the following lines of the middle ages, which in their quaint old French apply to-day as much as ever they did:

> "Basti si magnifiquement
> Il est debout, comme un géant,
> Dedans le lit de la rivière,
> C'est-à-dire dessus un pont
> Qui porte cent toises de long."

The part of the edifice which Bohier erected in 1515 is that through which the visitor makes his entrance, and is built upon the piers of an old mill which was destroyed at that time.

Catherine bequeathed Chenonceaux to the wife of Henri III., Louise de Vaudémont, who died here in 1601. For a hundred years it still belonged to royalty, but in 1730 it was sold to

M. Dupin, who, with his wife, enriched and repaired the fabric. They gathered around them a company so famous as to be memorable in the annals of art and literature. This is best shown by the citing of such names as Fontenelle, Montesquieu, Buffon, Bolingbroke, Voltaire, and Rousseau, all of whom were frequenters of the establishment, the latter being charged with the education of the only son of M. and Madame Dupin.

Considering Rousseau's once proud position among his contemporaries, and the favour with which he was received by the nobility, it is somewhat surprising that his struggle for life was so hard. The Marquise de Créquy wrote in her "Souvenirs:" "Rousseau left behind him his *Mémoires,* which I think for the sake of his memory and fame ought to be much curtailed." And undoubtedly she was right. Rousseau wrote in his "Confessions:" "In 1747 we went to spend the autumn in Touraine, at the Château of Chenonceaux, a royal residence upon the Cher, built by Henri II. for Diane de Poitiers, whose initials are still to be seen there. . . . We amused ourselves greatly in this fine spot; the living was of the best, and I became fat as a monk. We made a great deal of music and acted comedies."

One might imagine, from a stroll through the magnificent halls and galleries of Chenonceaux, that Rousseau's experiences might be repeated to-day if one were fortunate enough to be asked to sojourn there for a time. The nearest that one can get, however, to becoming personally identified with the château and its life is to sign his name in the great vellum quarto which ultimately will rest in the archives of the château.

It is doubtless very wrong to be covetous; but Chenonceaux is such a beautiful place and comes so near the ideal habitation of our imagination that the desire to possess it for one's own is but human.

In the "Galerie Louis XIV." were given the first representations of many of Rousseau's pieces.

One gathers from these accounts of the happenings in the Long Gallery that it formed no bridge of sighs, and most certainly it did not. Its walls resounded almost continually with music and laughter. Here in these rooms Henri II. danced and made love and intrigued, while Catherine, his queen, was left at Blois with her astrologer and his poisons, to eat out her soul in comparative neglect.

Before the time of the dwelling built by Bohier for himself and family on the foundations of the old mill, there was yet a manor-house belonging to the ancient family of Marques, from whom the Norman financier bought the site. The tower, seen to-day at the right of the entrance to the château proper, — an expressive relic of feudal times, — was a part of the earlier establishment. To-day it is turned into a sort of *kiosque* for the sale of photographs, post-cards, and an admirable illustrated guide to the château.

The interior of the château to-day presents the following remarkable features: The dining-room of to-day, formerly the Salle des Gardes, has a ceiling in which the cipher of Catherine de Medici is interwoven with an arabesque. To the left of this apartment is the entrance to the chapel, which to-day seems a bit incongruously placed, leading as it does from the dining-room. It is but a tiny chapel, but it is as gay and brilliant as if it were still the adjunct of a luxury-loving court, and it has some glass dating from 1521, which, if not remarkable for design or colouring, is quite choice enough to rank as an art treasure of real value.

According to Viollet-le-Duc each feudal seigneur had attached to his château a chapel, often served by a private chaplain, and in some instances by an entire chapter of prelates.

These chapels were not simple oratories surrounded by the domestic apartments, but were architectural monuments in themselves, and either entirely isolated, as at Amboise, or semi-detached, as at Chenonceaux.

Below, in the sub-basement, at Chenonceaux, are the original foundations upon which Bohier laid his first stones. Here, too, are various chambers, known respectively as the prison, the Bains de la Reine, the *boulangerie,* etc.

Chenonceaux to-day is no whited sepulchre. It is a real living and livable thing, and, moreover, when one visits it, he observes that the family burn great logs in their fireplaces, have luxurious bouquets of flowers on their diningtable, and use great wax candles instead of the more prosaic oil-lamps, or worse — acetylene gas. Chenonceaux evidently has no thoughts of descending to steam heat and electricity.

All this is as it should be, for when one visits a shrine like this he prefers to find it with as much as possible of the old-time atmosphere remaining. Chambord is bare and suggestive of the tomb, in spite of the splendour of its outline and proportions; Pierrefonds, in the north, is more so, and so would be Blois except for its restored or imitation decorations; but here at Chenonceaux all is different, and breathes the spirit of other days as well as that of to-day. It is, perhaps, not exactly as Diane left it, or as Rousseau knew it under the régime of the Dupins, since, after many changings of hands, it became the property of the *Credit Foncier,* by whom it was sold in 1891 to Mr. Terry, an American.

Chenonceaux has two other architectural monuments which are often overlooked under the spell of the more magnificent château. In the village is a small Renaissance church — in which the Renaissance never rose to any very great heights — which is here far more effective and beautiful than usually are Renaissance churches of any magnitude. There is also a sixteenth-century stone house in the same style and even more successful as an expression of the art of the time. It is readily found by inquiry, and is known as the "Maison des Pages de François I."

# CHAPTER IX.

### LOCHES

Much may be written of Loches, of its storied past, of its present-day quaintness, and of its wealth of architectural monuments. Its church is certainly the most curious religious edifice in all France, judging from a cross-section of the vaults and walls. More than all else, however, Loches is associated in our minds with the memory of Agnes Sorel.

Within the walls of the old collegiate church the lovely mistress of Charles VII. was buried in 1450; but later her remains and tomb were removed to one of the towers of the ancient castle of Loches, where they now are. She had amply endowed the church, but they would no longer give shelter to her remains, so her bones were removed five hundred years later. The statue which surmounts her tomb, as seen to-day, represents the " gentille Agnes " in all her loveliness, with folded hands on breast, a kneeling angel at her head and a couchant lamb at her feet,—a reminder of her innocence, said Henry James, but surely he nodded when he said it. Lovely she was, and good in her way, but innocent she was not, as we have come to know the word.

It is fitting to recall that Charles VII. was not the only monarch who sang her praises, for

*Loches*

it was François I. who, many years later, wrote those lines beginning:

"Gentille Agnes, plus de loz tu mérites."

Whether one comes to Loches by road or by rail, the first impression is the same; he enters at once into a sleepy, old-world town which has practically nothing of modernity about it except the electric lights.

There is but one way to realize the immense wealth of architectural monuments centred at Loches, and that is to see the city for the first time, as, perhaps, François Premier saw it when he journeyed from Amboise, and came upon it from the heights of the forest of Loches. The city has not grown much since that day. Then it had three thousand eight hundred souls, and now it has five thousand.

Here, in the Forêt de Loches, Henry II. of England built a monastery, — yet to be seen, — known as the Chartreuse du Liget, in repentance, or, perhaps, as a penance for the murder of Becket. Over the doorway of this monastery was graven:

ANGLORUM HENRICUS REX<br>
THOMÆ CŒDE CRUENTUS,<br>
LIGETICOS FUNDAT CARTUSIA MONAKOS.

To-day the monastery is the property of a M. de Marsay, and therefore not open to the public; but the Chapelle du Liget, near by, is a fine contemporary church of the thirteenth century, well worth the admiration too infrequently bestowed upon it.

The first view of Loches must really be much as it was in François's time, except, perhaps, that the roadway down from the forest has improved, as roads have all over France, and fruit-trees and vineyards planted out, which, however, in no way change the aspect when the town is first seen in the dim haze of an early November morning.

It is the sky-line *ensemble* of the châteaux of the Renaissance period which is their most varied feature. No two are alike, and yet they are all wonderfully similar in that they cut the sky with turret, tower, and chimney in a way which suggests nothing as much as the architecture of fairy-land.

The artists who illustrated the old fairy-tale books and drew castles wherein dwelt beautiful maidens could nowhere have found more real inspiration than among the châteaux of the Loire, the Cher, and the Indre.

Loches is a veritable mediæval town, and it is even more than that, for its history dates back into the earliest years of feudal times. Loches is one of those *soi-disant* French towns not great enough to be a metropolis, and yet quite indifferent to the affairs of the outside world.

The only false notes are those sounded by the various hawkers and cadgers for the visitor's money, who have hired various old mediæval structures, within the walls, and assure one that in the basement of their establishment there are fragments "recently discovered,"—this in English,—quite worth the price of admission which they charge you to peer about in a gloomy hole of a cellar, littered with empty wine-bottles and rubbish of all sorts.

All this is delightful enough to the simon-pure antiquarian; but even he likes to dig things out for himself, and the householders can't all expect to find *cachots* in their sub-cellars or iron cages in their garrets unless they manufacture them.

The old town, in spite of its lack of modernity, is full of surprises and contrasts that must make it very livable to one who cares to spend a winter within its walls. He may walk about on the ramparts on sunny days; may fish in the Indre, below the mill; and, if he is an artist, he will find, within a comparatively small area, much more that is exceedingly "paintable" than is usually found in the fishing-villages of Brittany or on the sand-dunes of the Pas de Calais, "artist's sketching-grounds" which have been pretty well worked of late.

The history of Loches is so varied and vivid that it is easy to account for the many remains of feudal and Renaissance days now existing. The derivation of its name is in some doubt. Loches was unquestionably the Luccæ of the

*Loches and Its Church*

Romans, but the Armorican Celts had the word *loc'h*, meaning much the same thing, — *un marais*, — which is also wonderfully like the *loch* known to-day in the place-names of Scotland and the *lough* of Ireland. Partisans may take their choice.

In the fifth century a monastery was founded here by St. Ours, which ultimately gave its name to the collegiate church which exists to-day. A château, or more probably a fortress, appeared in the sixth century. The city was occupied by the Franks in the seventh century, but by 630 it had become united with Aquitaine. Pepin sacked it in 742, and Charles le Chauve made it a seat of a hereditary government which, by alliance, passed to the house of Anjou in 886, to whom it belonged up to 1205. Jean-sans-Terre gave it to France in 1193. Richard Cœur de Lion apparently resented this, for he retook it in the year following. In 1204, Philippe-Auguste besieged Chinon and Loches simultaneously, and took the latter after a year, when he made it a fief, and gave it to Dreux de Mello, Constable of France, who in turn sold it to St. Louis.

The château of Loches became first a fortress, guarding the ancient Roman highway from the Blaisois to Aquitaine, then a prison, and then a royal residence, to which Charles VII. frequently repaired with Agnes Sorel, which calls up again the strangely contrasting influences of the two women whose names have gone down in history linked with that of Charles VII.

"Louis XI. aggrandized the château," says a French authority, "and perfected the prisons," whatever that may mean. He did, we know, build those terrible dungeons far down below the surface of the ground, where daylight never penetrated. They were perfect enough in all conscience as originally built, at least as perfect as the celebrated iron cage in which he imprisoned Cardinal Balue. The cage is not in its wonted place to-day, and only a ring in the wall indicates where it was once made fast.

Charles VIII. added the great round tower; but it was not completed until the reign of Louis XII. François I., in a not too friendly meeting, received Charles Quint here in 1539, just previous to his visit to Amboise. Marie de Medici, on escaping from Blois, stopped at the château at the invitation of the governor, the Duc d'Epernon, who sped her on her way, as joyfully as possible, to Angoulême.

The château itself is the chief attraction of interest, just as it is the chief feature of the landscape when viewed from afar. Of course it is understood that, when one speaks of the château at Loches, he refers to the collective châteaux which, in more or less fragmentary form, go to make up the edifice as it is to-day.

Whether we admire most the structure of Geoffroy Grise-Gonelle, the elegant edifice of the fifteenth century, or the additions of Charles VII., Louis XI., Charles VIII., Louis XII., or Henri III., we must conclude that to know this conglomerate structure intimately one must actually live with it. Nowhere in France — perhaps in no country — is there a château that suggests so stupendously the story of its past.

The chief and most remarkable features are undoubtedly the great rectangular keep or donjon, and the Tour Neuf or Tour Ronde. The first, in its immensity, quite rivals the best examples of the kind elsewhere, if it does not actually excel them in dimensions. It is, moreover, according to De Caumont, the most beautiful of all the donjons of France. As a state prison it confined Jean, Duc d'Alençon, Pierre de Brézé, and Philippe de Savoie.

The Tour Ronde is a great cylinder flanked with dependencies which give it a more or less irregular form. It encloses the prison where were formerly kept the famous cages, the invention of Cardinal Balue, who himself became their first victim. The Tour Ronde is reminiscent of two great female figures in the mediæval portrait gallery, — Agnes Sorel and Anne de Bretagne. The tomb of Agnes Sorel is here, and the Duchesse Anne made an oratory in this grim tower, from which she sent up her prayer for the success and unity of the political plans which inspired her marriage into the royal family of France. It is a daintily decorated chamber, with the queen's family device, the ermine with its twisted necklet, prominently displayed.

In the passage which conducts to the dungeons of this great round tower, one reads this ironical invitation: "*Entrés, messieurs, ches le Roy Nostre Mestre*" (*O. F.*).

That portion of the collective châteaux facing to the north is now occupied by the Sous-Préfecture, and is more after the manner of the residential châteaux of the Loire than of a fortress-stronghold or prison. Before this portion stands the famous chestnut-tree, planted, it is said, by François I., "and large enough to shelter the whole population of Loches beneath its foliage," says the same doubtful authority.

Under a fifteenth-century structure, called the Martelet, are the true dungeons of Loches. Here one is shown the cell occupied for nine years by the poor Ludovic Sforza, who died in 1510, from the mere joy of being liberated. More deeply hidden still is the famous Prison des Évêques of the era of François I. and the dungeon of Comte de St. Vallier, the father of the fascinating Diane, who herself was the means of securing his liberation by " fascinating the king," as one French writer puts it. This may be so. St. Vallier *was* liberated, we know, and the susceptible François *was* fascinated, though he soon tired of Diane and her charms. She had the perspicacity, however, to transfer her affections to his son, and so kept up a sort of family relationship.

Like the historic " prisoner of Gisors," the occupants of the dungeons at Loches whiled away their lonely hours by inscribing their sentiments upon the walls. Only one remains to-day, though fragmentary stone-carved letters and characters are to be seen here and there. He who wrote the following was certainly as cheerful as circumstances would allow:

> " Malgré les ennuis d'une longue souffrance,
> Et le cruel destin dont je subis la loy,

Il est encort des biens pour moy,
Le tendre amour et la douce espérance."

Most of these formidable dungeons of Loches were prisons of state until well into the sixteenth century.

Beneath, or rather beside, the very walls of the château is the bizarre collegiate church of

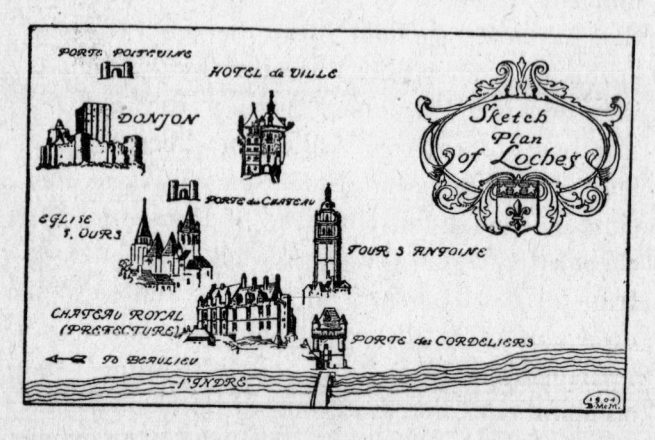

St. Ours. One says bizarre, simply because it is curious, and not because it is unchurchly in any sense of the word, for it is not. Its low nave is surmounted by an enormous tower with a stone spire, while there are two other pyramidal erections over the roof of the choir which make the whole look, not like an elephant, as a cynical Frenchman once wrote, but rather

*St. Ours, Loches*

like a camel with two humps. This strange architectural anomaly is, in parts, almost pagan; certainly its font, a fragment of an ancient altar on which once burned a sacred fire, *is* pagan.

There is a Romanesque porch of vast dimensions which is the real artistic expression of the fabric, dressed with extraordinary primitive sculptures of saints, demons, stryges, gnomes, and all manner of outré things. All these details, however, are chiselled with a masterly conception.

Behind this exterior vestibule the first bays of the nave form another, a sort of an inner vestibule, which carries out still further the unique arrangement of the whole edifice. This portion of the structure dates from a consecration of the year 965, which therefore classes it as of very early date, — indeed, few are earlier. Most of the church, however, is of the twelfth century, including another great pyramid which rises above the nave and the two smaller ones just behind the spire. The side-aisles of the nave were added between the twelfth and fifteenth centuries, while only the stalls and the tabernacle are as recent as the sixteenth. The eastern end is triapsed, an unusual feature in France. From this one realizes, quite to the fullest extent possible, the antiquity and individuality of the Église de St. Ours at Loches.

The quaint Renaissance Hôtel-de-Ville was built by the architect Jean Beaudoin (1535-1543), from sums raised, under letters patent from François I., by certain *octroi* taxes. From the fact that through its lower story passes one of the old city entrances, it has come to be known also as the Porte Picoys. In every way it is a worthy example of Renaissance civic architecture.

In the Rue de Château is a remarkable Renaissance house, known as the Chancellerie, which dates from the reign of Henri II. It has most curious sculptures on its façade interspersed with the devices of royalty and the inscription:

IVSTITIA REGNO, PRUDENTIA NUTRISCO.

The Tour St. Antoine serves to-day as the city's belfry. It is all that remains of a church, demolished long since, which was built in 1519-30, in imitation of St. Gatien's of Tours. Doubtless it was base in many of its details, as is its more famous compeer at Tours; but, if the old tower which remains is any indication, it must have been an elaborate and imposing work of the late Gothic and early Renaissance era.

As a literary note, lovers of Dumas's romances will be interested in the fact that in the Hôtel de la Couroirie at Loches a body of Protestants captured the celebrated Chicot, the jester of Henri III. and Henri IV.

Loches has a near neighbour in Beaulieu, which formerly possessed an ardent hatred for its more progressive and successful contemporary, Loches. Its very name has been perverted by local historians as coming from Bellilocus, "the place of war," and not "*le lieu d'un bel aspect.*"

The abbey church at Beaulieu was built by the warlike Foulques Nerra (in 1008-12), who usually built fortresses and left church-building to monks and bishops. It is a remarkable Romanesque example, though, since the fifteenth century, it has been mostly in ruins. Foulques Nerra himself, whose countenance had "*la majesté de celui d'un ange,*" found his last resting-place within its walls, which also sheltered much rich ornament, to-day greatly defaced, though that of the nave, which is still intact, is an evidence of its former worth.

The abbatial residence, still existent, has a curious exterior pulpit built into the wall, examples of which are not too frequent in France.

Agnes Sorel, the belle of belles, lived here for

a time in a house near the Porte de Guigné, which bears a great stone *panonceau,* from which the armorial bearings have to-day disappeared. It is another notable monument to "the most graceful woman of her times," and without doubt has as much historic value as many another more popular shrine of history.

In connection with Agnes Sorel, who was so closely identified with Loches and Beaulieu, it is to be recalled that she was known to the chroniclers of her time as "*la dame de Beauté-sur-Marne,*" — a place which does not appear in the books of the modern geographers. It may be noted, too, that it was the encouragement of the "*belle des belles*" of Charles VII. that, in a way, contributed to that monarch's success in politics and arms, for her sway only began with Jeanne d'Arc's supplication at Gien and Chinon. Tradition has it, indeed, that it was the "gentille Agnes" who put the sword of victory in his hands when he set out on his campaign of reconquest. Thus does the Jeanne d'Arc legend receive a damaging blow.

The château of Sausac, an elegant edifice of the sixteenth century, completely restored in later days, is near by.

*Tours*

## CHAPTER X.

#### TOURS AND ABOUT THERE

Tours, above all other of the ancient capitals of the French provinces, remains to-day a *ville de luxe,* the elegant capital of a land balmy and delicious; a land of which Dante sung:

> " Terra molle, e dolce e dilettosa. . . . "

It is not a very grand town as the secondary cities of France go; not like Rouen or Lyons, Bordeaux or Marseilles; but it is as typical a reflection of the surrounding country as any, and therein lies its charm.

One never comes within the influence of its luxurious, or, at least, easy and comfortable appointments, its distinctly modern and up-to-date railway station, its truly magnificent modern Hôtel de Ville, its well-appointed hotels and cafés and its luxurious shops, but that he realizes all this to a far greater extent than in any other city of France.

And again, referring to the material things

of life, everything is most comfortable, and the restaurants and hotels most attractive in their fare. Tours is truly one provincial capital where the *cuisine bourgeoise* still lives.

Touraine, and Tours in particular, besides many other things, is noted for its hotels. Their praises have been sung often and loudly, not forgetting Henry James's praise of the Hôtel de l'Univers, which is all one expects to find it and more. The same may be said of the Hôtel du Croissant, with the added opinion that it serves the most bountiful and excellent *déjeuner* to be had in all provincial France. It is difficult to say just what actually causes all this excellence and abundance, except that the catering there is an easy and pleasurable occupation.

The Rue Nationale — "*toujours et vraiment royale*" — is the great artery of Tours running riverwards. On it circulates all the life of the city.

To the right is the Quartier de la Cathédrale, where are assembled the great houses of the nobility — or such of them as are left — and of the old *bourgeoisie tourangelle*.

To the left are the streets of the workers, a silk-mill or two, and the printing-offices. Tours is and always has been celebrated for the number and size of its *imprimeries,* with which, in olden times, the name of the great Christopher Plantin, the master printer of Antwerp, was connected. To-day, Tours's greatest establishment is that of Alfred Mame et Fils, known throughout the Roman Catholic world.

The printers and booksellers of the middle ages were favoured persons, and their rank was high. In the days of solemn processions the booksellers led the way, followed by the paper-makers, the parchment-makers, the scribes, — who had not wholly died out, — the binders and the illuminators. In these days the printers were granted an emblazoned arms, which was characteristic and distinguished. The same was true of the *avocats,* who bore upon their escutcheon a gowned figure, with something very like a halo surrounding its head. The innkeepers went one better, and had a bishop with an undeniable halo. This is curious and inexplicable in the light of our modern conception of similar things, but it's better than a shield with quarterings representing half a canal-boat and half a locomotive, which was recently adopted by an enterprising watering-place which shall be nameless.

In the same ancient quarter are the old towers of Charlemagne and St. Martin. This part of the town is the nucleus of the old foundation, the site of the *oppidum* of the *Turones*, the *Cæsarodunum gallo-romain*, and of the life which centred around the old abbey of St. Martin, so venerated and so powerful in the middle ages.

To the inviolable refuge of this old abbey came multitudes of Christian pilgrims from the world over; the Merovingians to undergo the penances imposed upon them by the bishops and clerics in expiation of their crimes. Under Charlemagne, the Abbé Alcuin founded great schools of languages, history, astronomy, and music, from which founts of learning went forth innumerable and illustrious religious teachers.

All but the two towers of this old religious foundation are gone. The years of the Revolution saw the fall of the abbey; a street was cut through the nave of its church, and the two dismembered parts stand to-day as monuments to the sacrilege of modern times.

To-day a banal faubourg has sprung up around the site of the abbey, with here and there old tumble-down houses either of wood and stone, such as one reads of in the pages of Balzac, or sees in the designs of Doré, or with their sides covered with overlapping slates.

Amid all these is an occasional treasure of architectural art, such as the graceful Fountain of Beaune, the work of Michel Colombe, and some remains of early Renaissance houses of somewhat more splendid appointments than their fellows, particularly the Maison de Tristan l'Hermite, the Hôtel Xaincoings, and many exquisite fragments now made over into an *auberge* or a *cabaret,* which make one dream of Rabelais and his Gargantua.

It is uncertain whether Michel Colombe, who designed this fountain and also that masterwork, the tomb of the Duc François II. and Marguerite de Foix, at Nantes, was a Tourangeau or a Breton, but Tours claims him for her own, and settles once for all the spelling of his name by producing a "*papier des affaires*" signed plainly "Colombe." The proof lies in this document, signed in a notary's office at Tours, concerning payments which were made to him on behalf of the magnificent sepulchre which he executed for the church of St. Sauveur at La Rochelle. In his time — fifteenth century — Colombe had no rivals in the art of monumental sculpture in France, and with reason he has been called the Michel Ange of France.

The cathedral quarter has for its chief attraction that gorgeously florid St. Gatien, whose ornate façade was likened by a certain monarch to a magnificently bejewelled casket. It is an interesting and lovable Gothic-Renaissance church which, if not quite of the first rank among the masterpieces of its kind, is a marvel of splendour, and an example of the "*caprices d'une guipure d'art,*" as the French call it.

Bordering the Loire at Tours is a series of tree-lined quays and promenades which are the scenes, throughout the spring and summer months, of fêtes and fairs of many sorts. Here, too, at the extremity of the Rue Nationale, are statues of Descartes and Balzac.

The Tour de Guise on the river-bank recalls the domination of the Plantagenet kings of England, who were Counts of Anjou since it formed a part of the twelfth-century château built here by Henry II. of England.

At the opposite extremity of the city is another tower, the Tour de Foubert, which pro-

*Scene in the Quartier de la Cathédrale, Tours*

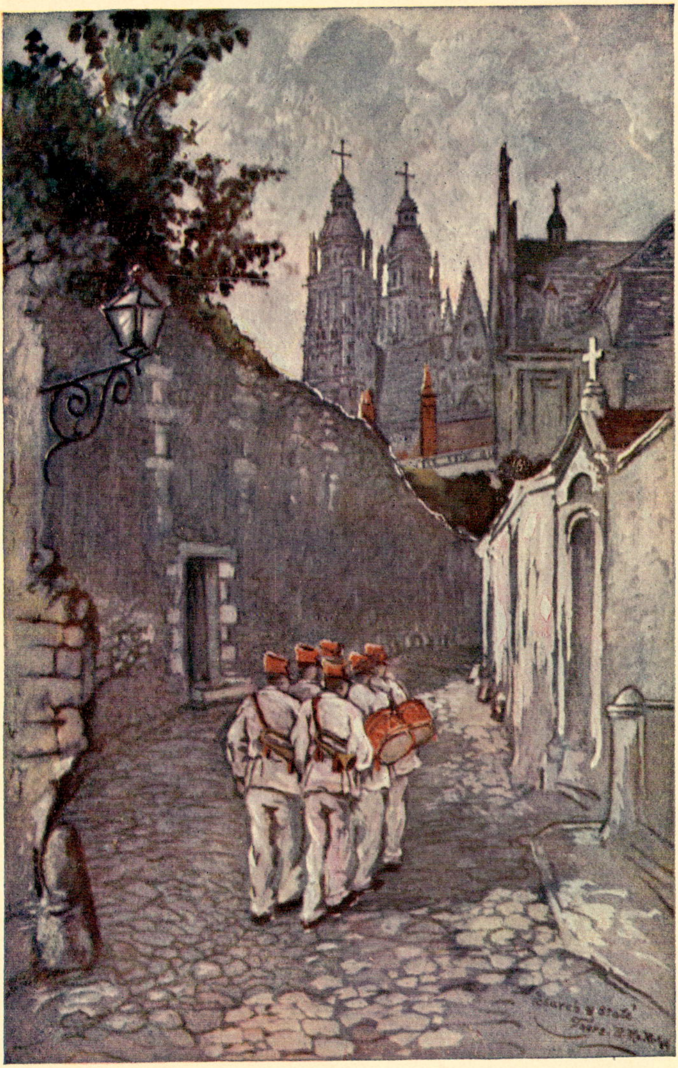

tected the feudal domain of the old abbey of St. Martin. The history of days gone by at Tours was more churchly than political.

Once only — during the reign of Louis XII. — did the States General meet at Tours (in 1506). Then the deputies of the *bourgeoisie* met alone for their deliberations, the chief outcome of which was to bestow upon the king the eminently fitting title of "Père du Peuple." One may question the righteousness of Louis XII. in throwing over his wife, Jeanne de France, in order to serve political ends by acquiring the estates of Anne of Brittany for the Crown of France for ever, but there is no doubt but that he did it for the "*good of his people.*"

The principal literary shrine at Tours is the house, in the Rue Nationale, where was born Honoré de Balzac.

One could not do better than to visit Tours during the "*été de St. Martin*," since it was the soldier-priest of Tours who gave his name to that warm, bright prolongation of summer which in France (and in England) is known as "St. Martin's summer," and which finds its counterpart in America's "Indian summer."

The legend tells us that somewhere in the dark ages lived a soldier named Martin. He was always of a charitable disposition, and none asked alms of him in vain. One November day, when the wind blew briskly and the snow fell fast, a beggar asked for food and clothing. Martin had but his own cloak, and this he forthwith tore in half and gave one portion to the beggar. Later on the same night there came a knocking at Martin's door; the snow had ceased falling and the stars shone brightly, and one of goodly presence stood with the cloak on his arm, saying, "I was naked and ye clothed me." Martin straightway became a priest of the church, and died an honoured bishop of Tours, and for ever after the anniversary of his conversion is celebrated by sunny skies.

We owe a double debt to St. Martin. We have to thank him for the saying, "*All my eye*" and the words "*chapel*" and "*chaplain.*" The full form of the phrase, "*All my eye and Betty Martin,*" which we all of us have often heard, is an obvious corruption of "*O mihi beate Martine,*" the beginning of an invocation to the saint. The cloak he divided with a naked beggar, which, by the way, took place at Amiens, not at Tours, was treasured as a relic by the Frankish kings, borne before them in battle, and brought forth when solemn oaths were to be taken. The guardians of this cloak

PLESSIS-LES-TOURS in the time of LOUIS XI

dedicated to Our Lady of Cléry, before whose altar the superstitious Louis made his inconstant devotions.

Once a great forest surrounded the château, and was, as Scott says, "rendered dangerous and well-nigh impracticable by snares and traps armed with scythe-blades, which shred off the unwary traveller's limbs . . . and calthrops that would pierce your foot through, and pitfalls deep enough to bury you in them for ever." To-day the forest has disappeared, "lost in the night of time," as a French historian has it.

The detailed description in "Quentin Durward" is, however, as good as any, and, if one has no reference works in French by him, he may well read the dozen or more pages which Sir Walter devotes to the further description of the castle.

Perhaps, after all, it is fitting that a Scot should have written so enthusiastically of it, for the castle itself was guarded by the Scottish archers, "to the number of three hundred gentlemen of the best blood of Scotland."

An anonymous poet has written of the ancient glory of this retreat of Louis's as follows:

> "Un imposant château se présente à la vue,
> Par des portes de fer l'entrée est défendue ;
> Les murs en sont épais et les fossés profonds ;
> On y voit des créneaux, des tours, des bastions,
> Et des soldats armés veillent sur ses murailles."

Frame this with such details as the surrounding country supplies, the Cher on one side, the Loire on the other, and the fertile hills of St. Cyr, of Ballon, and of Joué, and one has a picture worthy of the greatest painter of any time.

Louis XI. died at Plessis, after having lived there many years. Louis XII. made of it a *rendezvous de chasse,* but François II. confided its care to a governor and would never live in it. Louis XIV. gave the governorship as a hereditary perquisite to the widow of the Seigneur de Sausac.

In 1778 it was used as a sort of retreat for the indigent, though happily enough Touraine was never overburdened with this class of humanity. Under Louis XV. a Mademoiselle Deneux, a momentary rival of La Pompadour and Du Barry, found a retreat here. Later it became a *maison de correction,* and finally a *dépôt militaire.* At the time of the Revolution it was declared to be national property, and on the *nineteenth Nivoise, Year IV.,* Citizen Cormeri, justice of the peace at Tours, fixed its value at one hundred and thirty-one thousand francs.

To-day it is as bare and uncouth as a mere barracks or as a disused flour-mill, and its ruins are visited partly because of their former historical glories, as recalled by students of French history, and partly because of the glamour which was shed over it, for English readers, by Scott.

Sixty years ago a French writer deplored the fact that, on leaving these scanty remains of a so long gone past, he observed a notice nailed to a pillar of the *porte-cochère* reading:

>                         LA FERME DU PLESSIS
> O LOUER OU A VENDRE

To-day some sort of a division and rearrangement of the property has been made, but the result is no less mournful and sad, and thus a glorious page of the annals of France has become blurred.

It is interesting to recall what manner of persons composed the household of Louis XI. when he resided at Plessis-les-Tours. Commines, his historian, has said that habitually it consisted of a chancellor, a *juge de l'hôtel*, a private secretary, and a treasurer, each having under him various employees. In addition there was a master of the pantry, a cupbearer, a *chef de bouche* and a *chef de cuisine,* a *fruitier,* a master of the horse, a quartermaster or master-at-arms, and, in immediate control of these domestic servants, a *seneschal* or *grand maître.* In many respects the household was not luxuriously conducted, for the parsimonious Louis lived fully up to the false maxim: " *Qui peu donne, beaucoup recueille."*

Louis himself was fond of doing what the modern housewife would call " messing about in the kitchen." He did not dabble at cookery as a pastime, or that sort of thing; but rather he kept an eagle eye on the whole conduct of the affairs of the household.

One day, coming to the kitchen *en négligé,* he saw a small boy turning a spit before the fire.

" And what might you be called? " said he, patting the lad on the shoulder.

" Etienne," replied the *marmiton.*

" Thy *pays,* my lad? "

" Le Berry."

" Thy age? "

" Fifteen, come St. Martin's."

" Thy wish? "

"To be as great as the king" (he had not recognized his royal master).

"And what wishes the king?"

"His expenses to become less."

The reply brought good fortune for the lad, for Louis made him his *valet de chambre,* and took him afterward into his most intimate confidence.

Louis was fond of *la chasse,* and Scott does not overlook this fact in "Quentin Durward." When affairs of state did not press, it was the king's greatest pleasure. For the royal hunt no pains or expense were spared. The carriages were without an equal elsewhere in the courts of Europe, and the hunting establishment was equipped with *chiens courants* from Spain, *levriers* from Bretagne, *bassets* from Valence, mules from Sicily, and horses from Naples.

The attractions of the environs of Tours are many and interesting: St. Symphorien, Varennes, the Grottoes of Ste. Radegonde, and the site of that most famous abbey of Marmoutier, also a foundation of St. Martin. Here, under the name Martinus Monasterium, grew up an immense and superb establishment. From an old seventeenth-century print one quotes the following couplet:

" De quel côté que le vent vente
Marmoutier a cens et rente."

From this one infers that the abbey's original functions are performed no more.

## ENVIRONS of TOURS

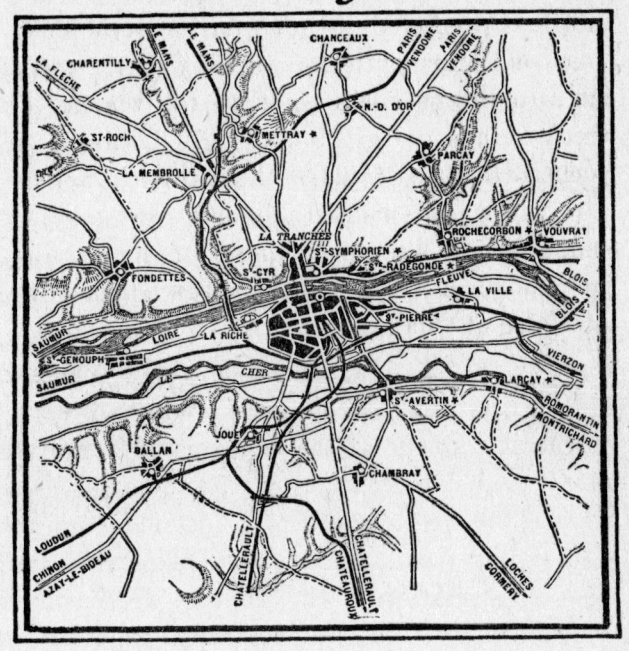

In the middle ages (thirteenth century) it was one of the most powerful institutions of its class, and its church one of the most beautiful in Touraine. The tower and donjon are the only substantial remains of this early edifice.

A curious chapel, called the "Chapelle des Sept Dormants," is here cut in the form of a cross into the rock of the hillside, where are buried the remains of the Seven Sleepers, the disciples of St. Martin, who, as the holy man had predicted, all died on the same day.

Beyond Marmoutier, a stairway of 122 steps, cut also in the rock, leads to the plateau on which stands the gaunt and ugly Lanterne de Rochecorbon, a fourteenth-century construction with a crenelated summit, an unlovely companion of that even more enigmatic erection known as "La Pile," a few miles down the Loire at Cinq-Mars.

# CHAPTER XI.

### LUYNES AND LANGEAIS

BELOW Tours, and before reaching Saumur, are a succession of panoramic surprises which are only to be likened to those of our imagination, but they are very real nevertheless.

As one leaves Tours by the road which skirts the right bank of the Loire, he is once more impressed by the fact that the *cailloux de Loire* are the river's chief product, though fried fish, of a similar variety to those found in the Seine, are found on the menus of all roadside taverns and restaurants.

Still, the effect of the uncovered bed of the Loire, with its variegated pebbles and mirror-like pools, is infinitely more picturesque than if it were mud flats, and its tree-bordered banks are for ever opening great alleyed vistas such as are only known in France.

The hills on either bank are not of the stupendous and magnificently scenic order of those of the Seine above and below Rouen; but, such as they are, they are of much the same composition, a soft talcy formation which here serves admirably the purposes of cliff-dwellings for the vineyard and wine-press workers, who form practically the sole population of the Loire villages from Vouvray, just above Tours, to Saumur far below.

On the hillsides are the vineyards themselves, growing out of the thin layer of soil in shades of red and brown and golden, which no artist has ever been able to copy, for no one has painted the rich colouring of a vineyard in a manner at all approaching the original.

Not far below Tours, on the right bank, rise the towers and turrets of the Château de Luynes, hanging perilously high above the lowland which borders upon the river. An unpleasant tooting tram gives communication a dozen times a day with Tours, but few, apparently, patronize it except peasants with market-baskets, and vineyard workers going into town for a jollification. It is perhaps just as well, for the fine little town of Luynes, which takes its name from the château which has been the residence of a Comte de Luynes since the days of Louis XIII., would be quite spoiled if it were on the beaten track.

*A Vineyard of Vouvray*

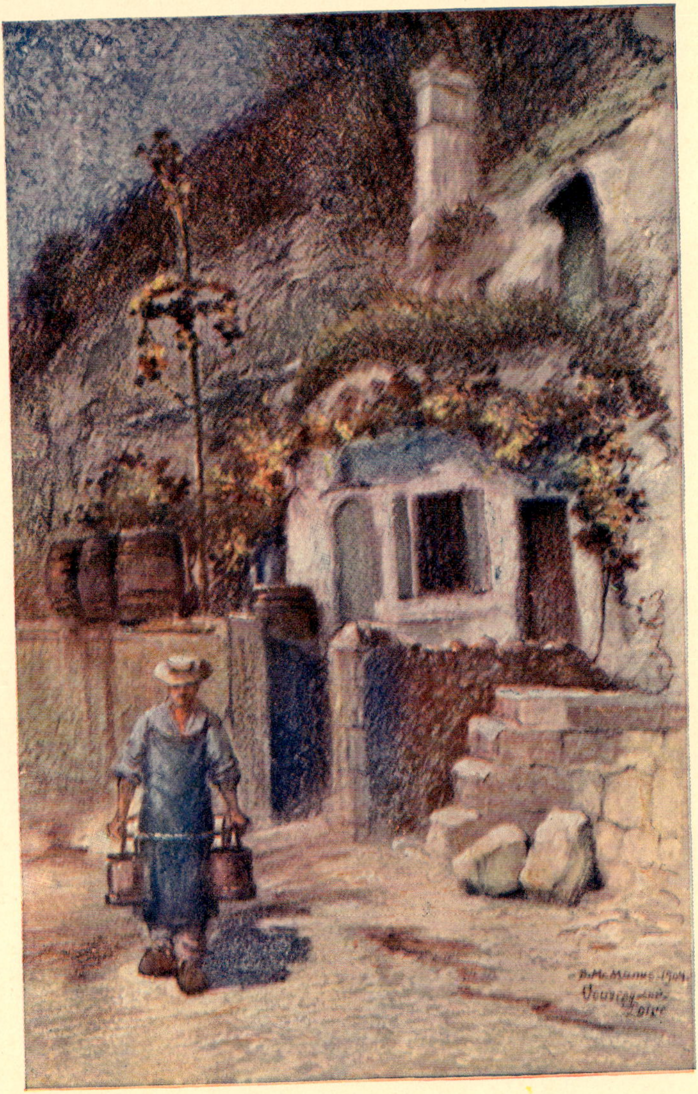

The brusque façade of the Château de Luynes makes a charming interior, judging from the descriptions and drawings which are to be met with in an elaborately prepared volume devoted to its history.

The stranger is allowed to enter within the gates of the courtyard, beneath the grim coiffed towers; but he may visit only certain apartments. He will, however, see enough to indicate that the edifice was something more than a mere *maison de campagne*. All the attributes of an important fortress are here, great, round, thickly built towers, with but few exterior windows, and those high up from the ground. There is nothing of luxurious elegance about it, and its aspect is forbidding, though imposing.

The château belies its looks somewhat, for it was built only in the fifteenth and sixteenth centuries, when, in most of its neighbours, the more or less florid Renaissance was in vogue. A Renaissance structure in stone and brick forms a part of that which faces on the interior court, and is flanked by a fine octagonal "*tour d'escalier.*"

From the terrace of the courtyard one gets an impressive view of the Loire, which glides by two or more kilometres away, and of the towers and roof-tops of Tours, and the vine-carpeted hills which stretch away along the river's bank in either direction.

The château of Luynes is still in the possession of a Duc de Luynes, through whose courtesy one may visit such of the apartments as his servants are allowed to show. It is not so great an exhibition, nor so good a one, as is to be had at Langeais; but it is satisfactory as far as it goes, and, when it is supplemented by the walks and views which are to be had on the plateau, upon which the grim-towered château sits, the memory of it all becomes most pleasurable.

The former Ducs de Luynes were continually appearing in the historic events of the later Renaissance period, but it was only with Louis XIII., he who would have put France under the protection of the Virgin, that the chatelain of Luynes came to a position of real power. Louis made Albert, the Gascon, both Duc de Luynes and Connétable de France, and thereby gave birth to a tyrant whom he hated and feared, as he did his mother, his wife, and his minister, Richelieu.

The site occupied by the château of Luynes is truly marvellous, though, as a matter of fact, there is no great magnificence about the pro-

*Mediæval Stairway and the Château de Luynes*

portions of the château itself. It is piled gracefully on the top of a table-land which rises abruptly from the Loire and has a charmingly quaint old town nestled confidingly below it, as if for protection.

One reaches the château by any one of a half-dozen methods, by the highroad which bends around in hairpin curves until it reaches the plateau above, by various paths across or around the vineyards of the hillside, or by a quaintly cut mediæval stairway, levelled and terraced in the gravelly soil until it ends just beneath the frowning walls of the château itself. From this point one gets quite the most imposing aspect of the château to be had, its towers and turrets piercing the sky high above the head, and carrying the mind back to the days when civilization meant something more — or less — than it does to-day, with the toot of a steam-tram down below on the river's bank and the midday whistles of the factories of Tours rending one's ears the moment he forgets the past and recalls the present.

To-day the Château de Luynes is modern, at least to the extent that it is lived in, and has all the refinements of a modern civilization; but one does not realize all this from an exterior contemplation, and only as one strolls through the apartments publicly shown, and gets glimpses of electrical conveniences and modern arrangements, does he wonder how far different it may have been before all this came to pass.

Built in early Renaissance times, the château has all the peculiarities of the feudal period, when window-openings were few and far between, and high up above the level of the pavement. In feudal and warlike times this often proved an admirable feature; but one would have thought that, with the beginning of the Renaissance, a more ample provision would have been made for the admission of sunshine.

The *chef-d'œuvre* of this really great architectural monument is undoubtedly the façade of the beautiful fifteenth-century courtyard. There is nothing even remotely feudal here, but a purely decorative effect which is as charming in its way as is the exterior façade of Azay-le-Rideau. "A poem," it has been called, "in weather-worn timber and stone," and the simile could hardly be improved upon.

The town, too, or such of it as immediately adjoins the château, is likewise charming and quaint, and sleepily indolent as far as any great activity is concerned.

Luynes was the seat of a seigneurie until

1619, when it became a possession of the Comte de Maillé. Finally it came to Charles d'Albert, known as "D'Albert de Luynes," a former page to Henri IV., who afterward became the favourite and the Guardian of the Seals of Louis XIV.; and thus the earlier foundation of Maillé became known as Luynes.

Except for its old houses of wood and stone, its old wooden market-house, and its tortuous streets of stairs, there are few features here, except the château, which take rank as architectural monuments of worth. The church is a modern structure, built after the Romanesque manner and wholly without warmth and feeling.

From the height on which stands the château of Luynes one sees, as his eye follows the course of the Loire to the southwestward, the gaunt, unbeautiful " Pile " of Cinq-Mars. The origin of this singular square tower, looking for all the world like a factory chimney or some great ventilating-shaft, is lost far back in Carlovingian, or perhaps Roman, times. It is a mystery to archæologists and antiquarians, some claiming it to be a military monument, others a beacon by land, and yet others believing it to be of some religious significance.

At all events, all the explanations ignore the

four *pyramidions* of its topmost course, and these, be it remarked, are quite the most curious feature of the whole fabric.

To many the name of the little town of Cinq-Mars will suggest that of the Marquis de Cinq-Mars, a court favourite of Louis XIII. It was the ambitious but unhappy career at court of this young gallant which ultimately resulted in his death on the scaffold, and in the razing, by Richelieu, of his ancestral residence, the castle of Cinq-Mars, "to the heights of infamy." The expression is a curious one, but history so records it. All that is left to-day to remind one of the stronghold of the D'Effiats of Cinq-Mars are its two crumbling gate-towers with an arch between and a few fragmentary foundation walls which follow the summit of the cliff behind "La Pile."

The little town of not more than a couple of thousand inhabitants nestles in a bend of the Loire, where there is so great a breadth that it looks like a long-drawn-out lake. The low hills, so characteristic of these parts, stretch themselves on either bank, unbroken except where some little streamlet forces its way by a gentle ravine through the scrubby undergrowth. Oaks and firs and huge limestone cliffs jut out from the top of the hillside on

*Ruins of Cinq-Mars*

the right bank and shelter the town which lies below.

Cinq-Mars is a miniature metropolis, though not a very progressive one at first sight; indeed, beyond its long main street and its houses, which cluster about its grim, though beautiful, tenth and twelfth century church, there are few signs of even provincial importance.

In reality Cinq-Mars is the centre of a large and important wine industry, where you may hear discussed, at the *table d'hôte* of its not very readily found little inn, the poor prices which the usually abundant crop always brings. The native even bewails the fact that he is not blessed with a poor season or two and then he would be able to sell his fine vintages for something more than three sous a litre. By the time it reaches Paris this *vin de Touraine* of commerce has aggrandized itself so that it commands two francs fifty centimes on the Boulevards, and a franc fifty in the University quarter.

The fall of Henri Cinq-Mars was most pathetic, though no doubt moralists will claim that because of his covetous ambitions he deserved nothing better.

He went up to Paris from Touraine, a boy of twenty, and was presented to the king, who was immediately impressed by his distinguished manners. From infancy Cinq-Mars had been a lover of life in the open. He had hunted the forests of Touraine, and had angled the waters of the Loire, and thus he came to give a new zest to the already sad life of Louis XIII. Honour after honour was piled upon him until he was made Grand Seneschal of France and Master of the King's Horse, at which time he dropped his natal patronymic and became known as "Monsieur le Grand."

Cinq-Mars fell madly in love with Marion Delorme and wished to make her "Madame la Grande," but the dowager Marquise de Cinq-Mars would not hear of it: Mlle. Marion Delorme, the Aspasia of her day, would be no honour to the ancestral tree of the Effiats of Cinq-Mars.

Headstrong and wilful, one early morning, Monsieur le Grand and his beloved, then only thirty, took coach from her hôtel in the Rue des Tournelles at Paris for the old family castle in Touraine, sitting high on the hills above the feudal village which bore the name of Cinq-Mars. In the chapel they were secretly married, and for eight days the proverbial marriage-bell rang true. Their Nemesis appeared on the ninth day in the person of the dowager,

and Cinq-Mars told his mother that the whole
affair was simply a *passe temps,* and that
Mlle. Delorme was still Mlle. Delorme. His
mother would not be deceived, however, and she
flew for succour to Richelieu, who himself was
more than slightly acquainted with the charms
of the fair Marion.

This was Cinq-Mars's downfall. He advised
the king " by fair means or foul, let Richelieu
die," and the king listened. A conspiracy was
formed, by Cinq-Mars and others, to do away
with the cardinal, *and even the king,* at whose
death Gaston of Orleans was to be proclaimed
regent for his nephew, the infant Louis XIV.

The court went to Narbonne, on the Mediter-
ranean, that it might be near aid from Spain;
all of which was a subterfuge of Cinq-Mars.
The rest moves quickly: Richelieu discovered
the plot; Cinq-Mars attempted to flee disguised
as a Spaniard, was captured and brought as a
prisoner to the castle at Montpellier.

Richelieu had proved the more powerful of
the two; but he was dying, and this is the reason, perhaps, why he hurried matters. Cinq-
Mars, " the amiable criminal," went to the tor-
ture-chamber, and afterward to the scaffold.

" Then," say the old chronicles, " Richelieu
ordered that the feudal castle of Cinq-Mars, in

the valley of the Loire, should be blown up, and the towers razed to the height of infamy."

From Cinq-Mars to Langeais, whose château is really one of the most appealing sights of the Loire, the characteristics of the country are topographically and economically the same; green hills slope, vine-covered, to the river, with here and there a tiny rivulet flowing into the greater stream.

As at Cinq-Mars, the chief commodity of Langeais is wine, rich, red wine and pale amber, too, but all of it wine of a quality and at a price which would make the city-dweller envious indeed.

There are two distinct châteaux at Langeais; at least, there is *the* château, and just beyond the ornamental stone-carpet of its courtyard are the ruins of one of the earliest donjons, or keeps, in all France. It dates from the year 990, and was built by the celebrated Comte d'Anjou, Foulques Nerra, "*un criminel dévoyé des hommes et de Dieu,*" whose hobby, evidently, was building châteaux, as his "follies" in stone are said to have encumbered the land in those old days.

Taken and retaken, dismantled and in part razed in the fifteenth century, it gave place to the present château by the orders of Louis XI.

*Château de Langeais*

The Château de Langeais of to-day is a robust example of its kind; its walls, flanked by great hooded towers, have a surrounding "*guette,*" or gallery, which served as a means of communication from one part of the establishment to another and, in warlike times, allowed boiling oil or melted lead, or whatever they may have used for the purpose, to be poured down upon the heads of any besiegers who had the audacity to attack it.

There is no glacis or moat, but the machicolations, sixty feet or more up from the ground, must have afforded a well-nigh perfect means of repelling a near attack.

Altogether Langeais is a redoubtable little château of the period, and its aspect to-day has changed but very little. "It is the swan-song of expiring feudalism," said the Abbé Bosseboeuf.

One gets a thrill of heroic emotion when he views its hardy walls for the first time: "a mountain of stone, a heroic poem of Gothic art," it has with reason been called.

Jean Bourré, the minister of Louis XI., built the present château about 1460. The chief events of its history were the drawing up within its walls of the "common law" of Touraine, by the order of Charles VII., and the marriage of Charles VIII. with Anne de Bretagne, on the 16th of December, 1491.

The land belonged, in 1276, to Pierre de Brosse, the minister of Philippe-le-Hardi; later, to François d'Orleans, son of the celebrated *Bâtard;* to the Princesse de Conti, daughter of the Duc de Guise; to the families Du Bellay and D'Effiats, Barons of Cinq-Mars; and, finally, to the Duc de Luynes, in whose hands it remained up to the Revolution.

Honoré de Balzac, who may well be called one of the historians of Touraine, gave to one of his heroines the name of Langeais. Today, however, the family of Langeais does not exist, and, indeed, according to the chronicles, never had any connection with either the donjon of Foulques Nerra or the château of the fifteenth century. The present owner is M. Jacques Siegfreid, who has admirably restored and furnished it after the Gothic style of the middle ages.

The château of Langeais, like that of Chenonceaux, is occupied, as one learns from a visit to its interior. A lackey of a superior order receives you; you pay a franc for an admission ticket, and the lackey conducts you through nearly, if not quite all, of the apartments. Where the family goes during this process it is hard to say, but doubtless they are willing to inconvenience themselves for the benefit of " touring " humanity.

The interior, no less than the exterior, impresses one as being something which has lived in the past, and yet exists to-day in all its original glory, for the present proprietor, with the aid of an admirable adviser, M. Lucien Roy, a Parisian architect, has produced a resemblance of its former furnishings which, so far as it goes, is beyond criticism.

There is nothing of bareness about it, nor is there an over-luxuriant interpolation of irrelevent things, such as a curator crowds into a museum. In short, nothing more has been done than to attempt to reconstitute a habitation of the fifteenth century. For seventeen years the work has gone on, and there have been collected many authentic furnishings contemporary with the fabric itself, great oaken beds, tables, chairs, benches, tapestries, and other articles. In addition, the decorations have been carried out after the same manner, copied in many cases from contemporary pictures and prints.

To-day, the general aspect is that of a peaceful household, with all recollections of feudal times banished for ever. All is tranquil, respectable, and luxurious, and it would take a chronic faultfinder not to be content with the manner with which these admirable restorations and refurnishings have been carried out.

One notes particularly the infinite variety and appropriateness of the tiling which goes to make up the floors of these great salons — modern though it is. The great chimneypieces, however, are ancient, and have not been retouched. Those in the Salle des Gardes and the Salle where was celebrated the marriage of Charles VIII. and Anne de Bretagne, with their ornamentation in the best of Gothic, are especially noteworthy.

This latter apartment is the chief attraction of the château and the room of which the present dwellers in this charming monument of history are naturally the most proud. To-day it forms the great dining-hall of the establishment. Mementos of this marriage, so momentous for France, are exceedingly numerous along the lower Loire, but this handsome room quite leads them all. This marriage, and the goods and lands it brought to the Crown, had but one stipulation connected with it, and that was that the Duchesse Anne should be privileged to marry the elderly king's successor, should she survive her royal husband.

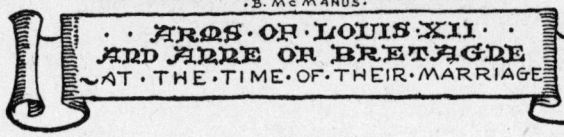

ARMS OF LOUIS XII
AND ANNE OF BRETAGNE
AT THE TIME OF THEIR MARRIAGE

Louis XII. was not at all opposed to becoming the husband of la Duchesse Anne after Charles VIII. had met his death on the tennis-court, because this second marriage would forever bind to France that great province ruled by the gentle Anne.

In the Salle des Gardes are six valuable tapestries representing such heroic figures as Cæsar and Charlemagne, surrounded by their companions in arms.

From the towers, on a clear day, one may see the pyramids of the cathedral at Tours rising on the horizon to the northward. Below is the Château de Villandry, where Philippe-Auguste met Henry II. of England to conclude a memorable peace. To the right is Azay-le-Rideau, and to the extreme right are the ruined towers of Cinq-Mars and its Pile. Nothing could be more delicious on a bright summer's day than the view from the ramparts of Langeais over the roof-tops of the charming little town in the foreground.

Some time after the Revolution there was found, in the gardens of the château, the remains of a *chapelle romaine* which historians, who have searched the annals of antiquity in Touraine, claim to have been the chapel in honour of St. Sauveur which Foulques V., called le Jeune, one of the five Counts of Anjou of that name, constructed upon his return from his voyage to Palestine in the twelfth century. To-day it is overgrown with a trellised grapevine and is practically not visible, still it is another architectural monument of the first rank with which the not very ample domain of the Château de Langeais is endowed.

From the courtyard the walls of the château take on a Renaissance aspect; a tiny doorway beside the great gate is manifestly Renaissance; so, too, are the polygonal towers, with their winding stairs, the pignons and gables of the roof, and what carved stone there is in evidence. Three stone stairways which mount by the slender *tourelles* serve to communicate with the various floors to-day as they did in the times of Charles VIII.

The courtyard itself, with its formal carpet design in stone, its shaded walls, its stone seats, and its Roman sarcophagus, is a pleasant retreat, but it has not the seclusion of the larger park, delightful though it is.

Just before the drawbridge of the old château, that mediæval gateway by which one enters to-day, one sees the Maison de Rabelais, who is the deity of Langeais and Chinon, as is Balzac that of Tours. It is a fine old-time house of a certain amplitude and grandeur among its less splendid fellows, now given over, on the ground floor, to a bakery and pastry-shop. Enough is left of its original aspect, and the Renaissance decorations of its façade are sufficiently well preserved to stamp it as a worthy abode for the "Curé de Chinon," who lived here for some years.

Two other names in literature are connected with Langeais: Ronsard, the poet, who lived here for a time, and César-Alexis-Chichereau, Chevalier de la Barre, who was a poet and a troubadour of repute.

The main street of Langeais is still flanked with good Gothic and Renaissance houses, neither pretentious nor mean, but of that order which sets off to great advantage the walls and towers and porches of the château and the church. This street follows the ancient Roman roadway which traversed the valley of the Loire through Gaul.

The river is here crossed by one of those too frequent, though useful, suspension-bridges, with which the Loire abounds. The guide-books call it *beau,* but it is not. One has to cross it to reach Azay-le-Rideau, which lies ten kilometres or more away across the Indre.

# CHAPTER XII.

### AZAY - LE - RIDEAU, USSÉ, AND CHINON

From Langeais, one's obvious route lies towards Chinon, via Azay-le-Rideau and Ussé. These latter are practically within the forest, though the Forêt de Chinon proper does not actually begin until one leaves Azay behind, when for twenty kilometres or more one of the most superb forest roads in France crosses many hills and dales until it finally descends into Chinon itself.

Like most forest roads in France, this highway is not flat; it rises and falls with a sheer that is sometimes precipitous, but always with a gravelled surface that gives little dust, and which absorbs water as the sand from the pounce-box of our forefathers dried up ink. This simile calls to mind the fact that in twentieth-century France the pounce-box is still in use, notably at wayside railway stations, where the agent writes you out your ticket and dries it off in a box, not of sand, but of sawdust.

To partake of the hospitality of Azay-le-Rideau one must arrive before four in the afternoon, and not earlier than midday. From the photographs and post-cards by which one has become familiar with Azay-le-Rideau, it appears like a great country house sitting by itself far away from any other habitation. In England this is often the case, in France but seldom.

Clustered around the walls of the not very great park which surrounds the château are all manner of shops and cafés, not of the tourist order, — for there is very little here to suggest that tourists ever come, though indeed they do, by twos and threes throughout all the year, — but for the accommodation of the population of the little town itself, which must approximate a couple of thousand souls, all of whom appear to be engaged in the culture of the vine and its attendant pursuits, as the wine-presses, the coopers' shops, and other similar establishments plainly show. There is, moreover, the pleasant smell of fermented grape-juice over all, which, like the odour of the hop-fields of Kent, is conducive to sleep; and there lies the charm of Azay-le-Rideau, which seems always half-asleep.

The Hôtel du Grand Monarque is a wonder-

# Azay-le-Rideau, Ussé, and Chinon 243

fully comfortable country inn, with a dining-room large enough to accommodate half a hundred persons, but which, most likely, will serve only yourself. One incongruous note is sounded, — convenient though it be, — and that is the electric light which illuminates the hotel and its dependencies, including the stables, which look as though they might once have been a part of a mediæval château themselves.

However, since posting days and tallow dips have gone for ever, one might as well content himself with the superior civilization which confronts him, and be comfortable at least.

The Château d'Azay-le-Rideau is one of the gems of Touraine's splendid collection of Renaissance art treasures, though by no means is it one of the grandest or most imposing.

A tree-lined avenue leads from the village street to the château, which sits in the midst of a tiny park; not a grand expanse as at Chambord or Chenonceaux, but a sort of green frame with a surrounding moat, fed by the waters of the Indre.

The main building is square, with a great coiffed round tower at each corner. The Abbé Chevalier, in his "Promenades Pittoresques en Touraine," called it the purest and best of French Renaissance, and such it assuredly is, if one takes a not too extensive domestic establishment of the early years of the sixteenth century as the typical example.

Undoubtedly the sylvan surroundings of the château have a great deal to do with the effectiveness of its charms. The great white walls of its façade, with the wonderful sculptures of Jean Goujon, glisten in the brilliant sunlight of Touraine through the sycamores and willows which border the Indre in a genuinely romantic fashion.

Somewhere within the walls are the remains of an old tower of the one-time fortress which was burned by the Dauphin Charles in 1418, after, says history, " he had beheaded its governor and taken all of the defenders to the number of three hundred and thirty-four." This act was in revenge for an alleged insult to his sacred person.

There are no remains of this former tower visible exteriorly to-day, and no other bloody acts appear to have attached themselves to the present château in all the four hundred years of its existence.

Gilles Berthelot erected the present structure early in the reign of François I. He was a man close to the king in affairs of state, first *conseiller-secrétaire,* then *trésorier-général des*

*Château d'Azay-le-Rideau*

*finances,* hence he knew the value of money. Among the succeeding proprietors was Guy de Saint Gelais, one of the most accomplished diplomats of his time. He was followed by Henri de Beringhem, who built the stables and ornamented the great room known as the Chambre du Roi from the fact that Louis XIV. once slept there, with the magnificent paintings which are shown to-day.

Everywhere is there a rich, though not gross, display of decoration, beginning with such constructive details as the pointed-roofed *tourelles,* which are themselves exceedingly decorative. The doors, windows, roof-tops, chimneypieces, and the semi-enclosed circular stairways are all elaborately sculptured after the best manner of the time.

The entrance portico is a wonder of its kind, with a strong sculptured arcade and arched window-openings and niches filled with bas-reliefs. Sculptured shells, foliage, and mythological symbols combine to form an arabesque, through which are interspersed the favourite ciphers of the region, the ermine and the salamander, which go to prove that François and other royalties must at one time or another have had some connection with the château.

History only tells us, however, that Gilles

Berthelot was a king's minister and Mayor of Tours. Perhaps he thought of handing it over as a gift some day in exchange for further honours. His device bore the words, "*Ung Seul Desir*," which may or may not have had a special significance.

The interior of the edifice is as beautiful as is its exterior, and is furnished with that luxuriance of decorative effect so characteristic of the best era of the Renaissance in France.

Until recently the proprietor was the Marquis de Biencourt, who, like his fellow proprietors of châteaux in Touraine, generously gave visitors an opportunity to see his treasure-house for themselves, and, moreover, furnished a guide who was something more than a menial and yet not a supercilious functionary.

Within a twelvemonth this "purest joy of the French Renaissance" was put upon the real estate market, with the result that it might have fallen into unappreciative hands, or, what a Touraine antiquarian told the writer would be the worse fate that could possibly befall it, might be bought up by some American millionaire, who through the services of the housebreaker would dismantle it and remove it stone by stone and set it up anew on some asphalted avenue in some western metropolis. This extraordinary fear or rumour, whatever it was, soon passed away and as a "*monument historique*" the château has become the property of the French government.

Less original, perhaps, in plan than Chenonceaux, less appealing in its *ensemble* and less fortunate in its situation, Azay-le-Rideau is nevertheless entitled to the praises which have been heaped upon it.

It is but a dozen kilometres from Azay-le-Rideau to Ussé, on the road to Chinon. The Château d'Ussé is indeed a big thing; not so grand as Chambord, nor so winsome as Langeais, but infinitely more characteristic of what one imagines a great residential château to have been like. It belongs to-day to the Comte de Blacas, and once was the property of Vauban, Maréchal of France, under Louis XIV., who built the terrace which lies between it and the river, a branch of the Indre.

Perched high above the hemp-lands of the river-bottom, which here are the most prolific in the valley of the Indre, the château with its park of seven hundred or more acres is truly regal in its appointments and surroundings. This park extends to the boundary of the national reservation, the Forêt de Chinon.

The Renaissance château of to-day is a reconstruction of the sixteenth century, which preserves, however, the great cylindrical towers of a century earlier. Its architecture is on the whole fantastic, at least as much so as Chambord, but it is none the less hardy and strong. Practically it consists of a series of *pavillons* bound to the great fifteenth-century donjon by smaller towers and turrets, all slate-capped and pointed, with machicolations surrounding them, and above that a sort of roofed and crenelated battlement which passes like a collar around all the outer wall.

The general effect of the exterior walls is that of a great feudal stronghold, while from the courtyard the aspect is simply that of a luxurious Renaissance town house, showing at least how the two styles can be pleasingly combined.

Crenelated battlements are as old as Pompeii, so it is doubtful if the feudality of France did much to increase their use or effectiveness. They were originally of such dimensions as to allow a complete shelter for an archer standing behind one of the uprights. The contrast to those of a later day, which, virtually nothing more than a course of decorative stonework, give no impression of utility, is great, though

*Château d'Ussé*

# Azay-le-Rideau, Ussé, and Chinon

here at Ussé they are more pronounced than in many other similar edifices.

The interior arrangements here give due prominence to a fine staircase, ornamented with a painting of St. John that is attributed to Michel Ange.

The Chambre du Roi is hung with ancient embroideries, and there is a beautiful Renaissance chapel, above the door of which is a sixteenth-century bas-relief of the Apostles. Most of the other great rooms which are shown are resplendent in oak-beamed ceilings and massive chimneypieces, always a distinct feature of Renaissance château-building, and one which makes modern imitations appear mean and ugly. To realize this to the full one has only to recall the dining-room of the pretentious hotel which huddles under the walls of Amboise. In a photograph it looks like a regal banqueting-hall; but in reality it is as tawdry as stage scenery, with its imitation wainscoted walls, its imitation beamed ceiling of three-quarter-inch planks, and its plaster of Paris fireplace.

Near Ussé is the Château de Rochecotte which recalls the name of a celebrated chieftain of the Chouans. It belongs to-day, though it is not their paternal home, to the family of

Castellane, a name which to many is quite as celebrated and perhaps better known.

The château contains a fine collection of Dutch paintings of the seventeenth century, and in its chapel there is a remarkably beautiful copy of the Sistine Madonna. The name of Talleyrand is intimately connected with the occupancy of the château, in pre-revolutionary times, by Rochecotte.

On the road to Chinon one passes through, or near, Huismes, which has nothing to stay one's march but a good twelfth-century church, which looks as though its doors were never opened. The Château de la Villaumère, of the fifteenth century, is near by, and of more than passing interest are the ruins of the Château de Bonneventure, built, it is said, by Charles VII. for Agnes Sorel, who, with all her faults, stands high in the esteem of most lovers of French history. At any rate this shrine of "*la belle des belles*" is worthy to rank with that containing her tomb at Loches.

As one enters Chinon by road he meets with the usual steep decline into a river-valley, which separates one height from another. Generally this is the topographic formation throughout France, and Chinon, with its silent guardians, the fragments of three non-contemporary castles, all on the same site, is no exception.

"We never went to Chinon," says Henry James, in his "Little Tour in France," written thirty or more years ago. "But one cannot do everything," he continues, "and I would rather have missed Chinon than Chenonceaux." A painter would have put it differently. Chenonceaux is all that fact and fancy have painted it, a gem in a perfect setting, and Chinon's three castles are but mere crumbling walls; but their environs form a *petit pays* which will some day develop into an "artists' sketching-ground," in years to come, beside which Etretat, Moret, Pont Aven, Giverny, and Auvers will cease to be considered.

At the base of the escarped rock on which sit the châteaux, or what is left of them, lies the town of Chinon, with its old houses in wood and stone and its great, gaunt, but beautiful churches. Before it flows the Vienne, one of the most romantically beautiful of all the secondary rivers of France.

From the *castrum romanum* of the emperors to the feudal conquest Chinon played its due part in the history of Touraine. There are those who claim that Chinon is a "*cité antédiluvienne*" and that it was founded by Cain, who after his crime fled from the paternal malediction and found a refuge here; and that its name, at first *Caynon,* became Chinon. Like the derivation of most ancient place-names, this claim involves a wide imagination and assuredly sounds unreasonable. *Caino* may, with more likelihood, have been a Celtic word, meaning an excavation, and came to be adopted because of the subterranean quarries from which the stone was drawn for the building of the town. The annalists of the western empire give it as *Castrum-Caino,* and whether its origin dates from antediluvian times or not, it was a town in the very earliest days of the Christian era.

The importance of Chinon's rôle in history and the beauty of its situation have inspired many writers to sing its praises.

> ". . . Chinon
> Petite ville, grand renom
> Assise sur pierre ancienne
> Au haute le bois, au bas la Vienne."

The disposition of the town is most picturesque. The winding streets and stairways are "foreign;" like Italy, if you will, or some of the steps to be seen in the towns bordering upon the Adriatic. At all events, Chinon is not

*The Roof-tops of Chinon*

# Azay-le-Rideau, Ussé, and Chinon

exactly like any other town in France, either with respect to its layout or its distinct features, and it is not at all like what one commonly supposes to be charactcristic of the French.

Dungeons of mediæval châteaux are here turned into dwellings and wine-cellars, and have the advantage, for both uses, of being cool in summer and warm in winter.

Already, in the year 371, Chinon's population was so considerable that St. Martin, newly elected Bishop of Tours, longed to preach Christianity to its people, who were still idolators. Some years afterward St. Mesme or Maxime, fleeing from the barbarians of the north, came to Chinon, and soon surrounded himself with many adherents of the faith, and in the year 402 consecrated the original foundation of the church which now bears his name.

Clovis made Chinon one of the strongest fortresses of his kingdom, and in the tenth century it came into the possession of the Comtes de Touraine. Later, in 1044, Thibaut III. ceded it to Geoffroy Martel. The Plantagenets frequently sojourned at Chinon, becoming its masters in the twelfth century, from which time it was held by the Kings of France up to Louis XI.

The most picturesque event of Chinon's history took place in 1428, when Charles VII. here assembled the States General, and Jeanne d'Arc prevailed upon him to march forthwith upon Orleans, then besieged by the English.

Memories of Charles VII., of Jeanne d'Arc, and of François Rabelais are inextricably mixed in the guide-book accounts of Chinon; but their respective histories are not so involved as would appear. There is some doubt as to whether the Pantagruelist was actually born at Chinon or in the suburbs, therefore there is no "*maison natale*" before which literary pilgrims may make their devotions. All this is a great pity, for Rabelais excites in the minds of most people a greater curiosity than perhaps any other mediæval man of letters that the world has known.

Though one cannot feast his eye upon the spot of Rabelais's birth, historians agree that it took place at Chinon in 1483. Much is known of the "Curé de Chinon;" but, in spite of his rank as the first of the mediæval satirists, his was not a wide-spread popularity, nor can one speak very highly of his appearance as a type of the Tourangeau of his time. His portraits make him appear a most supercilious character, and doubtless he was. He certainly was

# Azay-le-Rideau, Ussé, and Chinon 255

not an Adonis, nor had he the head of a god or the cleverness of a court gallant. Indeed there has been a tendency of late to represent him as a buffoon, a trait wholly foreign to his real character.

As for Charles VII. and Jeanne d'Arc, Chinon was simply the meeting-place between the inspired maid and her sovereign, when she urged him to put himself at the head of his troops and march upon Orleans.

Chinon is of the sunny south; here the grapes ripen early and cling affectionately, not only to the hillsides, but to the very house-walls themselves.

Chinon's attractions consist of fragments of three castles, dating from feudal times; of three churches, of more than ordinary interest and picturesqueness; and many old timbered and gabled houses; nor should one forget the Hôtel de France, itself a reminder of other days, with its vine-covered courtyard and tinkling bells hanging beneath its gallery, for all the world like the sort of thing one sees upon the stage.

There is not much else about the hotel that is of interest except its very ancient-looking high-posted beds and its waxed tiled floors, worn into smooth ruts by the feet of countless

thousands and by countless polishings with wax.
It is curious how a waxed tiled floor strikes
one as being something altogether superior to
one of wood. Though harder in substance, it is
infinitely pleasanter to the feet, and warm and
mellow, as a floor should be; moreover it seems
to have the faculty of unconsciously keeping
itself clean.

The Château de Chinon, as it is commonly
called, differs greatly from the usual Loire
château; indeed it is quite another variety altogether, and more like what we know elsewhere as a castle; or, rather it is three castles,
for each, so far as its remains are concerned,
is distinct and separate.

The Château de St. Georges is the most ancient and is an enlargement by Henry Plantagenet — whom a Frenchman has called "the
King Lear of his race" — of a still more ancient fortress.

The Château du Milieu is built upon the ruins
of the *castrum romanum,* vestiges of which are
yet visible. It dates from the eleventh, twelfth,
and thirteenth centuries, and was restored
under Charles VI., Charles VII., and Louis XI.

One enters through the curious Tour de
l'Horloge, to which access is given by a modern
bridge, as it was in other days by an ancient

drawbridge which covered the old-time moat.
The Grand Logis, the royal habitation of the
twelfth to fifteenth centuries, is to the right,
overlooking the town. Here died Henry II. of
England (1189) and here lived Charles VII.
and Louis XI. It was in the Grand Salle of this
château that Jeanne d'Arc was first presented
to her sovereign (March 8, 1429). From the
hour of this auspicious meeting until the hour
of the departure for Orleans she herself lived in
the tower of the Château de Coudray, a little
farther beyond, under guard of Guillaume
Bélier.

The meeting between the king and the
"Maid" is described by an old historian of
Touraine as follows: "The inhabitants of
Chinon received her with enthusiasm, the purpose of her mission having already preceded
her. . . . She appeared at court as *une
pauvre petite bergerette* and was received in
the Grande Salle, lighted by fifty torches and
containing three hundred persons." (This
statement would seem to point to the fact that
it was not the *salle* which is shown to-day; it
certainly could not be made to hold three hundred people unless they stood on each other's
shoulders!) "The seigneurs were all clad in
magnificent robes, but the king, on the contrary,

*Château de Chinon*

was dressed most simply. The 'Maid,' endowed with a spirit and sagacity superior to her education, advanced without hesitation. '*Dieu vous donne bonne vie, gentil roi,*' said she. . . ."

The Grand Logis is flanked by a square tower which is separated from the Château de Coudray and the Tour de Boissy by a moat. In the magnificent Tour de Boissy was the ancient Salle des Gardes, while above was a battlemented gallery which gave an outlook over the surrounding country. This watch-tower assured absolute safety from surprise to any monarch who might have wished to study the situation for himself.

The Tour du Moulin is another of the defences, more elegant, if possible, than the Tour de Boissy. It is taller and less rotund; the French say it is "svelt," and that describes it as well as anything. It also fits into the landscape in a manner which no other mediæval donjon of France does, unless it be that of Château Gaillard, in Normandy.

The primitive Château de Coudray was built by Thibaut-le-Tricheur in 954, and its bastion and sustaining walls are still in evidence.

The Vienne, which runs by Chinon to join the Loire above Saumur, is, in many respects, a remarkable river, although just here there is nothing very remarkable about it. It is, however, delightfully picturesque, as it washes the tree-lined quays which form Chinon's riverfront for a distance of upward of two kilometres. In general the waterway reminds one of something between a great traffic-bearing river and a mere pleasant stream.

The bridge between Chinon and its faubourg is typical of the art of bridge-building, at which, in mediæval times, the French were excelled by no other nation. To-day, in company with the Americans, they build iron and steel abominations which are eyesores which no amount of utility will ever induce one to really admire. Not so the French bridges of mediæval times, of the type of those at Blois on the Loire; at Chinon on the Vienne; at Avignon on the Rhône; or at Cahors on the Lot.

If Rabelais had not rendered popular Chinon and the Chinonais the public would have yet to learn of this delightful *pays,* in spite of that famous first meeting between Charles VII. and Jeanne d'Arc.

If the modern founders of " garden-cities " would only go as far back as the time of Richelieu they would find a good example to follow in the little Touraine town, the *chef-lieu* of the

## Azay-le-Rideau, Ussé, and Chinon

Commune, which bears the name of Richelieu. When Armand du Plessis first became the seigneur of this "*little land*" he resolutely set about to make of the property a town which should dignify his name. Accordingly he built, at his own expense, after the plans of Lemercier, "a city, regular, vast, and luxurious." At the same time the cardinal-minister replaced the paternal manor with a château elaborately and prodigally royal.

Richelieu was a sort of "petit Versailles," which was to be to Chinon what the real Versailles was to the capital.

To-day, as in other days, it is a "*ville vaste, régulière et luxueuse,*" but it is unfinished. One great street only has been completed on its original lines, and it is exactly 450 metres long. Originally the town was to have the dimensions of but six hundred by four hundred metres; modest enough in size, but of the greatest luxury. The cardinal had no desire to make it more grand, but even what he had planned was not to be. Its one great street is bordered with imposing buildings, but their tenants to-day have not the least resemblance to the courtiers of the cardinal who formerly occupied them.

Richelieu disappeared in the course of time, and work on his hobby stopped, or at least changed radically in its plan. Secondary streets were laid out, of less grandeur, and peopled with houses without character, low in stature, and unimposing. The plan of a *ville seigneuriale* gave way to a *ville de labeur*. Other habitations grew up until to-day twenty-five hundred souls find their living on the spot where once was intended to be only a life of luxury.

Of the monuments with which Richelieu would have ornamented his town there remains a curious market-hall and a church in the pure Jesuitic style of architecture, lacking nothing of pretence and grandeur.

Not much can be said for the vast Église Notre Dame de Richelieu, a heavy Italian structure, built from the plans of Lemercier. However satisfying and beautiful the style may be in Italy, it is manifestly, in all great works of church-building in the north, unsuitable and uncouth.

There was also a château as well, a great Mansart affair with an overpowering dome. Practically this remains to-day, but, like all else in the town, it is but a promise of greater things which were expected to materialize, but never did.

At the bottom of a little valley, in a fertile

plain, lies Fontevrault, or what there is left of it, for the old abbey is now nothing more than a matter-of-fact *" maison de détention "* for criminals. The abbey of yesterday is the prison of to-day.

Fontevrault is an enigma; it is, furthermore, what the French themselves call a *" triste et maussade bourg."* Its former magnificent abbey was one of the few shrines of its class which was respected by the Revolution, but now it has become a prison which shelters something like a thousand unfortunates.

For centuries the old abbey had royal princesses for abbesses and was one of the most celebrated religious houses in all France. It is a sad degeneration that has befallen this famous establishment.

In the eleventh century an illustrious man of God, a Breton priest, named Robert d'Arbrissel, outlined the foundation of the abbey and gathered together a community of monks. He died in the midst of his labours, in 1117, and was succeeded by the Abbess Petronille de Chemille.

For nearly six hundred years the abbey — which comprised a convent for men and another for women — grew and prospered, directed, not infrequently, by an abbess of the blood royal. It has been claimed that, as a religious establishment for men and women, ruled over by a woman, the abbey of Fontevrault was unique in Christendom.

It is an ample structure with a church tower of bistre which forms a most pleasing note of colour in the landscape. The basilica was begun in 1101, and consecrated by Pope Calixtus II. in 1119. Its interior showed a deep vaulting, with graceful and hardy arches supported by massive columns with quaint and curiously sculptured capitals.

The twelfth-century cloister was indeed a masterwork among those examples, all too rare, existing to-day. Its arcade is severely elegant and was rebuilt by the Abbess Renée de Bourbon, sister of François I., after the best of decorative Renaissance of that day. The chapter-house, now used by the director of the prison, has in a remarkable manner retained the mural frescoes of a former day. There are depicted a series of groups of mystical and real personages in a most curious fashion. The refectory is still much in its primitive state, though put to other uses to-day. Its tribune, where the lectrice entertained the sisters during their repasts, is, however, still in its place.

The curious, bizarre, kilnlike pyramid,

*Cuisines, Fontevrault*

known as the Tour d'Evrault, has ever been an enigma to the archæologist and antiquarian. Doubtless it formed the kitchens of the establishment, for it looks like nothing else that might have belonged to a great abbey. It has a counterpart at the Abbey of Marmoutier near Tours, and of St. Trinité at Vendôme; from which fact there would seem to be little doubt as to its real use, although it looks more like a blast furnace or a distillery chimney.

This curious pyramidal structure is like the collegiate church of St. Ours at Loches, one of those bizarre edifices which defy any special architectural classification. At Fontevrault the architect played with his art when he let all the light in this curious "*tour*" enter by the roof. At the extreme apex of the cone he placed a lantern from which the light of day filtered down the slope of the vaulting in a weird and tomblike manner. It is a most surprising effect, but one that is wholly lost to-day, since the Tour d'Evrault has been turned into the kitchen for the "*maison de détention*" of which it forms a part.

The nave of the church of the old abbey of Fontevrault has been cut in two and a part is now used as the dormitory of the prison, but the choir, the transepts, and the towers remain to suggest the simple and beautiful style of their age.

In the transepts, behind an iron grille, are buried Henry II., King of England and Count of Anjou, Éléanore of Guienne, Richard Cœur de Lion, and Isabeau of Angoulême, wife of Jean-sans-Terre. Four polychromatic statues, one in wood, the others in stone, lying at length, represent these four personages so great in English history, and make of Fontevrault a shrine for pilgrims which ought to be far less ignored than it is. The cemetery of kings has been shockingly cared for, and the ludicrous kaleidoscopic decorations of the statues which surmount the royal tombs are nothing less than a sacrilege. It is needless to say they are comparatively modern.

At Bourgueil, near Fontevrault, are gathered great crops of *réglisse,* or licorice. It differs somewhat in appearance from the licorice roots of one's childhood, but the same qualities exist in it as in the product of Spain or the Levant, whence indeed most of the commercial licorice does come. It is as profitable an industry in this part of France as is the saffron crop of the Gâtinais, and whoever imported the first roots was a benefactor. At the juncture of the Vienne and the Loire are two tiny towns which are noted for two widely different reasons.

These two towns are Montsoreau and Candes, the former noted for the memory of that bloodthirsty woman who gave a plot to Dumas (and some real facts of history besides), and the other noted for its prunes, Candes being the chief centre of the industry which produces the *pruneaux de Tours*.

Descending the Vienne from Chinon, one first comes to Candes, which dominates the confluence of the Vienne with the Loire from its imposing position on the top of a hill.

Candes was in other times surrounded by a protecting wall, and there are to-day remains of a château which had formerly given shelter to Charles VII. and Louis XI. It has, moreover, a twelfth-century church built upon the site of the cell in which died St. Martin in the fourth century. The native of the surrounding country cares nothing for churches or châteaux, but assumes that the prune industry of Candes is the one thing of interest to the visitor.

Be this as it may, it is indeed a matter of considerable importance to all within a dozen kilometres of the little town. All through the region round about Candes one meets with the fruit-pickers, with their great baskets laden with prunes, pears, and apples, to be sent ultimately to the great ovens to be desiccated and dried. Fifty years ago, you will be told, the cultivators attended to the curing process themselves, but now it is in the hands of the middleman.

At Montsoreau much the same economic conditions exist as at Candes, but there is vastly more of historic lore hanging about the town. In the fourteenth century, after a shifting career, the fief passed to the Vicomtes de Chateaudun; then, in the century following, to the Chabots and the family of Chambes, of which Jean IV., prominent in the massacre of St. Bartholomew's night, was a member. It was he who assassinated the gallant Bussy d'Amboise at the near-by Château of Coutancière (at Brain-sur-Allonnes), who had made a rendezvous with his wife, since become famous in the pages of Dumas and of history as "La Dame de Montsoreau."

To-day the old bourg is practically non-existent, and there is a smugness of prosperity which considerably discounts the former charm that it once must have had. But for all that, there is enough left to enable one to picture what the life here under the Renaissance must have been.

The parish church — that of the ancient Paroisse de Retz — still exists, though in ruins, and there are very substantial remains of an old priory, an old-time dependency of the Abbey of St. Florent, now converted into a farm.

Beside the highroad is the fifteenth-century château. It has a double façade, one side of which is ornamented with a series of *mâchicoulis,* great high window-openings, and flanking towers; and, in spite of its generally frowning aspect, looks distinctly livable even to-day.

The ornamental façade of the courtyard is somewhat crumbled but still elegant, and has incorporated within its walls a most ravishing Renaissance turret, smothered in exquisite *moulures* and *arabesques.* On the terminal gallery and on the panels which break up the flatness of this inner façade are a series of allegorical bas-reliefs, representing monkeys, surmounted with the inscription, " *Il le Feray.*"

The interior of this fine edifice is entirely remodelled, and has nothing of its former fitments, furnishings, or decorations.

Near Port Boulet, almost opposite Candes, is the great farm of a certain M. Cail. Communication is had with the Orleans railway by means of a traction engine, which draws its own broad-wheeled wagons on the regular highway between the *gare d'hommes* and the tall-chimneyed manor or château which forms the residence of this enterprising agriculturist.

The property consists of nearly two thousand acres, of which at least twelve hundred are under the process of intensive cultivation, and is divided into ten distinct farms, having each an overseer charged directly with the control of his part of the domain. These farms are wonderfully well kept, with sanded roadways like the courtyard of a château. There are no trees in the cultivated parts, and the great grain-fields are as the western prairies.

The estate bears the generic name of "La Briche." On one side it is bordered by the railroad for a distance of nearly forty kilometres, and it gives to that same railway an annual freight traffic of two thousand tons of merchandise, which would be considerably more if all the cattle and sheep sent to other markets were transported by rail.

As might be expected, this domain of "La Briche" has given to the neighbouring farmers a lesson and an example, and little by little its influence has resulted in an increased activity among the neighbouring landholders, who formerly gave themselves over to "*la chasse,*" and left the conduct of their farms to incompetent and more or less ignorant hirelings.

# CHAPTER XIII.

### ANJOU AND BRETAGNE

As one crosses the borderland from Touraine into Anjou, the whole aspect of things changes. It is as if one went from the era of the Renaissance back again into the days of the Gothic, not only in respect to architecture, but history and many of the conditions of every-day life as well.

Most of the characteristics of Anjou are without their like elsewhere, and opulent Anjou of ancient France has to-day a departmental etiquette in many things quite different from that of other sections.

A magnificent agricultural province, it has been further enriched by liberal proprietors; a land of aristocracy and the church, it has ever been to the fore in political and ecclesiastical matters; and to-day the spirit of industry and progress are nowhere more manifest than here in the ancient province of Anjou.

The Loire itself changes its complexion but

little, and its entrance into Saumur, like its entrance into Tours, is made between banks that are tinged with the rainbow colours of the growing vine. What hills there are near by are burrowed, as swallows burrow in a cliff, by the workers of the vineyards, who make in the rock homes similar to those below Saumur, in the Vallée du Vendomois, and at Cinq-Mars near Tours.

Anjou has a marked style in architecture, known as Angevin, which few have properly placed in the gamut of architectural styles which run from the Byzantine to the Renaissance.

The Romanesque was being supplanted everywhere when the Angevin style came into being, as a compromise between the heavy, flat-roofed style of the south and the pointed sky-piercing gables of the north. All Europe was attempting to shake off the Romanesque influence, which had lasted until the twelfth century. Germany alone clung to the pure style, and, it is generally thought, improved it. The Angevin builders developed a species that was on the borderland between the Romanesque and the Gothic, though not by any means a mere transition type.

The chief cities of Anjou are not very great

or numerous, Angers itself containing but slightly over fifty thousand souls. Cholet, of thirteen thousand inhabitants, is an important cloth-manufacturing centre, while Saumur carries on a great wine trade and was formerly the capital of a "*petit gouvernement*" of its own, and, like many other cities and towns of this and neighbouring provinces, was the scene of great strife during the wars of the Vendée.

In ancient times the *Andecavi*, as the old peoples of the province were known, shared with the *Turonii* of Touraine the honour of being the foremost peoples of western Gaul, though each had special characteristics peculiarly their own, as indeed they have to-day.

After one passes the junction of the Cher, the Indre, and the Vienne, he notices no great change in the conduct of the Loire itself. It still flows in and out among the banks of sand and those little round pebbles known all along its course, nonchalantly and slowly, though now and then one fancies that he notes a greater eddy or current than he had observed before. At Saumur it is still more impressed upon one, while at the Ponts de Cé — a great strategic spot in days gone by — there is evidence that at one time or another the Loire must be a raging torrent; and such it does become periodically, only travellers never seem to see it when it is in this condition.

When Candes and Montsoreau are passed and one comes under the frowning walls of Saumur's grim citadel, a sort of provincial Bastille in its awesomeness, he realizes for the first time that there is, somewhere below, an outlet to the sea. He cannot smell the salt-laden breezes at this great distance, but the general appearance of things gives that impression.

From Tours to Saumur by the right bank of the Loire — one of the most superb stretches of automobile roadway in the world — lay the road of which Madame de Sévigné wrote in "Lettre CCXXIV." (to her mother), which begins: "*Nous arrivons ici, nous avons quitté Tours ce matin.*" It was a good day's journey for those times, whether by *malle-post* or the private conveyance which, likely enough, Madame de Sévigné used at the time (1630). To-day it is a mere morsel to the hungry road-devouring maw of a twentieth-century automobile. It's almost worth the labour of making the journey on foot to know the charms of this delightful river-bank bordered with historic shrines almost without number, and peo-

*Château de Saumur*

pled by a class of peasants as picturesque and gay as the Neapolitan of romance.

"*Saumur est, ma foi! une jolie ville,*" said a traveller one day at a *table d'hôte* at Tours. And so indeed it is. Its quays and its squares lend an air of gaiety to its proud old *hôtel de ville* and its grim château. Old habitations, commodious modern houses, frowning machicolations, church spires, grand hotels, innumerable cafés, and much military, all combine in a blend of fascinating interest that one usually finds only in a great metropolis.

The chief attraction is unquestionably the old château. To-day it stands, as it has always stood, high above the Quai de Limoges, with scarce a scar on its hardy walls and never a crumbling stone on its parapet.

The great structure was begun in the eleventh century, replacing an earlier monument known as the Tour du Tronc. It was completed in the century following and rebuilt or remodelled in the sixteenth. Outside of its impressive exterior there is little of interest to remind one of another day.

To literary pilgrims Saumur suggests the homestead of the father of Eugenie Grandet, and the *bon-vivant* reveres it for its soft pleasant wines. Others worship it for its wonders of architecture, and yet others fall in love with it because of its altogether delightful situation.

Below Saumur are the cliff-dwellers, who burrow high in the chalk cliff and stow themselves away from light and damp like bottles of old wine. The custom is old and not indigenous to France, but here it is sufficiently in evidence to be remarked by even the traveller by train. Here, too, one sees the most remarkable of all the *coiffes* which are worn by any of the women along the Loire. This Angevin variety, like Angevin architecture, is like none of its neighbours north, east, south, or west.

Students of history will revere Saumur for something more than its artistic aspect or its wines, for it was a favourite residence of the Angevin princes and the English kings, as well as being the capital of the *pape des Huguenots*.

While Nantes is the real metropolis of the Loire, and Angers is singularly up-to-date and well laid out, neither of these fine cities have a great thoroughfare to compare with the broad, straight street of Saumur, which leads from the Gare d'Orleans on the left bank and crosses the two bridges which span the branches of the Loire, to say nothing of the island between, and finally merges into the great national highway which runs south into Poitou.

## Anjou and Bretagne

Fine houses, many, if not most of them, dating from centuries ago, line the principal streets of the town, which, when one has actually entered its confines, presents the appearance of being too vast and ample for its population. And, in truth, so it really is. Its population barely reaches fifteen thousand souls, whereas it would seem to have the grandeur and appointments of a city of a hundred thousand. The revocation of the Edict of Nantes cut its inhabitants down to the extent of twenty or twenty-five thousand, and it has never recovered from the blow.

In the neighbourhood of Saumur, for a considerable distance up and down the Loire, the hills are excavated into dwelling-houses and wine-caves, producing a most curious aspect. One continuous line of these cliff villages — like nothing so much as the habitations of the cliff-dwelling Indians of America — extends from the juncture of the Vienne with the Loire nearly up to the Ponts de Cé.

The most curious effect of it all is the multitude of openings of doorways and windows and the uprising of chimney-pots through the chalk and turf which form the roof-tops of these settlements.

In many of these caves are prepared the

famous *vin mousseux* of Saumur, of which the greater part is sold as champagne to an unsuspecting and indifferent public, not by the growers or makers, but by unscrupulous middlemen.

Saumur, like Angers, is fortunate in its climate, to which is due a great part of the prosperity of the town, for the "Rome of the Huguenots" is more prosperous — and who shall not say more content? — than it ever was in the days of religious or feudal warfare.

Near Saumur is one shrine neglected by English pilgrims which might well be included in their itineraries. In the Château de Moraines at Dampierre died Margaret of Anjou and Lancaster, Queen of England, as one reads on a tablet erected at the gateway of this dainty *"petit castel à tour et creneaux."*

---

Manoir de la Vignole - Souzay autrefois Dampierre
Asile et dernière demure
de l'heroine de la guerre des deux roses
Marguerite d'Anjou de Lancastre, reine d'Angleterre
La plus malheureuse des reines, des éspouses, et des mères
Qui Morut le 25 Aout 1482
Agée de 53 Ans.

The Salvus Murus of the ancients became the Saumur of to-day in the year 948, when the monk Absalom built a monastery here and surrounded it with a protecting wall. Up to the thirteenth century the city belonged to the "Angevin kings of Angleterre," as the French historians proudly claim them.

The city passed finally to the Kings of France, and to them remained constantly faithful. Under Henri IV. the city was governed by Duplessis-Mornay, the "*pape des Huguenots,*" becoming practically the metropolis of Protestantism. Up to this time the chief architectural monument was the château, which was commenced in the eleventh century and which through the next five centuries had been aggrandized and rebuilt into its present shape.

The church of Notre Dame de Nantilly dates from the twelfth century and was frequently visited by Louis XI. The oratory formerly made use of by this monarch to-day contains the baptismal fonts. One of the columns of the nave has graven upon it the epitaph composed by King René of Anjou for his foster-mother, Dame Thiephanie. Throughout, the church is beautifully decorated.

The Hôtel de Ville may well be called the chief artistic treasure of Saumur, as the château is its chief historical monument. It is a delightful *ensemble* of the best of late Gothic, dating from the sixteenth century, flanked on its façade by turrets crowned with *mâchicoulis,* and lighted by a series of elegant windows *à croisillons.* Above all is a gracious campanile, in its way as fine as the belfry of Bruges, to which, from a really artistic standpoint, rhapsodists have given rather more than its due.

The interior is as elaborate and pleasing as is the outside. In the Salle des Mariages and Salle du Conseil are fine fifteenth-century chimneypieces, such as are only found in their perfection on the Loire. The library, of something over twenty thousand volumes, many of them in manuscript, is formed in great part from the magnificent collection formerly at the abbeys of Fontevrault and St. Florent. Doubtless these old tomes contain a wealth of material from which some future historian will perhaps construct a new theory of the universe. This in truth may not be literally so, but it is a fact that there is a vast amount of contemporary historical information, with regard to the world in general, which is as yet unearthed, as witness the case of Pompeii alone, where the area of the discoveries forms but a small part of the entire buried city.

At Saumur numerous prehistoric and *galloromain* remains are continually being added to the museum, which is also in the Hôtel de Ville. A recent acquisition — discovered in a neighbouring vineyard — is a Roman "*trompette*," as it is designated, and a more or less complete outfit of tools, obviously those of a carpenter.

The notorious Madame de Montespan — "the illustrious penitent," though the former description answers better — stopped here, in a house adjoining the Church of St. John, today a *maison de retrait*, on her way to visit her sister, the abbess, at Fontevrault.

From Saumur to Angers the Loire passes an almost continuous series of historical guideposts, some in ruins, but many more as proudly environed as ever.

At Treves-Cunault is a dignified Romanesque church which would add to the fame of a more popular and better known town. It is not a grand structure, but it is perfect of its kind, with its crenelated façade and its sturdy arcaded towers curiously placed midway on the north wall.

Here one first becomes acquainted with *men-*

*hirs* and *dolmens,* examples of which are to be found in the neighbourhood, not so remarkable as those of Brittany, but still of the same family.

The Ponts de Cé follow next, still in the midst of vine-land, and finally appear the twin spires of Angers's unique Cathedral of St. Maurice. Here one realizes, if not before, that he is in Anjou; no more is the atmosphere transparent as in Touraine, but something of the grime of the commercial struggle for life is over all.

Here the Maine joins the Loire, at a little village called La Pointe: "the Charenton of Angers," it was called by a Paris-loving boulevardier who once wandered afield.

Much has been written, and much might yet be written, about the famous Ponts de Cé, which span the Loire and its branches for a distance considerably over three kilometres. This ancient bridge or bridges (which, with that at Blois, were at one time, the only bridges across the Loire below Orleans) formerly consisted of 109 arches, but the reconstruction of the mid-nineteenth century reduced these to a bare score.

As a vantage-point in warfare the Ponts de Cé were ever in contention, the Gauls, the Romans, the Franks, the Normans, and the Eng-

*The Ponts de Cé*

lish successively taking possession and defending them against their opponents. The Ponts de Cé is a weirdly strange and historic town which has lost none of its importance in a later day, though the famous *ponts* are now remade, and their antique arches replaced by more solid, if less picturesque piers and piling. They span the shallow flow of the Loire water for three-quarters of a league and produce a homogeneous effect of antiquity, coupled with the city's three churches and its château overlooking the fortified isle in mid-river, which looks as though it had not changed since the days when Marie de Medici looked upon it, as recalled by the great Rubens painting in the Louvre. Since the beginning of the history of these parts, battles almost without number have taken place here, as was natural on a spot so strategically important.

There is a tale of the Vendean wars, connected with the "Roche-de-Murs" at the Ponts de Cé, to the effect that a battalion, left here to guard any attack from across the river, was captured by the Vendeans. Many of the "*Bleus*" refused to surrender, and threw themselves into the river beneath their feet. Among these was the wife of an officer, to whom the Vendeans offered life if she surrendered. This was refused, and precipitately, with her child, she threw herself into the flood beneath.

On the largest isle, that lying between the Louet and the Loire, is one vast garden or orchard of cherry-trees, which produce a peculiarly juicy cherry from which large quantities of *guignolet,* a sort of "cherry brandy," is made. The Angevins will tell you that this was a well-known refreshment in the middle ages, and was first made by one of those monkish orders who were so successful in concocting the subtle liquors of the commerce of to-day.

It is with real regret that one parts from the Ponts de Cé, with La Fontaine's couplet on his lips:

> ". . . Ce n'est pas petite gloire
> Que d'être pont sur la Loire.

Some one has said that the provinces find nothing to envy in Paris as far as the transformation of their cities is concerned. This, to a certain extent, is so, not only in respect to the modernizing of such grand cities as Lyons, Marseilles, or Lille, but in respect to such smaller cities as Nantes and Angers, where the improvements, if not on so magnificent a scale, are at least as momentous to their immediate environment.

For the most part these second and third class cities are to-day transformed in exceedingly good taste, and, though many a noble monument has in the past been sacrificed, to-day the authorities are proceeding more carefully.

Angers, in spite of its overpowering château and its unique cathedral, is of a modernity and luxuriousness in its present-day aspect which is all the more remarkable because of the contrast. Formerly the Angevin capital, from the days of King John up to a much later time Angers had the reputation of being a town "*plus sombre et plus maussade*" than any other in the French provinces. In Shakespeare's "King John" one reads of "black Angers," and so indeed is its aspect to-day, for its roof-tops are of slate, while many of the houses are built of that material entirely. In the olden time many of its streets were cut in the slaty rock, leaving its sombre surface bare to the light of day. One sees evidences of all this in the massive walls of the great black-banded castle of Angers, and, altogether, this magpie colouring is one of the chief characteristics of this grandly historic town.

Both the new and the old town sit proudly on a height crowned by the two slim spires of the

cathedral. In front, the gentle curves of the
river Maine enfold the old houses at the base
of the hillside and lap the very walls of the
grim fortress-château itself, or did in the days
when the Counts of Anjou held sway, though
to-day the river has somewhat receded.

Beyond the ancient ramparts, up the hill,
have been erected the "*quartiers neufs,*" with
houses all admirably planned and laid out, with
gardens forming a veritable girdle, as did the
retaining walls of other days which surrounded
the old château and its faubourg. To-day
Angers shares with Nantes the title of metropolis of the west, and the Loire flows on its ample
way between the two in a far more imposing
manner than elsewhere in its course from
source to sea.

Angers does not lie exactly at the juncture
of the Maine and Loire, but a little way above,
but it has always been considered as one of
the chief Loire cities; and probably many of
its visitors do not realize that it is not on the
Loire itself.

The marvellous fairy-book château of Angers, with its fourteen black-striped towers, is
just as it was when built by St. Louis, save that
its chess-board towers lack, in most cases, their
coiffes, and all vestiges have disappeared of

*Château d'Angers*

the *charpente* which formerly topped them off.

Beyond the rocky formation of the banks of the Loire, which crop out below the juncture of the Maine and the Loire, below Angers, are Savennières and La Possonière, whence come the most famous vintages of Anjou, which, to the wines of these parts, are what Château Margaux and Château Yquem are to the Bordelais, and the Clos Vougeot is to the Bourguignons.

The peninsula formed by the Loire and the Maine at Angers is the richest agricultural region in all France, the nurseries and the kitchen-gardens having made the fortune of this little corner of Anjou.

Angers is the headquarters for nursery-garden stock for the open air, as Orleans is for ornamental and woodland trees and shrubs.

The trade in living plants and shrubs has grown to very great proportions since 1848, when an agent went out from here on behalf of the leading house in the trade and visited America for the purpose of searching out foreign plants and fruits which could be made to thrive on French soil.

Both the soil and climate are very favourable for the cultivation of many hitherto unknown fruits, the neighbourhood of the sea, which, not far distant, is tempered by the Gulf Stream, having given to Anjou a lukewarm humidity and a temperature of a remarkable equality.

Some of the nurseries of these parts are enormous establishments, the Maison Andre Leroy, for example, covering an extent of some six hundred acres. A catalogue of one of these establishments, located in the suburbs of Angers, enumerates over four hundred species of pear-trees, six hundred varieties of apple-trees, one hundred and fifty varieties of plums, four hundred and seventy-five of grapes, fifteen hundred of roses, and two hundred and nineteen of rhododendrons.

Each night, or as often as fifty railway wagons are loaded, trains are despatched from the *gare* at Angers for all parts. When the *choux-fleurs* are finished, then come the *petits pois,* and then the *artichauts* and other *légumes* in favour with the Paris *bon-vivants*.

Near Angers is one of those Cæsar's camps which were spread thickly up and down Gaul and Britain alike. One reaches it by road from Angers, and, until it dawns upon one that the vast triangle, one of whose equilateral sides is formed by the Loire, another by the Maine, and the third by a ridge of land stretching between the two, covers about fourteen kilometres square, it seems much like any other neck or peninsula of land lying between two rivers. One hundred thousand of the Roman legion camped here at one time, which is not so very wonderful until it is recalled that they lived for months on the resources of this comparatively restricted area.

Before coming to Nantes, Ancenis and Oudon should claim the attention of the traveller, though each is not much more than a typically interesting small town of France, in spite of the memories of the past.

Ancenis has an ancient château, remodelled and added to in the nineteenth century, which possesses some remarkably important constructive details, the chief of which are a great tower-flanked doorway and the *corps de logis*, each the work of an Angevin architect, Jean de Lespine, in the sixteenth century. Within the walls of this château François II., Duc de Bretagne, and Louis XI. signed one of the treaties which finally led up to the union of the Duché de Bretagne with the Crown of France.

Oudon possesses a fine example of a mediæval donjon, though it has been restored in our day.

One does not usually connect Brittany with

the Loire except so far as to recollect that Nantes was a former political and social capital. As a matter of fact, however, a very considerable proportion of Brittany belongs to the Loire country.

Anjou of the counts and kings and Bretagne of the dukes and duchesses embrace the whole of the Loire valley below Saumur, although the river-bed of the Loire formed no actual boundary. Anjou extended nearly as far to the southward as it did to the north of the vine-clad banks, and Bretagne, too, had possession of a vast tract south of Nantes, known as the Pays de Retz, which bordered upon the Vendée of Poitou.

All the world knows, or should know, that Nantes and St. Nazaire form one of the great ports of the world, not by any means so great as New York, London, or Hamburg, nor yet as great as Antwerp, Bordeaux, or Marseilles, but still a magnificent port which plays a most important part with the affairs of France and the outside world.

Nantes, la Brette, is tranquil and solid, with the life of the laborious bourgeois always in the foreground. It is of Bretagne, to which province it anciently belonged, only so far as it forms the bridge between the Vendée and the

## Anjou and Bretagne

old duchy; literally between two opposing feudal lords and masters, both of whom were hard to please.

The memoirs of this corner of the province of Bretagne of other days are strong in such names as the Duchesse Anne, the monk Abelard, the redoubtable Clisson, the infamous Gilles de Retz, the warrior Lanoue, surnamed "Bras de Fer," and many others whose names are prominent in history.

"*Ventre Saint Gris! les Ducs de Bretagne n'étaient pas de petits compagnons!*" cried Henri Quatre, as he first gazed upon the Château de Nantes. At that time, in 1598, this fortress was defended by seven curtains, six towers, bastions and caponieres, all protected by a wide and deep moat, into which poured the rising tide twice with each round of the clock.

To-day the aspect of this château is no less formidable than of yore, though it has been debased and the moat has disappeared to make room for a roadway and the railroad.

It was in the château of Nantes, the same whose grim walls still overlook the road by which one reaches the centre of the town from the inconveniently placed station, that Mazarin had Henri de Gondi, Cardinal de Retz and coadjutor of the Archbishop of Paris, imprisoned in 1665, because of his offensive partisanship. Fouquet, too, after his splendid downfall, was thrown into the donjon here by Louis XIV.

De Gondi recounts in his "Mémoires" how he took advantage of the inattention of his guards and finally evaded them by letting himself over the side of the Bastion de Mercœur by means of a rope smuggled into him by his friends. The feat does not look a very formidable one to-day, but then, or in any day, it must have been somewhat of an adventure for a portly churchman, and the wonder is that it was performed successfully. At any rate it reads like a real adventure from the pages of Dumas, who himself made a considerable use of Nantes and its château in his historical romances.

Landais, the minister and favourite of François II. of Bretagne, was arrested here in 1485, in the very chamber of the prince, who delivered him up with the remark: "*Faites justice, mais souvenez-vous que vous lui êtes redevable de votre charge.*"

There is no end of historical incident connected with Nantes's old fortress-château of mediæval times, and, in one capacity or another, it has sheltered many names famous in history, from the Kings of France, from Louis

XII. onward, to Madame de Sévigné and the Duchesse de Berry.

Nantes's Place de la Bouffai (which to lovers of Dumas will already be an old friend) was formerly the site of a château contemporary with that which stands by the waterside. The Château de Bouffai was built in 990 by Conan, first Duc de Bretagne, and served as an official residence to him and many of his successors.

In Nantes's great but imperfect and unfinished Cathedral of St. Pierre one comes upon a relic that lives long in the memory of those who have passed before it: the tomb of François II., Duc de Bretagne, and Marguerite de Foix. The cathedral itself is no mean architectural work, in spite of its imperfections, as one may judge from the following inscription graven over the sculptured figure of St. Pierre, its patron:

> "L'an mil quatre cent trente-quatre,
> A my-avril sans moult rabattre:
> Au portail de cette église,
> Fut la première pierre assise."

Within, the chief attraction is that masterwork of Michel Colombe, the before-mentioned tomb, which ranks among the world's art-treasures. The beauty of the emblematic figures which flank the tomb proper, the fine chiselling

of the recumbent effigies themselves, and the
general *ensemble* is such that the work is bound
to appeal, whatever may be one's opinion of
Renaissance sculpture in France. The tomb
was brought here from the old Église des
Carmes, which had been pillaged and burned in
the Revolution.

The mausoleum was — in its old resting-
place — opened in 1727, and a small, heart-
shaped, gold box was found, supposed to have
contained the heart of the Duchesse Anne. The
coffer was surmounted by a royal crown and
emblazoned with the order of the Cordelière,
but within was found nothing but a scapulary.
On the circlet of the crown was written in
relief:

"Cueur de vertus orné
Dignement couronné.

And on the box beneath one read:

" En ce petit vaisseau, de fin or pur et munde,
Repose un plus grand cueur que oncque dame eut au monde.
Anne fut le nom d'elle, en France deux fois Royne
. . . . . . . . . .
Et ceste parte terrestre en grand deuil nos demure.
  IX. Janvier M.V.XIII."

In one respect only has Nantes suffered
through the march of time. Its magnificent
Quai de la Fosse has disappeared, a long façade which a hundred or more years ago was

bordered by the palatial dwellings of the great ship-owners of the Nantes of a former generation. The whole, immediately facing the river

*ENVIRONS of NANTES*

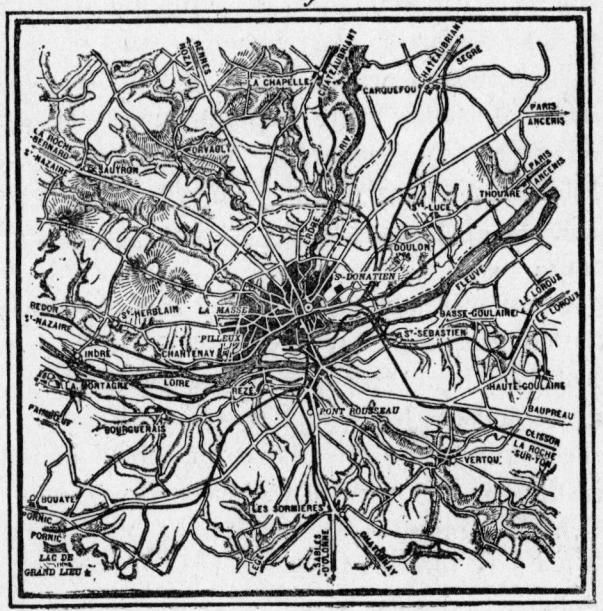

where formerly swung many ships at anchor, has disappeared entirely to make way for the railway.

The islands of the Loire opposite Nantes are an echo of the life of the metropolis itself. The

Ile Feydeau is monumental, the Ile Gloriette
hustling and nervous with "*affaires*," and
Prairie-au-Duc busy with industries of all
sorts.

Couëron, below Nantes on the right bank, is
sombre with gray walls surrounding its numberless factories, and chimney-stacks belching
forth clouds of dense smoke. Behind are great
walls of chalky-white rock crowned with verdure. Nearly opposite is the little town of Le
Pellerin graciously seated on the river's bank
and marking the lower limit of the Loire Nantaise.

Another hill, belonging to the domain of Bois-
Tillac and La Martinière, where was born
Fouché, the future Duc d'Otranta, comes to
view, and the basin of the Loire enlarges into
the estuary, and all at once one finds himself
in the true "Loire Maritime."

At Martinière is the mouth of the Canal Maritime à la Loire, which, from Paimbœuf to Le
Pellerin, is used by all craft ascending the
river to Nantes, drawing more than four metres
of water.

At the entrance of the Acheneau is the Canal
de Buzay, which connects that stream with the
more ambitious Loire, and makes of the Lac de
Grand Lieu a public domain, instead of a pri-

vate property as claimed by the "marquis" who holds in terror all who would fish or shoot over its waters. All this immediate region formerly belonged to the monks of the ancient Abbey of Buzay, and it was they who originally cut the waterway through to the Loire. About half-way in its length are the ruins of the ancient monastery, clustered about the tower of its old church. It is a most romantically sad monument, and for that very reason its grouping, on the bank of the busy canal, suggests in a most impressive manner the passing of all great works.

The prosperity of Nantes as a deep-sea port is of long standing, but recent improvements have increased all this to a hitherto unthought-of extent. Progress has been continuous, and now Nantes has become, like Rouen, a great deep-water port, one of the important seaports of France, the realization of a hope ever latent in the breast of the Nantais since the days and disasters of the Edict and its revocation.

Below Nantes, in the actual "Loire Maritime," the aspect of all things changes and the green and luxuriant banks give way to sand-dunes and flat, marshy stretches, as salty as the sea itself. This gives rise to a very considerable development of the salt industry which at Bourg de Batz is the principal, if not the sole, means of livelihood.

St. Nazaire, the real deep-water port of Nantes, dates from the fifteenth and sixteenth centuries, when it was known as Port Nazaire. It is a progressive and up-to-date seaport of some thirty-five thousand souls, but it has no appeal for the tourist unless he be a lover of great smoky steamships and all the paraphernalia of longshore life.

Pornichet, a "*station de bains de mer très fréquentée;*" Batz, with its salt-works; Le Croisic, with its curious waterside church, and the old walled town of Guérande bring one to the mouth of the Loire. The rest is the billowy western ocean whose ebb and flow brings fresh breezes and tides to the great cities of the estuary and makes possible that prosperity with which they are so amply endowed.

# CHAPTER XIV.

### SOUTH OF THE LOIRE

The estuary of the Loire belongs both to Brittany and to the Vendée, though, as a matter-of-fact, the southern bank, opposite Nantes, formed a part of the ancient Pays de Retz, one of the old seigneuries of Bretagne.

It was Henri de Gondi, Cardinal de Retz, who was the bitter rival of Mazarin. French historians have told us that when the regency under Anne of Austria began, Mazarin, who had been secretary to the terrible Richelieu, was just coming into his power. He was a subtle, insidious Italian, plodding and patient, but false as a spring-time rainbow. Gondi was bold, liberal, and independent, a mover of men and one able to take advantage of any turn of the wind, a statesman, and a great reformer, — or he would have been had he but full power. It was Cromwell who said that De Retz was the only man in Europe who saw through his plans.

Gondi had entered the church, but he had no

talents for it. His life was free, too free even for the times, it would appear, for, though he was ordained cardinal, it was impossible for him to supplant Mazarin in the good graces of the court. As he himself had said that he preferred to be a great leader of a party rather than a partisan of royalty, he was perhaps not so very greatly disappointed that he was not able to supplant the wily Italian successor of Richelieu in the favour of the queen regent. Gondi was able to control the parliament, however, and, for a time, it was unable to carry through anything against his will. Mazarin rose to power at last, barricaded the streets of Paris, and decided to exile Gondi — as being the too popular hero of the people. Gondi knew of the edict, but stuck out to the last, saying: "To-morrow, I, Henri de Gondi, before midday, will be master of Paris." Noon came, and he *was* master of Paris, but as he was still Archbishop-Coadjutor of Paris his hands were tied in more ways than one, and the plot for his supremacy over Mazarin, "the plunderer," fell through.

The whole neighbouring region south of the Loire opposite Nantes, the ancient Pays de Retz, is unfamiliar to tourists in general, and for that reason it has an unexpected if not a superlative charm. It was the bloodiest of the battle-grounds of the Vendean wars, and, though its monumental remains are not as numerous or as imposingly beautiful as those in many other parts, there is an interest about it all which is as undying as is that of the most ornate or magnificent château or fortress-peopled land that ever existed.

Not a corner of this land but has seen bloody warfare in all its grimness and horror, from the days when Clisson was pillaged by the Normans in the ninth century, to the guerilla warfare of the Vendean republicans in the eighteenth century. The advent of the railway has changed much of the aspect of this region and brought a twentieth-century civilization up to the very walls of the ruins of Clisson and Maulévrier, the latter one of the many châteaux of this region which were ruined by the wars of Stofflet, who, at the head of the insurgents, obliged the nobility to follow the peasants in their uprising.

Now and then, in these parts, one comes upon a short length of railway line not unlike that at which our forefathers marvelled. The line may be of narrow gauge or it may not, but almost invariably the two or three so-called carriages are constructed in the style (or lack of style) of the old stage-coach, and they roll along in much the same lumbering fashion. The locomotive itself is a thing to be wondered at. It is a pigmy in size, but it makes the commotion of a modern decapod, or one of those great flyers which pull the Southern Express on the main line via Poitiers and Angoulême, not fifty kilometres away.

There is a little tract of land lying just south of the Loire below Angers which is known as "le Bocage Vendéen." One leaves the Loire at Chalonnes and, by a series of gentle inclines, reaches the plateau where sits the town of Cholet, the very centre of the region, and a town whose almost only industry is the manufacture of pocket-handkerchiefs.

The aspect of the Loire has changed rapidly and given way to a more vigorous and varied topography; but, for all that, Cholet and the surrounding country depend entirely upon the great towns of the Loire for their intercourse with the still greater markets beyond. Like Angers, Cholet and all the neighbouring villages are slate-roofed, with only an occasional red tile to give variety to the otherwise gray and sombre outlook.

*En route* from Chalonnes one passes Chemillé almost the only market-town of any size

in the district. It is very curious, with its
Romanesque church and its old houses distributed
around an amphitheatre, like the *loges* in
an opera-house.

This is the very centre of the Bocage, where,
in Revolutionary times, the Republican armies
so frequently fought with the bands of Vendean
fanatics.

The houses of Cholet are well built, but always
with that grayness and sadness of tone
which does not contribute to either brilliancy
of aspect or gaiety of disposition. Save the
grand street which traverses the town from
east to west, the streets are narrow and uncomfortable;
but to make up for all this there are
hotels and cafés as attractive and as comfortable
as any establishments of the kind to be
found in any of the smaller cities of provincial
France.

The handkerchief industry is very considerable,
no less than six great establishments
devoting themselves to the manufacture.

Cholet is one of the greatest cattle markets,
if not the greatest, in the land. The farmers
of the surrounding country buy *bœufs maigres*
in the southwest and centre of France and
transform them into good fat cattle which in
every way rival what is known in England as

"best English." This is accomplished cheaply and readily by feeding them with cabbage stalks.

On Saturdays, on the Champ de Foire, the aspect is most animated, and any painter who is desirous of emulating Rosa Bonheur's "Horse Fair" (painted at the great cattle market of Bernay, in Normandy) cannot find a better vantage-ground than here, for one may see gathered together nearly all the cattle types of Poitou, the Vendée, Anjou, Bas Maine, and of Bretagne Nantaise.

In earlier days Cholet was far more sad than it is to-day; but there remain practically no souvenirs of its past. The wars of the Vendée left, it is said, but three houses standing when the riot and bloodshed was over. Two of the greatest battles of this furious struggle were fought here.

On the site of the present railroad station Kleber and Moreau fought the royalists, and the heroic Bonchamps received the wound of which he died at St. Florent, just after he had put into execution the order of release for five thousand Republican prisoners. This was on the 17th October, 1793. Five months later Stofflet possessed himself of the town and burned it nearly to the ground. Not much is

*Donjon of the Château de Clisson*

left to remind one of these eventful times, save the public garden, which was built on the site of the old château.

La Moine, a tiny and most picturesque river, still flows under the antique arches of the old bridge, which was held in turn by the Vendeans and the Republicans.

To the west of Cholet runs another line of railway, direct through the heart of the Sèvre-Nantaise, one of those *petits pays* whose old-time identity is now all but lost, even more celebrated in bloody annals than is that region lying to the eastward. Here was a country entirely sacked and impoverished. Mortagne was completely ruined, though it has yet left substantial remains of its fourteenth and fifteenth century château. Torfou was the scene of a bloody encounter between the Vendean hordes and Kleber's two thousand *héroiques de Mayence*. The able Vendean chiefs who opposed him, Bonchamps, D'Elbée, and Lescure, captured his artillery and massacred all the wounded.

At the extremity of this line was the stronghold of Clisson, which itself finally succumbed, but later gave birth to a new town to take the place of that which perished in the Vendean convulsion.

Throughout this region, in the valleys of the Moine and the Sèvre-Nantaise, the rocks and the verdure and the admirable, though ill preserved, ruins, all combine to produce as unworldly an atmosphere as it is possible to conceive within a short half-hundred kilometres of the busy world-port of Nantes and the great commercial city of Angers. One continually meets with ruins that recall the frightful struggle of Revolutionary times; hence the impression that one gets from a ramble through or about this region is well-nigh unique in all France.

The coast southward, nearly to La Rochelle, is a vast series of shallow gulfs and salt marshes which form weirdly wonderful outlooks for the painter who inclines to vast expanses of sea and sky.

Pornic is a remarkably picturesque little seaside village, where the inflowing and outflowing tides of the Bay of Biscay temper the southern sun and make of it — or would make of it if the tide of fashion had but set that way — a watering-place of the first rank.

It is an entrancing bit of coast-line which extends for a matter of fifty kilometres south of the juncture of the Loire with the ocean, with an aspect at times severe with a waste of sand, and again gracious with verdure and tree-clad and rocky shores.

The great Bay of Bourgneuf and its enfolding peninsula of Noirmoutier form an artist's sketching-ground that is not yet overrun with mere dabblers in paint and pencil, and is accordingly charming.

The Bay of Bourgneuf has most of the characteristics of the Morbihan, without that severity and sternness which impress one so deeply when on the shores of the great Breton inland sea.

The little town of Bourgneuf-en-Retz, with its little port of Colletis, is by no means a city of any artistic worth; indeed it is nearly bare of most of those things which attract travellers who are lovers of old or historic shrines; but it is a delightful stopping-place for all that, provided one does not want to go farther afield, to the very tip of the Vendean "land's end" at Noirmoutier across the bay.

Three times a day a steamer makes the journey to the little island town which is a favourite place of pilgrimage for the Nantais during the summer months. Once it was not even an island, but a peninsula, and not so very long ago either. The alluvial deposits of the Loire made it in the first place, and the sea, backing in from the north, made a strait which just barely separates it to-day from the mainland.

On this out-of-the-way little island there are still some remains of prehistoric monuments, the dolmen of Chiron-Tardiveau, the menhirs of Pinaizeaux and Pierre-Levée, and some others. In the speech of the inhabitants the isle is known as Noirmoutier, a contraction of "*Nigrum Monasterium,*" a name derived from the monastery founded here in the seventh century by St. Philibert.

In the town is an old château, the ancient fortress-refuge of the Abbé of Her. It is a great square structure flanked at the angles with little towers, of which two are roofed, one uncovered, and the fourth surmounted by a heliograph for communicating with the Ile de Yeu and the Pointe de Chenoulin. The view from the heights of these château towers is fascinating beyond compare, particularly at sundown on a summer's evening, when the golden rays of the sinking sun burnish the coast of the Vendée and cast lingering shadows from the roof-tops and walls of the town below. To the northwest one sees the Ilot du Pilier, with its lighthouse and its tiny coast-guard fortress; to the north is clearly seen Pornic and the neighbouring coasts of the Pays de Retz and of

Bouin with its encircling dikes,— all reminiscent of a little Holland. To the south is the narrow neck of Fromentin, the jagged Marguerites, which lift their fangs wholly above the surface of the sea only at low water, and the towering cliffs of the Ile de Yeu, which rise above the mists.

Just south of the Loire, between Nantes and Bourgneuf, is the Lac de Grand-Lieu, in connection with which one may hear a new rendering of an old legend. At one time, it is said, it was bordered by a city, whose inhabitants, for their vices, brought down the vengeance of heaven upon them, even though they cried out to the powers on high to avert the threatened flood which rose up out of the lake and overflowed the banks and swallowed the city and all evidences of its past. In this last lies the flaw in the legend; but, like the history of Sodom, of the Ville d'Ys in Bretagne, and of Ars in Dauphiné, tradition has kept it alive.

This wicked place of the Loire valley was called *Herbauge* or *Herbadilla*, and, from St. Philibert at the southern extremity of the lake, one looks out to-day on a considerable extent of shallow water, which is as murderous-looking and as uncanny as a swamp of the Everglades.

From the central basin flow two tiny rivers, the Ognon and the Boulogne, which are charming enough in their way, as also is the route by highroad from Nantes, but the gray monotonous lake, across which the wind whistles in a veritable tempest for more than six months of the year, is most depressing.

There are various hamlets, with some pretence at advanced civilization about them, scattered around the borders of the lake, St. Leger, St. Mars, St. Aignan, St. Lumine, Bouaye, and La Chevrolière; but in the whole number you will not get a daily paper that is less than forty-eight hours old, and nothing but the most stale news of happenings in the outside world ever dribbles through. St. Philibert is the metropolis of these parts, and it has no competitors for the honour.

At the entrance of the Ognon is the little village of Passay, built at the foot of a low cliff which dominates all this part of the lake. It is a picturesque little village of low houses and red roofs, with a little sandy beach in the foreground, through which little rivulets of soft water trickle and go to make up the greater body.

# CHAPTER XV.

### BERRY AND GEORGE SAND'S COUNTRY

Whether one enters Berry through the valley of the Cher or the Indre or through the gateway of Sancerre in the mid-Loire, the impression is much the same. The historic province of Berry resounds again and again with the echoes of its past, and no province adjacent to the Loire is more prolific in the things that interest the curious, and none is so little known as the old province which was purchased for the Crown by Philippe I. in 1101.

With the interior of the province, that portion which lies away from the river valleys, this book has little to do, though the traveller through the region would hardly omit the episcopal city of Bourges, and its great transeptless cathedral, with its glorious front of quintupled portals. With the cathedral may well be coupled that other great architectural monument, the Maison de Jacques Cœur. At Paris one is asked, *" Avez-vous vu le Louvre? "* but at Bourges it is always, *" Etes-vous allé à Jacques Cœur? "* even before one is asked if he has seen the cathedral.

From the hill which overlooks Sancerre, and forms a foundation for the still existing tower of the château belonging to the feudal Counts of Sancerre, one gets one of the most wonderfully wide-spread views in all the Loire valley. The height and its feudal tower stand isolated, like a rock rising from the ocean. From Cosne and beyond, on the north, to La Charité, on the south, is one vast panorama of vineyard, wheatfield, and luxuriant river-bottom. At a lesser distance, on the right bank, is the line of the railroad which threads its way like a serpent around the bends of the river and its banks.

Below the hill of Sancerre is a huge overgrown hamlet — and yet not large enough to be called a village — surrounding a most curious church (St. Satur), without either nave or apse. The old Abbey of St. Satur once possessed all the lands in the neighbourhood that were not in the actual possession of the Counts of Sancerre, and was a power in the land, as were most of the abbeys throughout France. The church was begun in 1360-70, on a most elaborate plan, so extensive in fact (almost approaching that great work at La Charité) that it has for ever remained uncompleted. The history of this little churchly suburb of Sancerre has been most interesting. The great Benedictine church was never finished and has since come to be somewhat of a ruin. In 1419 the English sacked the abbey and stole its treasure to the very last precious stone or piece of gold. A dozen flatboats were anchored or moored to the banks of the river facing the abbey, and the monks were transported thither and held for a ransom of a thousand crowns each. As everything had already been taken by their captors, the monks vainly protested that they had no valuables with which to meet the demand, and accordingly they were bound hand and foot and thrown into the river, to the number of fifty-two, eight only escaping with their lives. A bloody memory indeed for a fair land which now blossoms with poppies and roses.

Sancerre, in spite of the etymology of its name (which comes down from Roman times — Sacrum Cæsari), is of feudal origin. Its fortress, and the Comté as well, were under the suzerainty of the Counts of Champagne, and it was the stronghold and refuge of many a band of guerilla warriors, adventurers, and marauding thieves.

At the end of the twelfth century a certain Comte de Sancerre, at the head of a coterie of bandits called Brabaçons, marched upon Bourges and invaded the city, killing all who crossed their path, and firing all isolated dwellings and many even in the heart of the city.

Sancerre was many times besieged, the most memorable event of this nature being the attack of the royalists in 1573 against the Frondeurs who were shut up in the town. The defenders were without artillery, but so habituated were they to the use of the *fronde* that for eight months they were able to hold the city against the foe. From this the *fronde* came to be known as the "*arquebuse de Sancerre.*"

Sancerre is to-day a ruined town, its streets unequal and tortuous, all up and down hill and

*La Tour*, Sancerre

blindly rambling off into *culs-de-sac* which
lead nowhere. Above it all is the fine château,
built in a modern day after the Renaissance
manner, of Mlle. de Crussol, proudly seated on
the very crest of the hill. Within the grounds,
the only part of the domain which is free to the
public, are the ruins of the famous citadel
which was bought by St. Louis, in 1226, from
the Comte Thibaut. The only portion of this
feudal stronghold which remains to-day is
known as the "Tour des Fiefs."

One may enter the grounds and, in the company
of a *concierge,* ascend to the platform
of this lone tower, whence a wonderful view
of the broad "*ruban lumineux*" of the Loire
spreads itself out as if fluttering in the wind,
northward and southward, as far as the eye
can reach. Beside it one sees another line of
blue water, as if it were a strand detached from
the broader band. This is the Canal Latéral
de la Loire, one of those inland waterways of
France which add so much to the prosperity
of the land.

Above Sancerre is Gien, another gateway to
Berry, through which the traveller from Paris
through the Orléannais is bound to pass.

At a distance of five kilometres or more,
coming from the north, one sees the towers of

Château de Gien

the château of Gien piercing the horizon. The château is a most curious affair, with its chain-built blocks of stone, and its red and black — or nearly black — *brique,* crossed and recrossed in quaint geometrical designs. It was built in 1494 for Dame Anne de Beaujeau, who was regent of the kingdom immediately after the death of Charles VIII. This building replaced another of a century before, built by Jean-sans-Peur, where was celebrated the marriage of his daughter with the Comte de Guise. Gien's château, too, may be said to be a landmark on Jeanne d'Arc's route to martyrdom and fame, for here she made her supplication to Charles VII. to march on Reims. In Charlemagnian times this old castle had a predecessor, which, however, was more a fortress than a habitable château; but all remains of this had apparently disappeared before the later structure made its appearance. Louis XIV. and Anne of Austria, regent, held a fugitive, impoverished court in this château, and heard with fear and trembling the cannon-shots of the armies of Turenne and Condé at Bleneau, five leagues distant.

At Nevers or at La Charité one does not get the view of the Loire that he would like, for, in one case, the waterway is masked by a row of houses, and in the other by a series of walled gardens; but at Gien, where everything is splendidly theatrical, there is a tree-bordered quay and innumerable examples of those coquettish little houses of brick which are not beautiful, but which set off many a French riverside landscape as nothing else will.

In Gien's main street there are a multitude of rare mellowed old houses with sculptured fronts and high gables. This street twists and turns until it reaches the old stone and brick château, with its harmoniously coloured walls, making a veritable symphony of colour. Each turn in this old high-street of Gien gives a new vista of mediævalism quite surprising and eerielike, as fantastic as the weird pictures of Doré.

Gien and its neighbour Briare are chiefly noted commercially for their pottery. Gien makes crockery ware, and Briare inundates the entire world with those little porcelain buttons which one buys in every land.

Crossing the Sologne and entering Berry from the capital of the Orléannais, or coming out from Tours by the valley of the Cher, one comes upon the little visited and out-of-the-way château of Valençay, in the charming dainty valley of the Nahon.

There is some reason for its comparative neglect by the tourist, for it is on a cross-country railway line which demands quite a full day of one's time to get there from Tours and get away again to the next centre of attraction, and if one comes by the way of the Orléannais, he must be prepared to give at least three days to the surrounding region.

This is the gateway to George Sand's country, but few English-speaking tourists ever get here, so it may be safely called unknown.

It is marvellous how France abounds in these little corners all but unknown to strangers, even though they lie not far off the beaten track. The spirit of exploration and travel in unknown parts, except the Arctic regions, Thibet, and the Australian desert, seems to be dying out.

The château of Valençay was formerly inhabited by Talleyrand, after he had quitted the bishopric of Autun for politics. It is seated proudly upon a vast terrace overlooking one of the most charming bits of the valley of the Nahon, and is of a thoroughly typical Renaissance type, built by the great Philibert Delorme for Jacques d'Étampes in 1540, and only acquired by the minister of Napoleon and Louis XVIII. in 1805.

The architect, in spite of the imposing situation, is not seen at his best here, for in no way does it compare with his masterwork at Anet, or the Tuileries. The expert recognizes also the hands of two other architects, one of the Blaisois and the other of Anjou, who in some measure transformed the edifice in the reign of François I.

The enormous donjon, — if it is a donjon, — with its great, round corner tower with a dome above, which looks like nothing so much as an observatory, is perhaps the outgrowth of an earlier accessory, but on the whole the edifice is fully typical of the Renaissance.

The court unites the two widely different terminations in a fashion more or less approaching symmetry, but it is only as a whole that the effect is highly pleasing.

Beyond a *balustrade à jour* is the Jardin de la Duchesse, communicating with the park by a graceful bridge over an ornamental water. In general the apartments are furnished in the style of the First Empire, an epoch memorable in the annals of Valençay.

By the orders of Napoleon many royalties and ambassadors here received hospitality, and in 1808-14 it became a gilded cage — or a "golden prison," as the French have it — for

Château de Valençay

the Prince of the Asturias, afterward Ferdinand VII. of Spain, who consoled himself during his captivity by constructing wolf-traps in the garden and planting cauliflowers in the great urns and vases with which the terrace was set out.

There is a great portrait gallery here, where is gathered a collection of portraits in miniature of all the sovereigns who treated with Talleyrand during his ministerial reign, among others one of the Sultan Selim, painted from life, but in secret, since the reproduction of the human form is forbidden by the Koran.

In the Maison de Charité, in the town, beneath the pavement of the chapel, is found the tomb of the family of Talleyrand, where are interred the remains of Talleyrand and of Marie Thérèse Poniatowska, sister of the celebrated King of Poland who served in the French army in 1806. In this chapel also is a rare treasure in the form of a chalice enriched with precious stones, originally belonging to Pope Pius VI., the gift of the Princess Poniatowska.

The Pavillon de la Garenne, — what in England would be called a "shooting-box," — a rendezvous for the chase, built by Talleyrand, is some distance from the château on the edge of the delightful little Forêt de Gatine.

Varennes, just above Valençay, is thought by the average traveller through the long gallery of charms in the château country to be wholly unworthy of his attention. As a matter of fact, it does not possess much of historical or artistic interest, though its fine old church dates from the twelfth century.

Ascending the Cher from its juncture with the Loire, one passes a number of interesting places. St. Aignan, with its magnificent Gothic and Renaissance château; Selles; Romorantin, a dead little spot, dear as much for its sleepiness as anything else; Vierzon, a rich, industrial town where they make locomotives, automobiles, and mechanical hay-rakes, copying the most approved American models; and Mehun-sur-Yevre, all follow in rapid succession.

Mehun-sur-Yevre, which to most is only a name and to many not even that, is possessed of two architectural monuments, a grand ruin of a Gothic fortress of the time of Charles VII. and a feudal gateway of two great rounded cone-roofed towers, bound by a ligature through which a port-cullis formerly slid up and down like an act-drop in a theatre.

Wonderfully impressive all this, and the

*Gateway of Mehun-sur-Yevre*

*Porte de Mehun-sur-Yèvre*

*Le Carrior Dore, Romorantin*

more so because these magnificent relics of other days are unspoiled and unrestored.

Charles VII. was by no means constant in his devotions, it will be recalled, though he seems to have been seriously enamoured of Agnes Sorel — at any rate while she lived. Afterward he speedily surrounded himself with a galaxy of "*belles demoiselles vêtues comme reines.*" They followed him everywhere, and he spent all but his last sou upon them, as did some of his successors.

One day Charles VII. took refuge in the strong towers of the château of Mehun-sur-Yevre, which he himself had built and which he had frequently made his residence. Here he died miserable and alone, — it is said by history, of hunger. Thus another dark chapter in the history of kings and queens was brought to a close.

If one has the time and so desires, he may follow the Indre, the next confluent of the Loire south of the Cher, from Loches to "George Sand's country," as literary pilgrims will like to think of the pleasant valleys of the ancient province of Berry.

The history of the province before and since Philippe I. united it with the Crown of France was vivid enough to make it fairly well known,

# Berry and George Sand's Country

but on the whole it has been very little travelled. It is essentially a pastoral region, and, remembering George Sand and her works, one has refreshing memories of the idyls of its prairies and the beautiful valleys of the Indre and the Cher, which join their waters with the Loire near Tours.

If one would love Berry as one loves a greater and more famous haunt of a famous author, and would prepare in advance for the pleasure to be received from threading its highways and byways, he should read those " *petits chefs-d'œuvre* of sentiment and rustic poesy, the romances of George Sand. If he has done this, he will find almost at every turning some long familiar spot or a peasant who seems already an old friend.

Chateauroux is the real gateway to the country of George Sand.

Nohant is the native place of the great authoress, Madame Dudevant, whom the world best knows as George Sand; a little by-corner of the great busy world, loved by all who know it. Far out in the open country is the little station at which one alights if he comes by rail. Opposite is a " *petite route* " which leads directly to the banks of the Indre, where it joins the highway to La Châtre.

Nohant itself, as a dainty old-world village, is divine. Has not George Sand expressed her love of it as fervidly as did Marie Antoinette for the Trianon? The French call it a *"bon et honnête petit village berrichon."* Nude of artifice, it is deliciously unspoiled. A delightful old church, with a curious wooden porch and a parvise as rural as could possibly be, not even a cobblestone detracting from its rustic beauty, is the principal thing which strikes one's eye as he enters the village. Chickens and geese wander about, picking here and there on the very steps of the church, and no one says them nay.

The house of George Sand is just to the right of the church, within whose grounds one sees also the pavilion known to her as the *"théâtre des marionettes."*

In a corner of the poetic little cemetery at Nohant, one sees among the humble crosses emerging from the midst of the verdure, all weather-beaten and moss-grown, a plain, simple stone, green with mossy dampness, which marks the spot where reposes all that was mortal of George Sand. Here, in the midst of this land which she so loved, she still lives in the memory of all; at the house of the well-lettered for her abounding talent — second only to that of Balzac — and in the homes of the peasants for her generous fellowship.

Through her ancestry she could and did claim relationship with Charles X. and Louis XVIII.; but her life among her people had nought of pretence in it. She was born among the roses and to the sound of music, and she lies buried amid all the rusticity and simple charm of what may well be called the greenwood of her native land.

# CHAPTER XVI.

### THE UPPER LOIRE

The gateway to the upper valley may be said to be through the Nivernais, and the capital city of the old province, at the juncture of the Allier and the Loire.

After leaving Gien and Briare, the Loire passes through quite the most truly picturesque landscape of its whole course, the great height of Sancerre dominating the view for thirty miles or more in any direction.

Cosne is the first of the towns of note of the Nivernais, and is a gay little bourg of eight or nine thousand souls who live much the same life that their grandfathers lived before them. As a place of residence it might prove dull to the outsider, but as a house of call for the wearied and famished traveller, Cosne, with its charming situation, its tree-bordered quays, and its Hôtel du Grand Cerf, is most attractive.

Pouilly-sur-Loire is next, with three thou-

*Eglise S. Aignan, Cosne*

sand or more inhabitants wholly devoted to
wine-growing, Pouilly being to the upper river
what Vouvray is to Touraine. It is not a tourist point in any sense, nor is it very picturesque
or attractive.

Some one has said that the pleasure of contemplation is never so great as when one views
a noble monument, a great work of art, or a
charming French town for the first time.
Never was it more true indeed than of the
two dissimilar towns of the upper Loire,
Nevers, and La Charité-sur-Loire. The old
towers of La Charité rise up in the sunlight
and give that touch to the view which marks
it at once as of the Nivernais, which all archæologists tell one is Italian and not French, in
motive as well as sentiment.

It is remarkable, perhaps, that the name La
Charité is so seldom met with in the accounts
of English travellers in France, for in France
it is invariably considered to be one of the
most picturesque and famous spots in all mid-France.

It is an unprogressive, sleepy old place, with
streets mostly unpaved, whose five thousand
odd souls, known roundabout as Les Caritates,
live apparently in the past.

Below, a stone's throw from the windows of

*Pouilly-sur-Loire*

your inn, lies the Loire, its broad, blue bosom scarcely ruffled, except where it slowly eddies around the piers of the two-century-old *dos d'ane* bridge; a lovely old structure, built, it is recorded, by the regiment known as the "Royal Marine" in the early years of the eighteenth century.

The town is terraced upon the very edge of the river, with views up and down which are unusually lovely for even these parts. Below, almost within sight, is Nevers, while above are the heights of Sancerre, still visible in the glowing western twilight.

Beyond the bridge rises a giant column of blackened stone, festooned by four ranges of arcades, the sole remaining relic of the ancient church standing alone before the present structure which now serves the purposes of the church in La Charité.

The walls which surrounded the ancient town have disappeared or have been built into house walls, but the effect is still of a self-contained old burg.

In the fourteenth century, during the Hundred Years' War, the town was frequently besieged. In 1429 Jeanne d'Arc, coming from her success at St. Pierre-le-Moutier, here met with practically a defeat, as she was able to sustain the siege for only but a month, when she withdrew.

La Charité played an important part in the religious wars of the sixteenth century, and Protestants and Catholics became its occupants in turn. Virtually La Charité-sur-Loire became a Protestant stronghold in spite of its Catholic foundation.

In 1577 it bade defiance to the royal arms of the Duc d'Alençon, as is recounted by the following lines:

> "Ou allez-vous, hélas! furieux insensés
> Cherchant de Charité la proie et la ruine,
> Qui sans l'ombre de Foy abbatre la pensez!
>
> . . . . . . . . .
>
> Le canon ne peut rien contre la Charité,
> Plus tot vous détruira la peste et la famine,
> Car jamais sans Foy n'aurez la Charité."

In spite of this defiance it capitulated, and, on the 15th of May, at the château of Plessis-les-Tours on the Loire, Henri III. celebrated the victory of his brother by a fête *"ultra-galante,"* where, in place of the usual pages, there were employed *"des dames vestues en habits d'hommes. . . ."* Surely a fantastic and immodest manner of celebrating a victory against religious opponents; but, like many of the customs of the time, the fête was simply a fanatical debauch.

*Porte du Croux, Nevers*

At Nevers one meets the Canal du Nivernais, which recalls Daudet's "La Belle Nivernaise" to all readers of fiction, who may accept it without question as a true and correct guide to the region, its manners, and customs.

The chief characteristic of Nevers is that it is Italian in nearly, if not quite all, its aspects; its monuments and its history. Its ancient ducal château, part of which dates from the feudal epoch, was the abode of the Italian dukes who came in the train of Mazarin, the last of whom was the nephew of the cardinal, "who himself was French if his speech was not."

Nevers has also a charming Gothic cathedral (St. Cyr) with a double Romanesque apse (in itself a curiosity seldom, if ever, seen out of Germany), and, in addition to the cathedral, can boast of St. Etienne, one of the most precious of all the Romanesque churches of France.

The old walls at Nevers are not very complete, but what remain are wonderfully expressive. The Tour Gouguin and the Tour St. Eloi are notable examples, but they are completely overshadowed by the Porte du Croux, which is one of the best examples of the city gates which were so plentiful in the France of another day.

Above Nevers, Decize, Bourbon-Lancy, Gilly, and Digoin are mere names which mean nothing to the traveller by rail. They are busy towns of central France, where the bustle of their daily lives is of quite a different variety from that of the Ile de France, of Normandy, or of the Pas de Calais.

From Digoin to Roanne the Loire is followed by the Canal Latéral. Roanne is a not very pleasing, overgrown town which has become a veritable *ville des ouvriers,* all of whom are engaged in cloth manufacture.

Virtually, then, Roanne is not much more than a guide-post on the route to Le Puy — "the most picturesque place in the world" — and the wonderfully impressive region of the Cevennes and the Vivaris, where shepherds guard their flocks amid the solitudes.

Far above Le Puy, in a rocky gorge known as the Gerbier-de-Jonc, near Ste. Eulalie, in the Ardeche, rises the tiny Liger, which is the real source of the mighty Loire, that natural boundary which divides the north from the south and forms what the French geographers call "*la bassin centrale de France.*"

THE END.

# INDEX

Abbeville, 107.
*Abd-el-Kader, Emir,* 165.
*Abelard,* 293.
*Absalom,* 281.
Acheneau, The, 298.
*Adams, John,* 124.
*Alaric,* 149.
*Alcuin, Abbé,* 206.
*Alençon, Ducs d',* 195, 334.
*Alençon, Marguerite d',* 97, 150, 151-152.
Allier, The, 330.
Amboise and Its Château, 3, 20, 82, 96, 100, 123, 130-131, 137, 140, 148-169, 172, 181, 186, 194, 249.
*Amboise, Family of,* 118, 120-122.
Amboise, Forêt d', 169.
Amiens, 210.
Ancenis and Its Château, 11, 21-23, 291.
*Andrelini, Fausto,* 66.
Anet, Château d', 107, 177, 322.
*Ange, Michel,* 208, 249.
Angers and Its Château, 7, 10-13, 15, 21-23, 40, 84, 275, 278, 280, 283-284, 286-290, 304, 308.
Angoulême, 194, 304.
*Angoulême, Isabeau d',* 267.
*Angoulême, Jean d',* 89.
*Angoulême, Louise de Savoie, Duchesse d'* (See *Savoie, Louise de*).

Anjou, 15, 26, 142, 161, 273, 274, 284, 289-290, 292, 306, 322.
*Anjou, Counts of,* 150, 193, 208, 232, 239, 267, 288.
*Anjou, Foulques Nerra, Comte d'* (See *Foulques Nerra*).
*Anjou, Margaret of,* 280.
*Anne of Austria,* 301-302, 319.
Aquitaine, 18, 193.
*Arbrissel, Robert d',* 263.
*Arc, Jeanne d',* 202, 254-256, 258-260.
*Ardier, Paul,* 115.
*Arques, Château d',* 9.
*Aumale, Duc d',* 165.
*Aussigny, Thibaut d',* 48.
Authion, The, 13.
Autun, 321.
Auvergne, 15.
Auvers, 251.
Auxerre, 17, 119.
Avignon, 51, 260.
Azay-le-Rideau and Its Château, 10, 63, 140, 226, 238, 240-247.

Bacon, 40.
Ballon, 215.
*Balue, Cardinal,* 194, 196.
*Balzac, Honoré de,* 3, 6, 20, 128-129, 137-138, 143, 207-209, 234, 239, 329.
*Bardi, Comte de,* 108.

## Index

Barre, De la, 144, 240.
Barry, Madame du, 169, 215.
Beaudoin, Jean, 200.
Beaufort, A., 138.
Beaugency and Its Château, 9, 41, 48-53.
Beaujeau, Anne de, 319.
Beaulieu, 201-202.
Beauregard, Château de, 114-116.
Beauvron, The, 114.
Becket, 190.
Bélier, Guillaume, 258.
Bellanger, Stanislas, 135.
Bellay Family, Du, 5, 128, 234.
Belleau, Remy, 128.
Beringhem, Henri de, 245.
Bernay, 306.
Bernier, 57.
Berry, 7, 15, 56, 123, 313-314, 318, 320, 326-329.
Berry, Counts of, 150.
Berry, Duchesse de, 295.
Berthelot, Gilles, 244, 246.
Berthier, Maréchal, 108.
Beuvron, 87-88.
Biencourt, Marquis de, 246.
Blacas, Comte de, 247.
Blaisois, The, 52, 54, 56-84, 102, 123-124, 136, 148, 193, 322.
Bleneau, 319.
Blésois, The (See Blaisois, The).
Blois and Its Château, 3, 9, 11, 20, 40, 52-54, 56-84, 88, 94-95, 98, 100, 107, 110-112, 116-117, 119, 123, 125-126, 136, 139, 149, 156, 160, 164, 167, 174, 184, 186, 194, 260, 284.
Blois, Comtes de, 57-59, 62, 84, 87, 98, 118.
Blois, Forêt de, 54.
Blondel, 99.
Bocage, The, 304-305.

Bohier, Thomas, 174, 182, 184-186.
Bois-Tillac, 298.
Bolingbroke, 42, 183.
Bonchamps, 306-307.
Bonheur, Rosa, 306.
Bonneventure, Château de, 250.
Bontemps, Pierre, 105.
Bordeaux, 133, 171, 203, 292.
Bordeaux, Duc de, 108.
Bossebœuf, Abbé, 233.
Bouaye, 312.
Bouin, 311.
Boulogne, The, 312.
Bourbon, Cardinal de, 164.
Bourbon, Renée de, 264.
Bourbon-Lancy, 336.
Bourbonnais, 15.
Bourdaisière, Château de la, 169.
Bourg de Batz, 300.
Bourges, 15, 314, 316.
Bourgneuf-en-Retz, 309, 311.
Bourgogne, 4, 15, 142.
Bourgueil, 267.
Bourré, Jean, 233.
Boyer, 111.
Bracieux, 110.
Brain-sur-Allonnes, 269.
Brantôme, 101, 155, 157, 158.
Brenne, 135.
Bretagne, 15, 26, 35-36, 57, 192, 218, 284, 291-293, 301.
Bretagne, Anne de, 63, 97, 120, 168, 196, 209, 234, 236-238, 293, 296.
Bretagne, Conan, Duc de, 295.
Bretagne, François II., Duc de, 291, 294-296.
Bréze, Pierre de, 195.
Briare, 320, 330.
Briçonnet, Cardinal, 42.
Brinvilliers, 144.

## Index

Brittany (*See* Bretagne).
*Broglie, Princesse de*, 120.
*Brosse, Pierre de*, 234.
Bruges, 282.
*Brunyer, Abel*, 80, 81.
Buffon, 61, 183.
Bullion, 119.
*Bussy d'Amboise, De*, 269.
Buzay, Abbey of, 299.
Byron, 138.

*Cæsar*, 18, 290.
Cahors, 260.
*Cail, M.*, 270-272.
*Cain*, 251.
*Calixtus II.*, 264.
Canal de Brest à Nantes, 24.
Canal de Buzay, 298.
Canal d'Orleans, 36-37.
Canal du Nivernaise, 17, 335.
Canal Lateral, 12, 17, 318, 336.
Canal Maritime, 298.
Candes, 268-270, 276.
*Castellane Family*, 250.
*Caumont, De*, 195.
*Cellini*, 152.
Chalonnes, 24, 304.
Chambord and Its Château, 2-3, 20, 53, 79, 82, 84, 86, 94-110, 123, 139, 174, 186, 243, 247-248.
*Chambord, Comte de*, 109.
Chambris, 10.
*Champagne, Counts of*, 316.
Champeigne, 135.
Champtocé, 24.
Chanteloup, 154, 169.
Charlemagne, 206.
Charles I. (the Bald), 18, 193.
Charles II. of England, 82.
Charles V., Emperor, 130-131, 155, 194.
Charles VI., 257.
Charles VII., 150, 188-189, 194-195, 202, 233, 250, 254-256, 257-260, 268, 319, 324, 326.
Charles VIII., 45, 98, 130, 150, 165, 194-195, 234, 236, 238-239, 319.
Charles IX., 107, 122, 180.
Charles X., 329.
Charles Martel, 5.
Charles the Bold of Burgundy, 44.
Chartres, 22, 133.
Chartreuse du Liget, 190.
*Châteaubriand, Comtesse de*, 101, 130.
Château Chevigné, 22.
Château de la Fontaine, 43.
Château de la Source, 42-43.
Châteaudun and Its Castle, 21-22.
*Châteaudun, Vicomtes de*, 269.
Château Gaillard, 259.
Château l'Epinay, 22.
Châteauneuf-sur-Loire, 36, 84.
Châteauroux, 327.
Château Serrand, 22.
Chatillon, 12, 17, 19.
*Chatillon, Cardinal de*, 160.
*Chatillon, Comtes de*, 61, 68.
Chaumont and Its Château, 11, 20, 107, 110, 116-126, 140.
*Chaumont, Charles de*, 120.
*Chaumont, Donatien Le Ray de*, 123-125.
Chemillé, 304-305.
*Chemille, Petronille de*, 263.
Chenonceaux and Its Château, 10, 63, 107, 118, 140, 148, 165, 169, 171-187, 234, 243, 247, 251.
Cher, The, 10, 21, 91, 171-173, 177-178, 180, 183, 191, 215, 275, 313, 320, 324, 326-327.

# 340  Index

*Chevalier, Abbé,* 243.
Cheverny and Its Château, 82, 110-114, 133.
*Cheverny, Philippe Hurault, Comte de,* 111.
*Chicot,* 201.
Chinon and Its Châteaux, 10, 92, 140, 171, 193, 202, 239, 241, 247, 250-261, 268.
Chinon, Forêt de, 241, 247.
Chiron-Tardiveau, 310.
*Choiseul, Duc de,* 164, 169.
Cholet, 275, 304-307.
*Cholet, Comte de,* 115.
Cinq-Mars and Its Ruins, 7, 21, 137, 220, 227-232, 238, 274.
*Cinq-Mars, Henri, Marquis de,* 228, 229-231, 234.
*Cinq-Mars, Marquise de,* 230, 231.
*Claude of France,* 72, 80, 97, 155.
*Clément, Jacques,* 78.
Clermont-Ferrand, 15.
Cléry, 32, 41, 44-46, 214.
Clisson and Its Château, 8, 303, 307.
*Clisson,* 293.
*Clopinel, Jehan* (See *Jean de Meung*).
*Clouet,* 112.
*Clovis,* 43, 149, 253.
Cœuvres, 170.
Coligny, 160-161.
Colletis, 309.
*Colombe, Michel,* 207-208, 295.
*Commines, De,* 45.
*Condé, Prince de,* 119, 160-161, 168, 319.
*Conti, Princesse de,* 234.
*Cormeri, Citizen,* 215.
Cormery, 133.
Cosne, 18, 314, 330.
Cosson, The, 2, 97-98, 101.
Coteau de Guignes, 52.

Couëron, 298.
*Coulanges, M. de,* 18.
Coulmiers, 40.
Cour-Cheverny, 110, 114, 133.
*Cousin, Jean,* 105.
Coutancière, Château of, 269.
*Coxe, Miss,* 125.
*Créquy, Marquise de,* 183.
Croix de Monteuse, 16.
*Cromwell,* 301.
*Crussol, Mlle. de,* 318.

*Dalahaide,* 77.
Dampierre, 280.
*Dante,* 203.
*Danton,* 144.
*Daudet,* 17, 335.
Decize, 336.
*Delavigne, Casimir,* 34.
*Delorme, Marion,* 230-231.
*Delorme, Philibert,* 321.
*Deneux, Mlle.,* 215.
*Descartes,* 3, 208.
Digoin, 336.
Dijon, 15.
*Dino, Duc de,* 115.
Dive, The, 13.
Domfront, Château de, 9.
*Doré,* 207, 320.
*Duban,* 73.
*Ducos, Roger,* 164-165.
*Dudevant, Madame* (See *Sand, George*).
*Duguesclin,* 49.
*Dumas,* 3, 6, 47, 82, 201, 268-269, 294-295.
Dunois, The, 56.
*Dupin, M. and Mme.,* 183, 187.
*Duplessis-Mornay,* 281.

*Eckmühl, Prince,* 42.
Effiats Family, D' (See *Cinq-Mars*).
Elbée, D', 307.

## Index

*Eleanor of Portugal*, 155.
*Éléanore of Guienne*, 267.
Embrun, 44, 45.
*Epernon, Duc d'*, 194.
*Este, Cardinal d'*, 180.
*Estrées, Gabrielle d'*, 164, 169-170.
*Étampes, Duchesse d'*, 101, 130-131, 155.
*Étampes, Jacques d'*, 321.
Etretat, 251.
Eure et Loir, Department of, 35.

Falaise, Château de, 9.
Ferdinand VII. of Spain, 323.
Finistère, 35.
*Flaubert*, 6.
*Foix, Marguerite de*, 295-296.
Folie-Siffait, 26.
Fontainebleau, 97.
Fontaine des Sables Mouvants, 52.
*Fontenelle*, 183.
Fontenoy, 107.
Fontevrault, Abbey of, 3, 263-267, 282.
*Force, Piganiol de la*, 106.
Forez, Plain of, 17.
*Fouché*, 298.
*Foulques Nerra*, 93, 201, 232, 234.
*Foulques V.*, 238.
*Fouquet*, 164, 294.
*François I.*, 60-64, 69-70, 72-73, 75, 89, 94-99, 101, 104-107, 109, 114, 118, 130, 148, 151-156, 171-172, 174-176, 189-190, 194, 196-197, 200, 244-245, 264, 322.
*François II.*, 156-162, 168, 181, 215.
*Franklin, Benjamin*, 123-124, 125.
Freiburg, 22.
Fromentin, 311.

*Galles, Prince de*, 49.
Gaston of Orleans, 59-60, 62, 68-70, 79-82.
Gatanais, The, 36.
Gatine, Forêt de, 324.
*George IV.*, 169.
Gerbier-de-Jonc, 16, 336.
Gien and Its Château, 8, 18, 19, 202, 318-320, 330.
Gilly, 336.
Giverny, 251.
*Gondi, Henri de*, 293-294, 301-302.
*Goujon, Jean*, 105, 179, 244.
*Gregory of Tours*, 57.
*Grise-Gonelle, Geoffroy*, 195.
Grottoes of Ste. Radegonde, 218.
Guérande, 300.
*Guise, Henri, Duc de (Le Balafré)*, 67, 69-70, 73-78, 157, 160, 162, 164, 168, 180, 234.

Haute Loire, Department of, 11.
*Henri II.*, 69, 99, 107, 109, 115, 156, 158, 171-172, 174-177, 183-184, 197, 200.
*Henri III.*, 69-70, 73, 75-78, 182, 195, 201, 334.
*Henri IV. (de Navarre)*, 78, 164, 170, 201, 281, 293.
Henry II. of England, 190, 208, 238, 257-258, 267.
Henry VIII. of England, 107.
*Holbein*, 152.
*Hugo, Victor*, 37.
Huismes, 250.
*Hurault, Philippe*, 111, 112.

Ile de Yeu, 310-311.
Ile Feydeau, 298.
Ile Gloriette, 298.
Ile St. Jean, 149.
Ilot du Pilier, 310.

Indre, The, 10, 21, 191-192, 240, 243-244, 247, 275, 313, 326-327.
Indre et Loire, Département d', 142.

Jahel, Miss, 125.
James V. of Scotland, 157.
James, Henry, 14, 189, 204, 251.
Jargeau, 36.
Jean de Meung, 46-47.
Jean-sans-Peur, 319.
Jean-sans-Terre, 193, 267.
Jeanne d'Arc, 33-35, 38, 49, 319, 333.
Jeanne of France, 209.
John, King, 287.
Joué, 215.
Juvenet, 34.

Kleber, 306, 307.

La Beauce, 38, 41, 53, 87, 141.
"La Briche," 270-272.
Lac de Grand Lieu, 298-299, 311-312.
Lac d'Issarles, 16.
La Chapelle, 43.
La Charité, 17-18, 314-315, 319, 332-334.
La Châtre, 327.
La Chevrolière, 312.
Lafayette, Madame de, 109.
La Fontaine, 128, 286.
La Martinière, 298.
La Motte, 87-88.
Landais, 294.
Landes, Houdon des, 137.
Langeais and Its Château, 7, 21, 82, 133, 140, 165, 174, 224, 232-241, 247.
Languedoc, 15.
Lanoue, 293.
Lanterne de Rochecorbon, 220.
La Pointe, 13, 22-23, 284.

La Possonière, 289.
Larçay, 10.
La Rochelle, 208, 308.
Lauzun, 164.
Lavedan, 31-32.
Layon, The, 13.
Le Croisic, 300.
Le Havre, 27.
Lemaitre, Jules, 34.
Lemercier, 261-262.
Lenoir, 57.
Lenôtre, 43.
Lepage, 35.
Le Pellerin, 298.
Le Puy, 4-5, 10, 16, 137, 336.
Leray, M., 120.
Les Andelys, Château de, 9.
Lescure, 307.
Lespine, Jean de, 291.
Liger, The, 336.
Lille, 286.
Lille, Abbé de, 107.
"Limieul, La Demoiselle de" (See Tour, Isabelle de la).
Limousin, The, 109.
Lisieux, 92.
Loches and Its Châteaux, 3, 9-10, 130, 133, 140, 142, 188-202, 250, 266, 326.
Loches, Forêt de, 190.
Loir, The, 13, 21.
Loir et Cher, Department of the, 35, 57.
Loire, The, 1, 3-30, 32, 34-38, 40-41, 43, 50-51, 53-54, 56, 58, 64-65, 68, 92, 95-97, 101-102, 110, 116-118, 120-122, 124, 129, 133, 134, 137, 140-142, 148-149, 156, 163, 171, 173, 177-178, 191, 196, 208, 215, 220-223, 225, 227-228, 232, 236, 240, 257, 259-260, 267, 273, 275-276, 278-279, 282-286, 288-290, 292-293, 297-302, 304, 308-309, 311, 313-314, 318-319,

# Index

324, 326-327, 330, 332-334, 336.
Loiret, The, 41-43.
Loiret, Department of the, 35-36.
*Lorraine, Cardinal de,* 157, 180.
*Lorraine, Marie de,* 157.
Lorris, 37.
*Lorris, Guillaume de,* 37, 46.
Lot, The, 260.
Louet, The, 286.
*Louis II. (Le Bègue),* 150.
*Louis IX.* (See *St. Louis*).
*Louis XI.,* 5, 32, 41, 44-46, 48, 69, 130-131, 150, 154, 194, 195, 211-212, 214-218, 232-233, 253, 257-258, 268, 281, 291.
*Louis XII.,* 60-61, 64, 66, 83, 97, 120, 122, 151, 167, 194-195, 209, 215, 238, 294.
*Louis XIII.,* 63, 99, 107, 139, 222, 224, 228, 230-231.
*Louis XIV.,* 32, 82-83, 98-99, 107, 109, 111, 164, 215, 227, 232, 245, 247, 294, 319.
*Louis XV.,* 54, 84, 107, 164, 169, 215.
*Louis XVI.,* 32, 123.
*Louis XVIII.,* 321, 329.
*Louis Philippe,* 165.
Louvre, The, 130, 285.
*Lubin, M.,* 126.
Luynes and Its Château, 21, 222-227.
*Luynes Family,* 222, 224, 227, 234.
Lyonnais, 15.
Lyons, 16, 203, 286.
Lyons, Forêt de, 87.

Madon, 126.
*Maillé, Comte de,* 227.
Maine, The, 12-13, 21-23, 284, 288-290.

*Maintenon, Madame de,* 109.
*Malines,* 77.
*Mame et Fils, Alfred,* 205.
*Mansart* (elder), 62, 79.
Marguerites, The, 311.
*Marie Antoinette,* 328.
*Marigny, De,* 54.
Marmoutier, Abbey of, 218-220, 266.
*Marques, Family of,* 185.
*Marsay, M. de,* 190.
Marseilles, 27, 136, 203, 286, 292.
*Martel, Geoffroy,* 253.
Maulévrier, Château of, 303.
Mauves, Plain of, 26.
Mayenne, 21.
Mayenne, The, 21.
*Mazarin,* 6, 293, 301-302, 335.
*Medici, Catherine de,* 73-79, 107, 118-119, 122-123, 156-157, 160-162, 168, 175-182, 184-185.
*Medici, Marie de,* 194, 285.
Mehun-sur-Yevre and Its Château, 324-326.
*Mello, Dreux de,* 193.
Menars and Its Château, 53-54.
Mer, 52-53.
Metz, 40.
Meung-sur-Loire, 41, 44, 46-48.
Micy, Abbaye de, 43.
*Mignard,* 112.
Moine, The, 307-308.
*Molière,* 108.
Montbazon, 10.
*Montespan, Madame de,* 283.
*Montesquieu,* 183.
*Montgomery,* 158, 175.
Montjean, 24.
Montlivault, 53.
*Montmorency, Connétable de,* 174.
Montpellier, Castle of, 231.

# Index

*Montpensier, Charles de,* 154-155.
Montrichard and its Donjon, 9-10, 91-93.
Montsoreau, 268-270, 276.
Moraines, Château de (*See* Dampierre).
*Moreau,* 306.
*Moret,* 251.
*Morrison,* 81.
Mortagne, 307.
*Mosnier,* 112.
Moulins, 15.
Muides, 53.

Nahon, The, 320-321.
Nantes and Its Château, 3, 7-8, 12-13, 23, 25-28, 40, 59, 84, 133, 207, 278-279, 286, 288, 291-302, 308, 311-312.
*Napoleon I.,* 83, 138, 164, 321-322.
*Napoleon III.,* 88.
*Napoleon, Louis,* 165.
Narbonne, 231.
*Navarre, Marguerite of* (See *Alençon, Marguerite d'*).
*Nemours, Duc de,* 157.
*Nepveu, Pierre,* 104.
Nevers, 4, 6, 11, 15, 17, 137, 319, 332-333, 335-336.
*Nini,* 125.
Nivernais, The, 15, 330, 332.
Nohant, 327-329.
Noirmoutier, 309-310.
Normandy, 85, 92, 306.

Ognon, The, 312.
Onzain, 116.
Orléannais, The, 4, 10, 15, 19, 23, 30-57, 318, 320-321.
Orléans, 7-8, 10-12, 15, 17, 19, 30-35, 37-41, 43, 52, 133, 137, 256, 258, 270, 284, 289.

Orleans Family, 63, 65-66, 69, 140, 165, 231, 234 (See also *Gaston of Orleans*).
Orleans, Forêt d', 39-40.
Oudon, 25-26, 291.

Paimbœuf, 298.
Paris, 13, 30, 33, 42, 79, 119, 124, 136, 139-140, 229-230, 284, 302, 314.
*Parme, Duc de,* 108.
*Parmentier,* 80.
Pas de Calais, 192.
Passay, 312.
Passy-sur-Seine, 124.
Pays de Retz, 292, 301-302, 310.
*Penthièvre, Duc de,* 164.
*Pepin,* 193.
*Philippe I.,* 313, 326.
*Philippe II.* (*Auguste*), 93, 193, 238.
*Philippe III.* (*Le Hardi*), 234.
*Philippe IV.* (*Le Bel*), 49.
Pierrefonds, Château of, 186.
Pierre-Levée, 310.
*Pilon, Germain,* 105.
Pinaizeaux, 310.
*Pius VI.,* 323.
*Plantagenet, Henry* (See *Henry II. of England*).
*Plantin, Christopher,* 205.
*Plessis, Armand du* (See *Richelieu, Cardinal*).
Plessis-les-Tours, 7, 150, 211-218, 334.
Pointe de Chenoulin, 310.
Poitiers, 304.
*Poitiers, Diane de,* 118, 123, 130, 155, 172, 174-178, 183, 187, 197.
Poitou, 278, 292, 306.
*Pompadour, La,* 215.
*Poniatowska, Marie Thérèse,* 323.
Pont Aven, 251.

# Index

Ponts de Cé, 21-22, 275, 279, 284-286.
Pornic, 308, 310.
Pornichet, 300.
Port Boulet, 270.
Pouilly, 18, 330-332.
Prairie-au-Duc, 298.
*Primaticcio,* 152.
*Primatice,* 99.
Puy-de-Dôme, 16.

*Rabelais, François,* 3, 128, 143-144, 239-240, 254-256, 260.
Rambouillet, Forêt de, 87.
Reims, 319.
*Renaudie, Jean Barri de la,* 161.
*René, King,* 23, 281.
Rennes, 15.
*Retz, Cardinal de* (See Gondi, Henri de).
*Retz, Gilles de,* 24, 293.
Rhine, The, 13, 26.
Rhône, The, 13, 23, 260.
*Richard Cœur de Lion,* 93, 193, 267.
Richelieu, 260-262.
*Richelieu, Cardinal,* 224, 228, 231-232, 260-262, 301-302.
Roanne, 12, 16-17, 336.
Rochecotte, 250.
Rochecotte, Château de, 249-250.
Romorantin and Its Château, 85, 88-89, 324.
*Ronsard,* 128, 157, 180, 240.
Rouen, 92, 119, 121-122, 203, 221, 299.
*Rousseau, Jean Jacques,* 172, 183-184, 187.
*Roy, Lucien,* 235.
*Royale, Madame,* 109.
*Rubens,* 285.
*Ruggieri, Cosmo,* 78-79, 122-123.
Russy, Forêt de, 114.
*Saint Gelais, Guy de,* 245.

Sancerre and Its Châteaux, 18, 137, 313-318, 330, 333.
*Sancerre, Counts of,* 314-316.
*Sand, George,* 7, 321, 326-329.
San Juste, Monastery of, 131.
Saône, The, 23.
*Sardini, Scipion,* 119.
Sarthe, The, 13, 21.
Saumur and Its Château, 21, 119-120, 142, 171, 221-222, 259, 274-283, 292.
Sausac, Château of, 202.
*Sausac, Seigneur de,* 215.
Savennières, 289.
*Savoie, Louise de,* 151.
*Savoie, Philippe de,* 195.
*Saxe, Maurice de,* 107-108.
*Scott, Sir Walter,* 166, 211, 216, 218.
Sedan, 40.
Seine, The, 4, 13, 25, 36, 121, 221.
Selles, 10, 324.
*Sertio,* 100.
*Sévigné, Madame de,* 18, 276, 295.
*Sforza, Ludovic,* 197.
*Shenstone,* 106.
*Siegfried, Jacques,* 234.
Sologne, The, 38, 52-53, 56, 84-94, 97, 101, 110, 148, 320.
*Sorel, Agnes,* 152, 188-189, 194, 196, 201-202, 250, 326.
*Staël, Madame de,* 119-120.
St. Aignan and Its Château, 10, 312, 324.
*Stanislas of Poland, King,* 107-108.
St. Ay, 43-44.
St. Benoit-sur-Loire, 10, 19.
St. Claude, 54.
St. Cyr, 215.
St. Die, 53.
Ste. Eulalie, 336.

## Index

Stendahl, 128.
St. Etienne, 5, 16.
St. Florent, Abbey of, 282, 306.
St. Galmier, 16.
St. Georges-sur-Loire, 22.
St. Leger, 312.
*St. Liphard,* 48.
*St. Louis,* 37, 193, 288, 318.
St. Lumine, 312.
St. Mars, 312.
*St. Martin,* 5, 149, 209-211, 218, 220, 253, 268.
*St. Mesme,* 253.
St. Mesmin, 41, 43.
St. Nazaire, 23, 28, 292, 300.
*Stofflet,* 303, 306.
*St. Ours,* 193.
St. Philibert, 311-312.
*St. Philibert,* 310.
St. Pierre-le-Moutier, 333.
St. Rambert, 17.
*St. Sauveur,* 238.
Strasburg, 22.
St. Symphorien, 218.
St. Trinité, Abbey of, 266.
*Stuart, Mary,* 157-162, 168, 181.
*St. Vallier, Comte de,* 175, 197.
Suèvres, 53.
Sully, 19.

*Talleyrand,* 250, 321, 323.
*Tasso,* 180.
Tavers, 52.
*Terry, Mr.,* 187.
*Texier,* 22.
Thézée, 10.
*Thibaut-le-Tricheur,* 259.
*Thibaut III.,* 253.
*Thiephanie, Dame,* 281.
*Thouet, The,* 13.
*Thoury, Comtesse,* 105.
Torfou, 307.
Toulouse, 15.
*Tour, Isabelle de la,* 119.
Touraine, 1-4, 6-9, 15, 19-21, 23, 32, 54, 56, 79, 85, 92, 102, 105, 121, 128-148, 161, 164, 169, 172-173, 176, 183, 204, 215, 220, 229-230, 233-234, 238, 243-244, 246, 251, 260, 273, 275, 284, 332.
*Touraine, Comtes de,* 253.
Tours, 3, 4, 7, 8, 10-11, 20-21, 40, 57, 84, 116-117, 120, 132-133, 137, 148-149, 166, 171-172, 200, 203-211, 215, 221-222, 224-225, 238-239, 246, 253, 266, 274, 276-277, 320-321, 327.
Treves-Cunault, 283-284.
*Turenne,* 319.
*Turner,* 12.

Ussé and Its Château, 241, 247-249.

Valençay and Its Château, 320-324.
*Valentine de Milan,* 66.
*Valentinois, Duchesse de* (See *Poitiers, Diane de*).
Vallée du Vendomois, 274.
*Valois, Marguerite de (sister of François I.)* (See *Alençon, Marguerite d'*).
*Valois, Marguerite de (de Navarre),* 180.
*Van Eyck,* 152.
Varennes, 218, 324.
Varennes, The, 135.
*Vasari,* 153.
*Vauban,* 247.
*Vaudémont, Louise de,* 182.
Vendôme, 22, 266.
*Vendôme, César de,* 164.
Vendomois, The, 56-57.
Veron, 135.
Versailles, 43, 60, 86, 98, 139, 261.
*Vibraye, Marquis de,* 111.
Vienne, The, 10, 21, 251, 259-260, 267-268, 275, 279.

Vierzon, 84-85, 324.
*Vigny, Alfred de,* 128-129.
Villandry, Château de, 238.
Villaumère, Château de la, 250.
*Villon, François,* 48.
*Vinci, Leonardo da,* 59, 72, 100, 152-153, 166, 169, 174.
*Viollet-le-Duc,* 185.

Vivarais Mountains, 16.
*Voltaire,* 42, 142, 183.
Vorey, 11, 16.
Vouvray, 222, 332.

Yonne, The, 17.
*Young, Arthur,* 86.

*Zamet, Sebastian,* 170.

## Date Due

| | | | |
|---|---|---|---|
| DEC 4 '5 | DEC. 02 1992 | | |
| FEB 23 '56 | | | |
| DEC 19 '57 | | | |
| MAR 1 '61 | | | |
| DEC 11 '66 | | | |
| MAY 20 '67 | | | |
| JUL 16 '69 | | | |
| DEC 8 '70 | | | |
| MAR 14 '71 | | | |
| NOV. -1 1971 | | | |
| APR. 24 1972 | | | |
| SEP. 16 1972 | | | |
| DEC. -1 1977 | | | |
| MAR 14 1983 | | | |
| MAY 13 1984 | | | |
| APR -3 | | | |
| MAR 10 199? | | | |